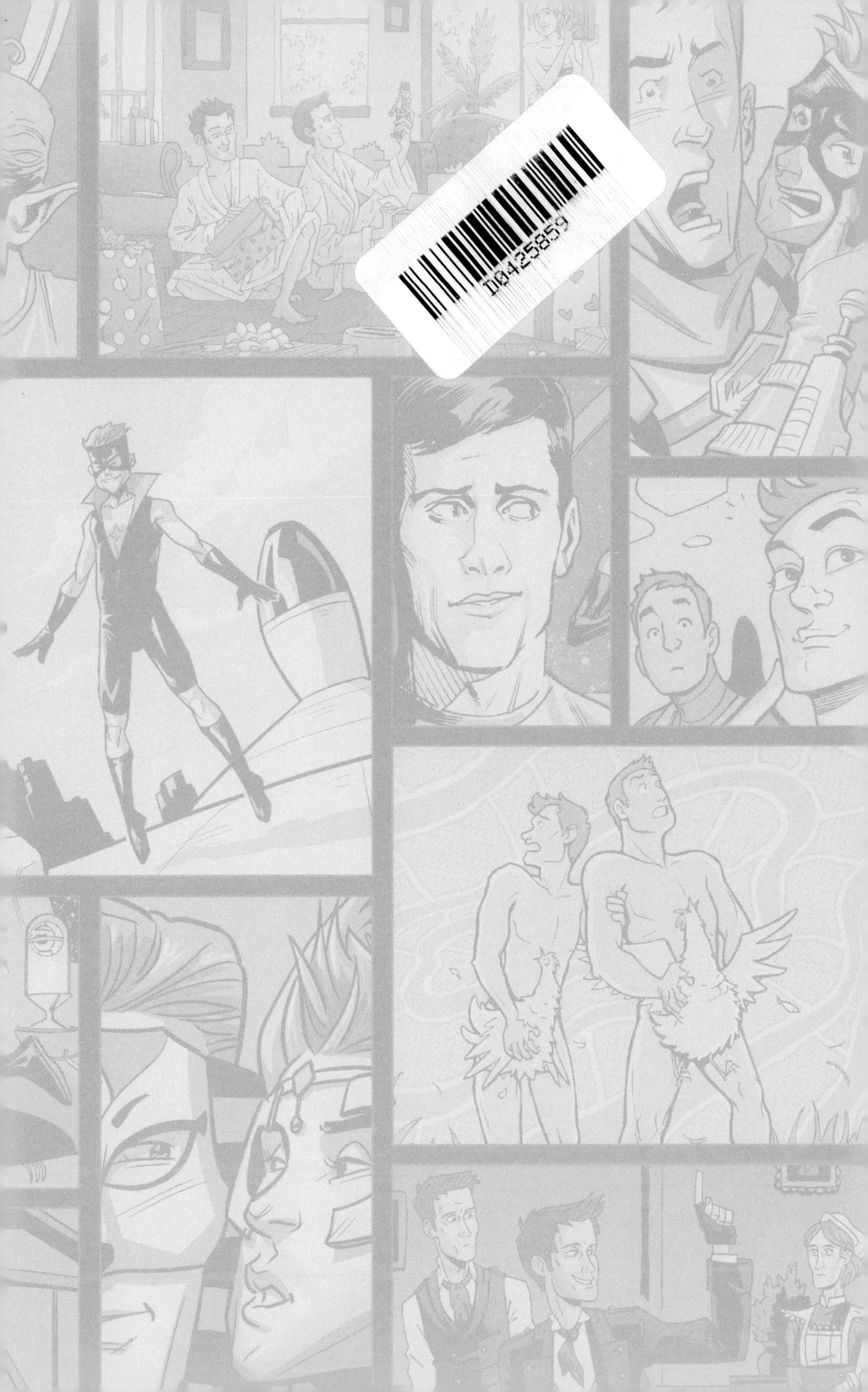

HUSBANDS™

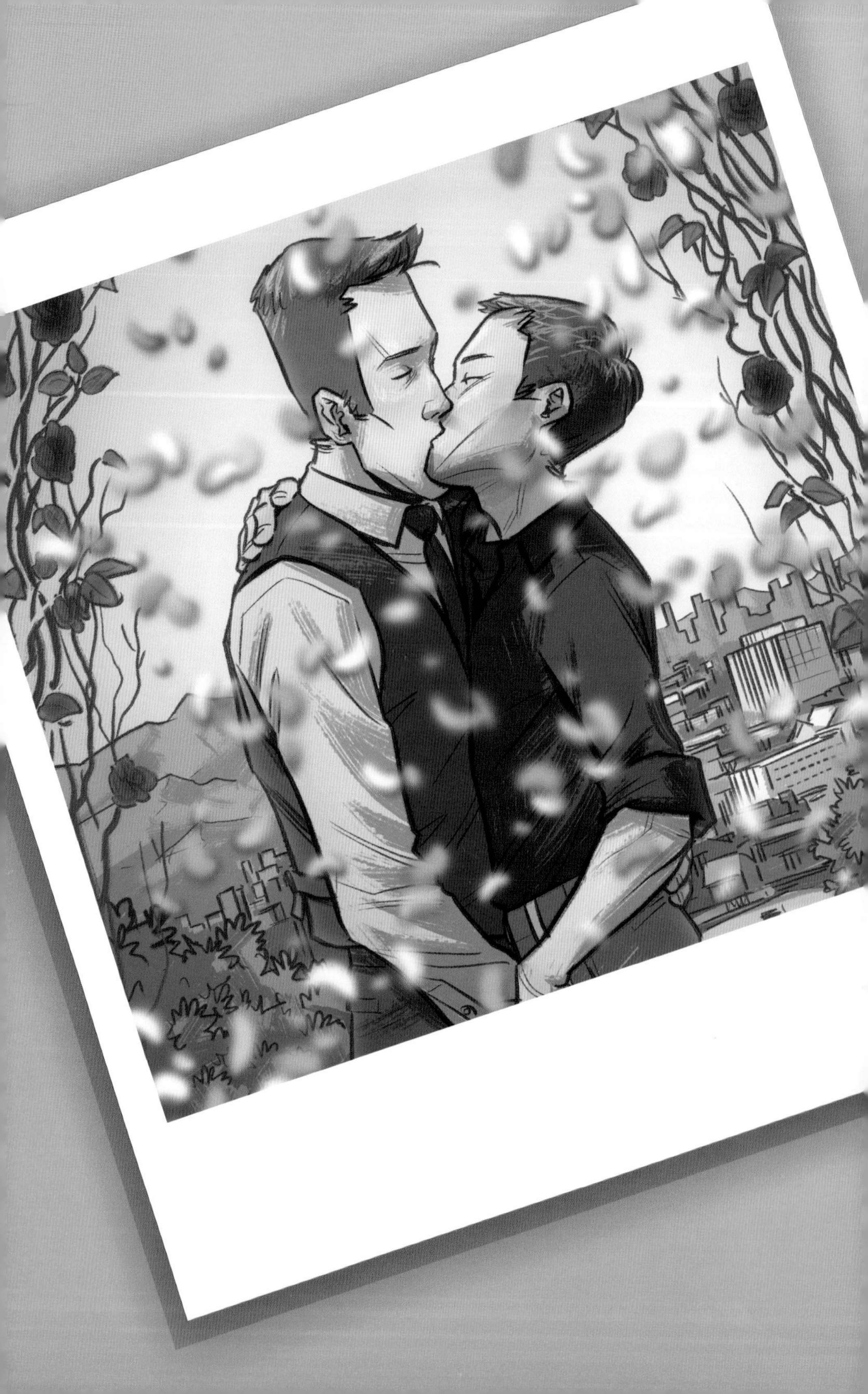

HUSBANDS™

Written and Created by
Brad Bell & **Jane Espenson**

Art by
Ron Chan
Natalie Nourigat
M. S. Corley
Ben Dewey
Tania del Rio

Lettering by
Nate Piekos of Blambot®
Richard Starkings &
Comicraft's Jimmy Betancourt

Cover art by
Ron Chan

Introduction by
Neil Gaiman

Afterword by
Russell T. Davies

DARK HORSE BOOKS

president and publisher
Mike Richardson

editor
Sierra Hahn

assistant editor
Freddye Lins

collection designer
Tina Alessi

Special thanks to Nate Atcheson, Jeff Greenstein, Sean Hemeon,
M. Elizabeth Hughes, Benjamin Kantor, Melanie Marquez,
Alessandra Torresani, Joss Whedon, and all of the wonderfully
supportive and enthusiastic fans who make *Husbands* possible.

*This volume collects Husbands #1–#6, originally published by
Dark Horse Digital.*

Published by Dark Horse Books
A division of Dark Horse Comics, Inc.
10956 SE Main Street
Milwaukie, OR 97222

DarkHorse.com / LoveHusbands.com

International Licensing: (503) 905-2377

To find a comics shop in your area, call the Comic
Shop Locator Service toll-free at 1-888-266-4226.

First edition: March 2013
ISBN 978-1-61655-130-8

10 9 8 7 6 5 4 3 2 1
Printed in China

Mike Richardson President and Publisher / Neil Hankerson
Executive Vice President / Tom Weddle Chief Financial Officer /
Randy Stradley Vice President of Publishing / Michael Martens
Vice President of Book Trade Sales / Anita Nelson Vice President
of Business Affairs / Scott Allie Editor in Chief / Matt Parkinson
Vice President of Marketing / David Scroggy Vice President of
Product Development / Dale LaFountain Vice President of
Information Technology / Darlene Vogel Senior Director of Print,
Design, and Production / Ken Lizzi General Counsel / Davey
Estrada Editorial Director / Chris Warner Senior Books Editor /
Diana Schutz Executive Editor / Cary Grazzini Director of Print
and Development / Lia Ribacchi Art Director / Cara Niece
Director of Scheduling / Tim Wiesch Director of International
Licensing / Mark Bernardi Director of Digital Publishing

CONTENTS

INTRODUCTION

I am not entirely certain how Jane Espenson entered my life. So we aren't friends. Honestly, I'm just a fan.

She's one of the few television writers who are smart and deep and funny and sometimes scary at the same time, which is my favorite kind of television.

I do know exactly how I discovered *Husbands*, though. Jane Espenson tweeted me and told me to watch it. So I watched it.

I'm not a big fan of newlywed comedies (except the first season of *Bewitched*, obviously), but I loved what Jane and Brad Bell were doing with it. The humanness. The love in spite of awkwardness, in spite of everything. So when Jane told me I could have a sneak preview of the *Husbands* comic, I was thrilled.

Husbands the graphic novel is a fun, loving romp through genre. It's smart, gentle, and silly. The jokes are good, the people are human, and I hope they do it again . . .

—Neil Gaiman

Drawn In

1

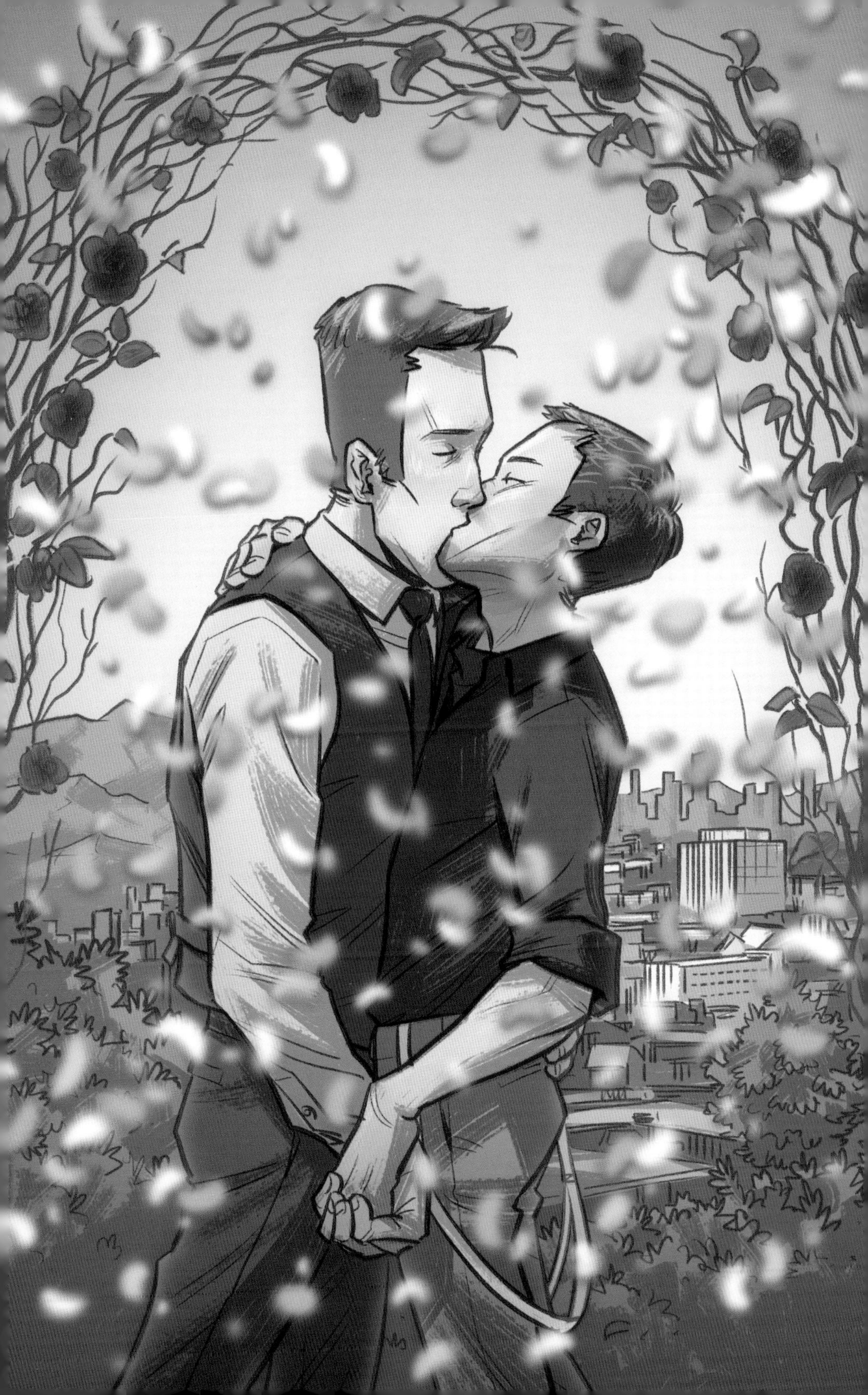

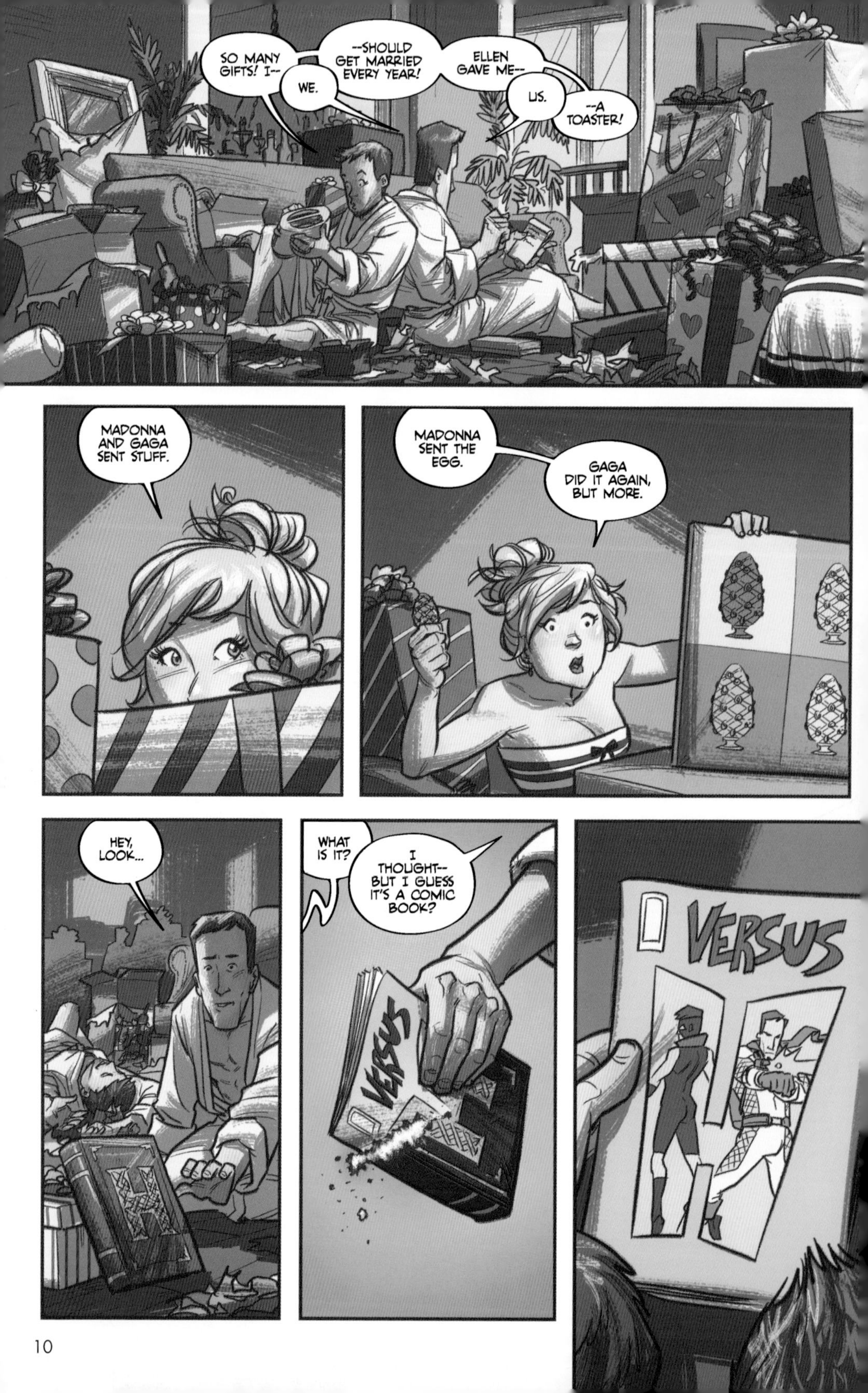
SO MANY GIFTS! I--
WE.
--SHOULD GET MARRIED EVERY YEAR!
ELLEN GAVE ME--
US.
--A TOASTER!
MADONNA AND GAGA SENT STUFF.
MADONNA SENT THE EGG.
GAGA DID IT AGAIN, BUT MORE.
HEY, LOOK...
WHAT IS IT?
I THOUGHT-- BUT I GUESS IT'S A COMIC BOOK?
VERSUS
VERSUS

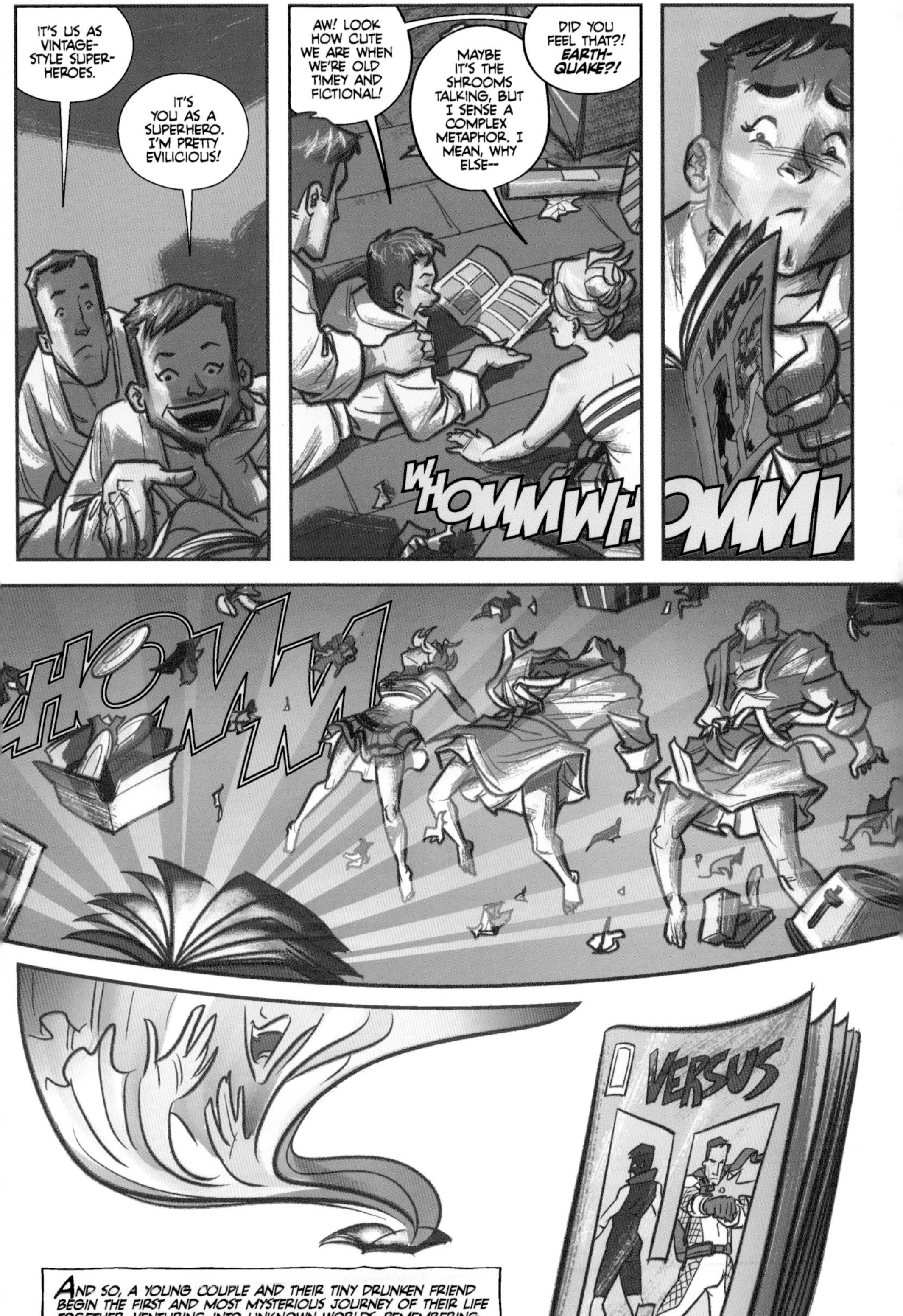

IT'S US AS VINTAGE-STYLE SUPER-HEROES.
IT'S YOU AS A SUPERHERO. I'M PRETTY EVILICIOUS!
AW! LOOK HOW CUTE WE ARE WHEN WE'RE OLD TIMEY AND FICTIONAL!
MAYBE IT'S THE SHROOMS TALKING, BUT I SENSE A COMPLEX METAPHOR. I MEAN, WHY ELSE--
DID YOU FEEL THAT?! EARTH-QUAKE?!
WHOMM WHOMM
WHOMM
VERSUS
VERSUS
AND SO, A YOUNG COUPLE AND THEIR TINY DRUNKEN FRIEND BEGIN THE FIRST AND MOST MYSTERIOUS JOURNEY OF THEIR LIFE TOGETHER, VENTURING INTO UNKNOWN WORLDS, REMEMBERING NOTHING OF THEIR LIVES BEFORE. WHAT MUST THEY LEARN TO RETURN HOME AGAIN?

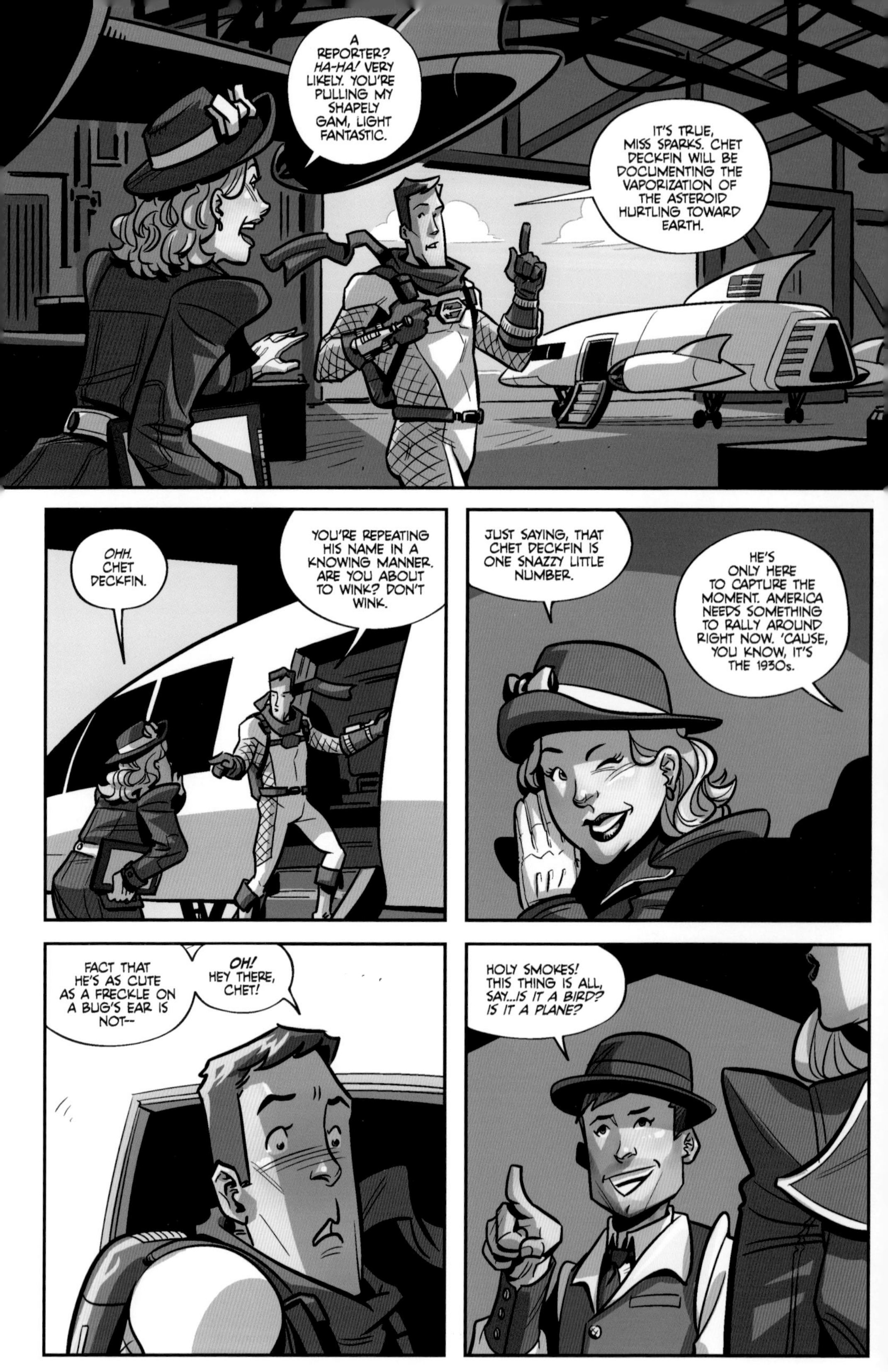
A REPORTER? *HA-HA!* VERY LIKELY. YOU'RE PULLING MY SHAPELY GAM, LIGHT FANTASTIC.
IT'S TRUE, MISS SPARKS. CHET DECKFIN WILL BE DOCUMENTING THE VAPORIZATION OF THE ASTEROID HURTLING TOWARD EARTH.
OHH. CHET DECKFIN.
YOU'RE REPEATING HIS NAME IN A KNOWING MANNER. ARE YOU ABOUT TO WINK? DON'T WINK.
JUST SAYING, THAT CHET DECKFIN IS ONE SNAZZY LITTLE NUMBER.
HE'S ONLY HERE TO CAPTURE THE MOMENT. AMERICA NEEDS SOMETHING TO RALLY AROUND RIGHT NOW. 'CAUSE, YOU KNOW, IT'S THE 1930s.
FACT THAT HE'S AS CUTE AS A FRECKLE ON A BUG'S EAR IS NOT--
OH! HEY THERE, CHET!
HOLY SMOKES! THIS THING IS ALL, SAY...*IS IT A BIRD? IS IT A PLANE?*

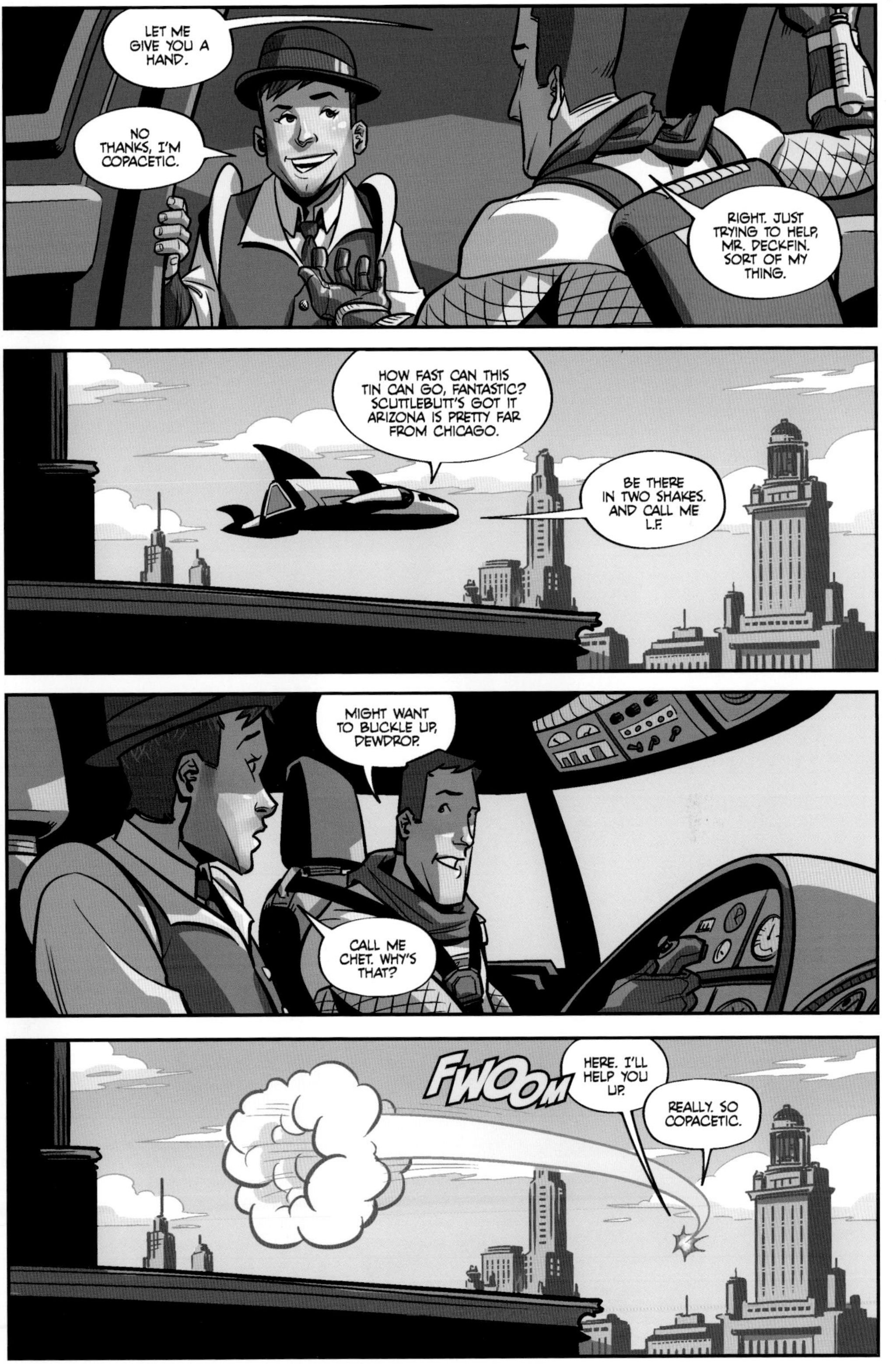
LET ME GIVE YOU A HAND.
NO THANKS, I'M COPACETIC.
RIGHT. JUST TRYING TO HELP, MR. DECKFIN. SORT OF MY THING.
HOW FAST CAN THIS TIN CAN GO, FANTASTIC? SCUTTLEBUTT'S GOT IT ARIZONA IS PRETTY FAR FROM CHICAGO.
BE THERE IN TWO SHAKES. AND CALL ME L.F.
MIGHT WANT TO BUCKLE UP, DEWDROP.
CALL ME CHET. WHY'S THAT?
FWOOM
HERE. I'LL HELP YOU UP.
REALLY. SO COPACETIC.

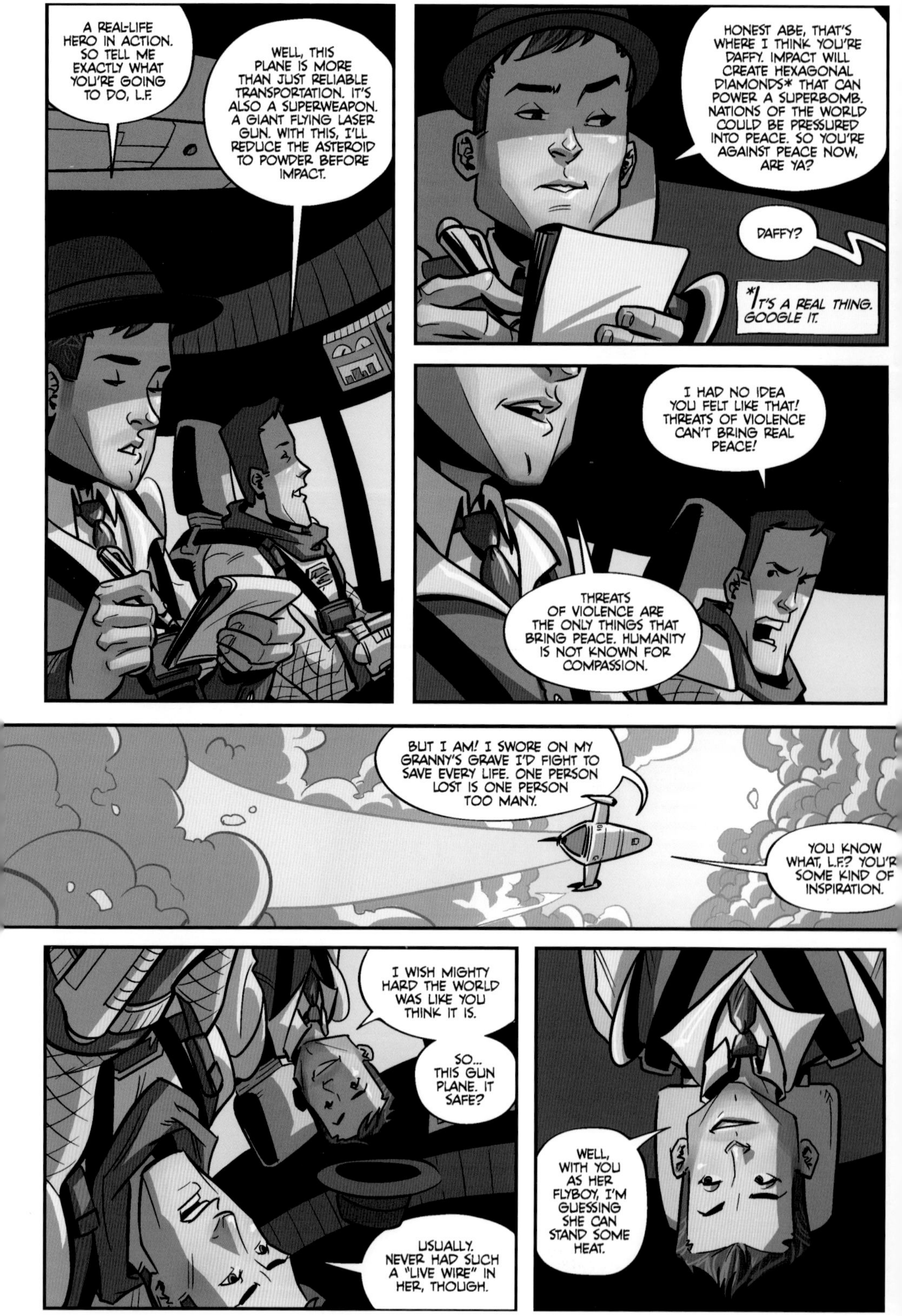
A REAL-LIFE HERO IN ACTION. SO TELL ME EXACTLY WHAT YOU'RE GOING TO DO, L.F.
WELL, THIS PLANE IS MORE THAN JUST RELIABLE TRANSPORTATION. IT'S ALSO A SUPERWEAPON. A GIANT FLYING LASER GUN. WITH THIS, I'LL REDUCE THE ASTEROID TO POWDER BEFORE IMPACT.
HONEST ABE, THAT'S WHERE I THINK YOU'RE DAFFY. IMPACT WILL CREATE HEXAGONAL DIAMONDS* THAT CAN POWER A SUPERBOMB. NATIONS OF THE WORLD COULD BE PRESSURED INTO PEACE. SO YOU'RE AGAINST PEACE NOW, ARE YA?
DAFFY?
*IT'S A REAL THING. GOOGLE IT.
I HAD NO IDEA YOU FELT LIKE THAT! THREATS OF VIOLENCE CAN'T BRING REAL PEACE!
THREATS OF VIOLENCE ARE THE ONLY THINGS THAT BRING PEACE. HUMANITY IS NOT KNOWN FOR COMPASSION.
BUT I AM! I SWORE ON MY GRANNY'S GRAVE I'D FIGHT TO SAVE EVERY LIFE. ONE PERSON LOST IS ONE PERSON TOO MANY.
YOU KNOW WHAT, L.F.? YOU'R SOME KIND OF INSPIRATION.
I WISH MIGHTY HARD THE WORLD WAS LIKE YOU THINK IT IS.
SO... THIS GUN PLANE. IT SAFE?
USUALLY. NEVER HAD SUCH A "LIVE WIRE" IN HER, THOUGH.
WELL, WITH YOU AS HER FLYBOY, I'M GUESSING SHE CAN STAND SOME HEAT.

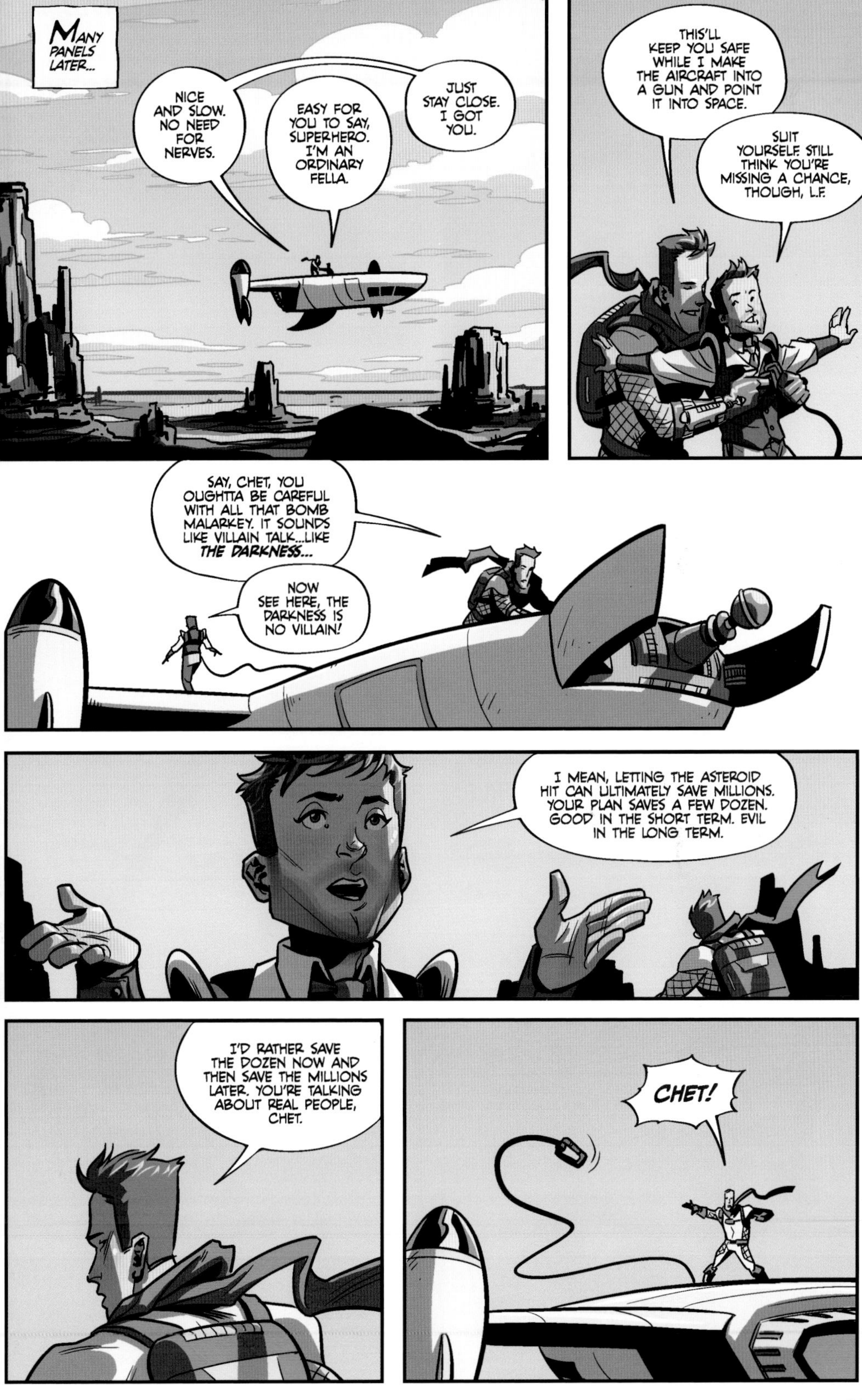
MANY PANELS LATER...
NICE AND SLOW. NO NEED FOR NERVES.
EASY FOR YOU TO SAY, SUPERHERO. I'M AN ORDINARY FELLA.
JUST STAY CLOSE. I GOT YOU.
THIS'LL KEEP YOU SAFE WHILE I MAKE THE AIRCRAFT INTO A GUN AND POINT IT INTO SPACE.
SUIT YOURSELF. STILL THINK YOU'RE MISSING A CHANCE, THOUGH, L.F.
SAY, CHET, YOU OUGHTTA BE CAREFUL WITH ALL THAT BOMB MALARKEY. IT SOUNDS LIKE VILLAIN TALK...LIKE *THE DARKNESS...*
NOW SEE HERE, THE DARKNESS IS NO VILLAIN!
I MEAN, LETTING THE ASTEROID HIT CAN ULTIMATELY SAVE MILLIONS. YOUR PLAN SAVES A FEW DOZEN. GOOD IN THE SHORT TERM. EVIL IN THE LONG TERM.
I'D RATHER SAVE THE DOZEN NOW AND THEN SAVE THE MILLIONS LATER. YOU'RE TALKING ABOUT REAL PEOPLE, CHET.
CHET!

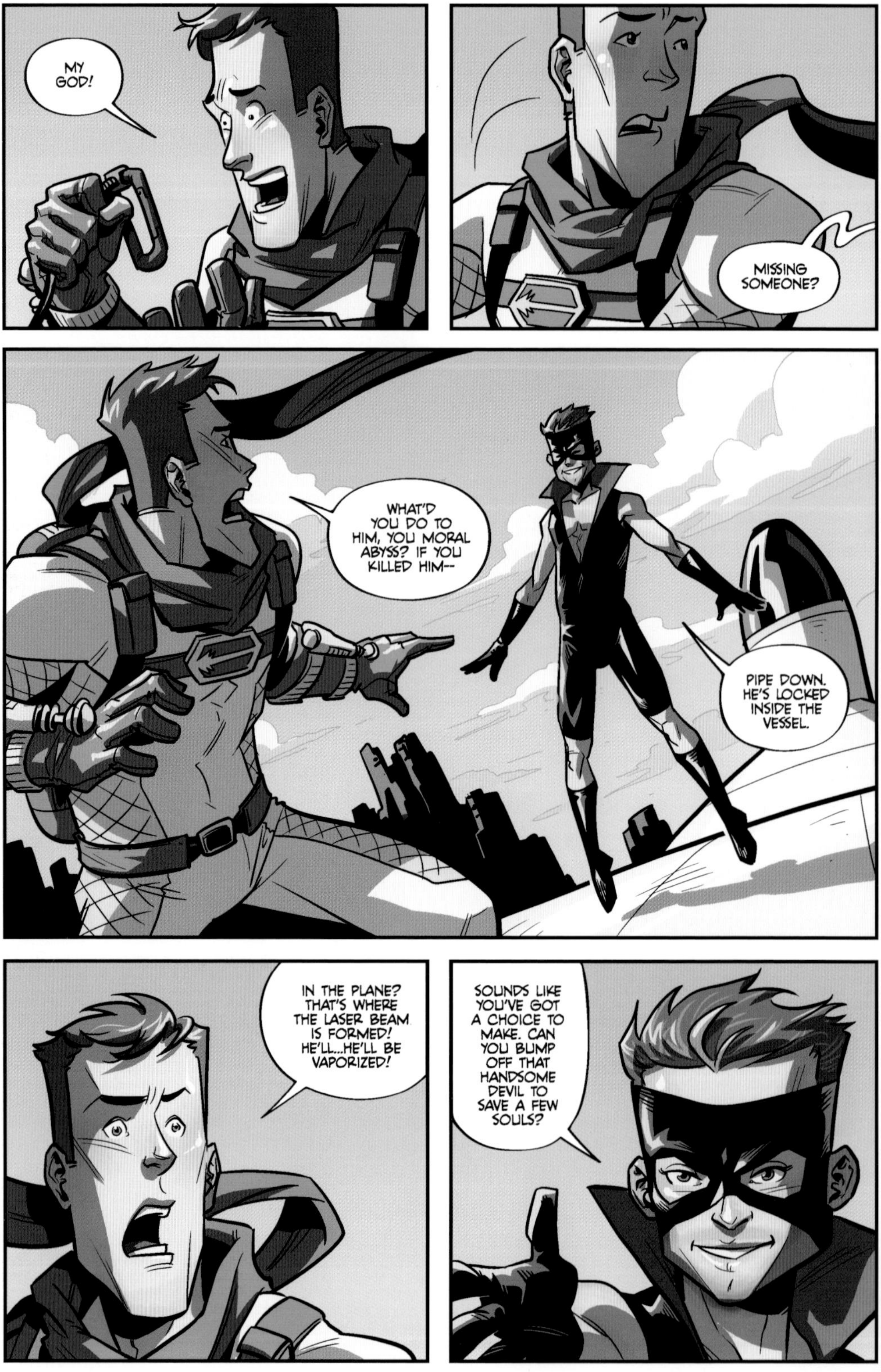
MY GOD!
MISSING SOMEONE?
WHAT'D YOU DO TO HIM, YOU MORAL ABYSS? IF YOU KILLED HIM--
PIPE DOWN. HE'S LOCKED INSIDE THE VESSEL.
IN THE PLANE? THAT'S WHERE THE LASER BEAM IS FORMED! HE'LL...HE'LL BE VAPORIZED!
SOUNDS LIKE YOU'VE GOT A CHOICE TO MAKE. CAN YOU BUMP OFF THAT HANDSOME DEVIL TO SAVE A FEW SOULS?

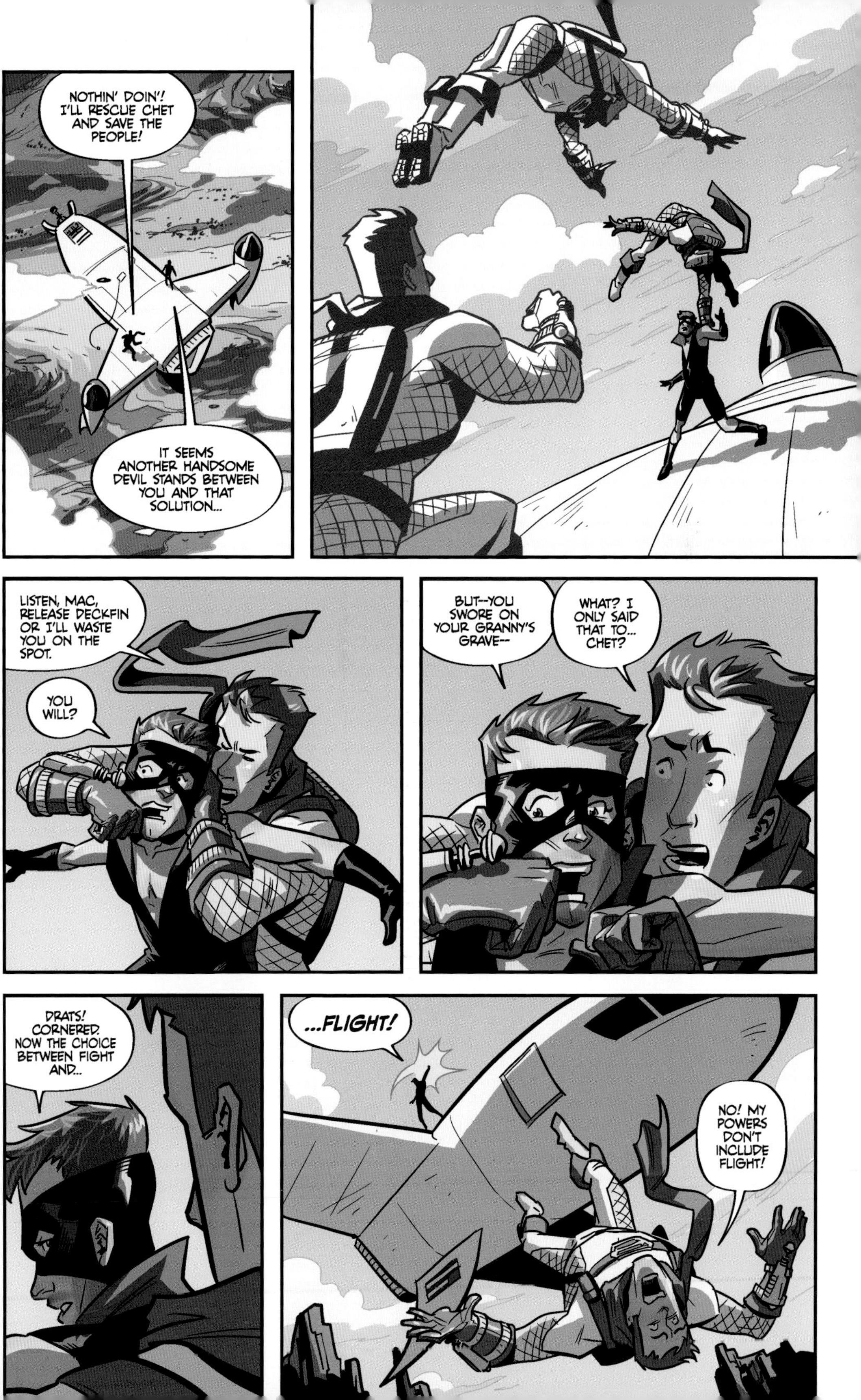
NOTHIN' DOIN'! I'LL RESCUE CHET AND SAVE THE PEOPLE!
IT SEEMS ANOTHER HANDSOME DEVIL STANDS BETWEEN YOU AND THAT SOLUTION...
LISTEN, MAC, RELEASE DECKFIN OR I'LL WASTE YOU ON THE SPOT.
YOU WILL?
BUT--YOU SWORE ON YOUR GRANNY'S GRAVE--
WHAT? I ONLY SAID THAT TO... CHET?
DRATS! CORNERED. NOW THE CHOICE BETWEEN FIGHT AND...
...FLIGHT!
NO! MY POWERS DON'T INCLUDE FLIGHT!

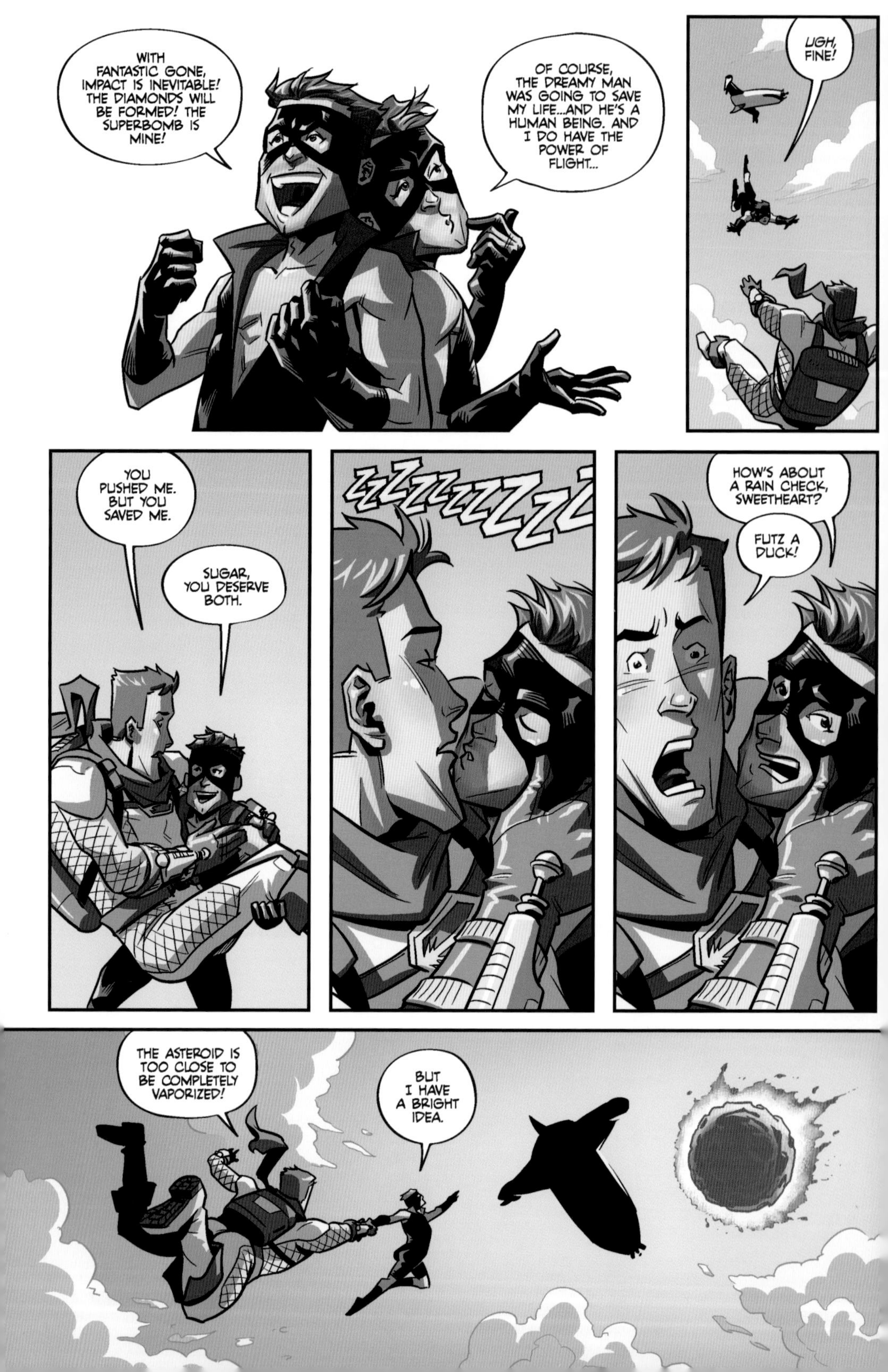
WITH FANTASTIC GONE, IMPACT IS INEVITABLE! THE DIAMONDS WILL BE FORMED! THE SUPERBOMB IS MINE!
OF COURSE, THE DREAMY MAN WAS GOING TO SAVE MY LIFE...AND HE'S A HUMAN BEING. AND I DO HAVE THE POWER OF FLIGHT...
UGH, FINE!
YOU PUSHED ME. BUT YOU SAVED ME.
SUGAR, YOU DESERVE BOTH.
ZZZZZZZZZZZZ
HOW'S ABOUT A RAIN CHECK, SWEETHEART?
FUTZ A DUCK!
THE ASTEROID IS TOO CLOSE TO BE COMPLETELY VAPORIZED!
BUT I HAVE A BRIGHT IDEA.

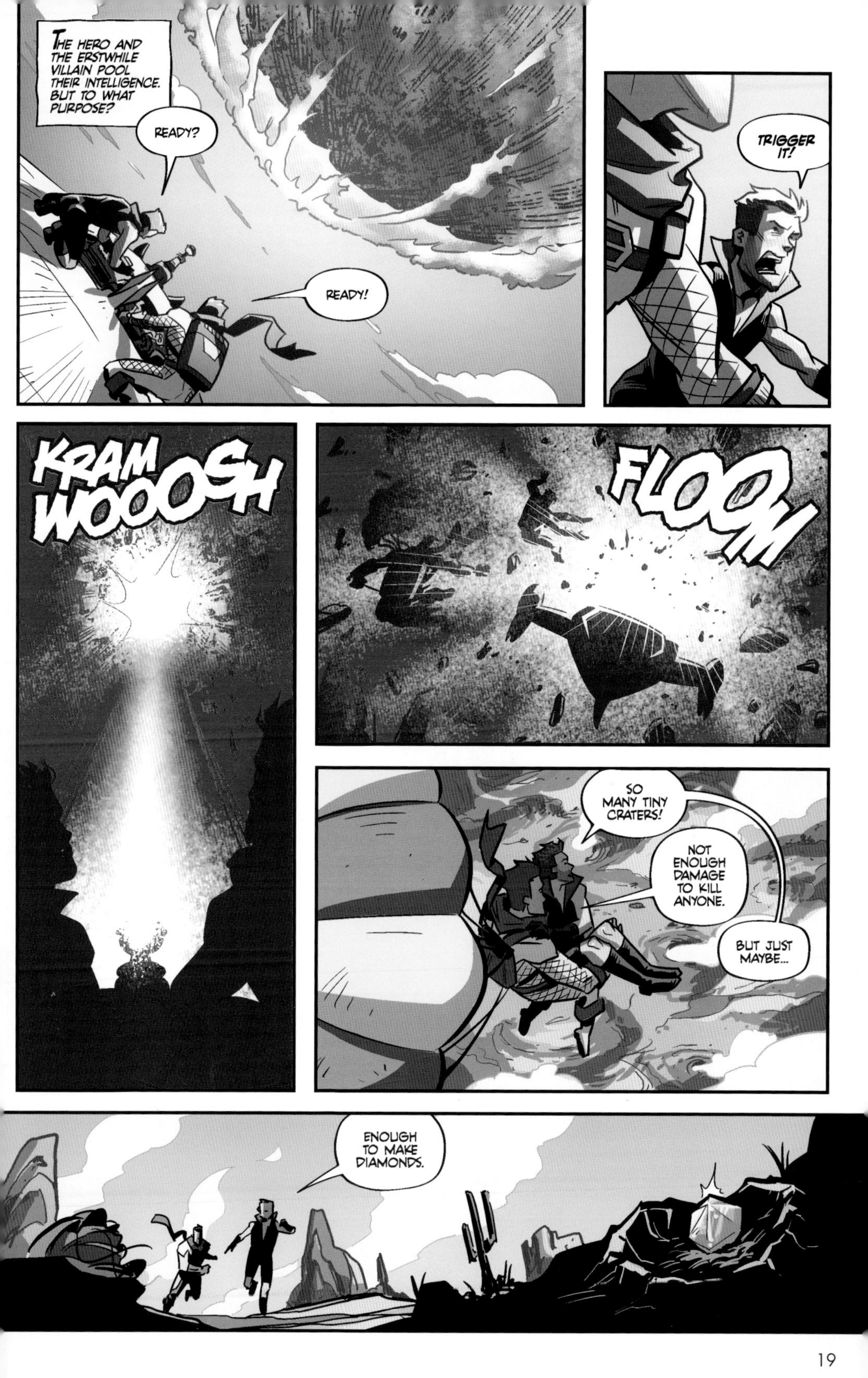
THE HERO AND THE ERSTWHILE VILLAIN POOL THEIR INTELLIGENCE. BUT TO WHAT PURPOSE?
READY?
READY!
TRIGGER IT!
KRAM WOOOSH
FLOOM
SO MANY TINY CRATERS!
NOT ENOUGH DAMAGE TO KILL ANYONE.
BUT JUST MAYBE...
ENOUGH TO MAKE DIAMONDS.

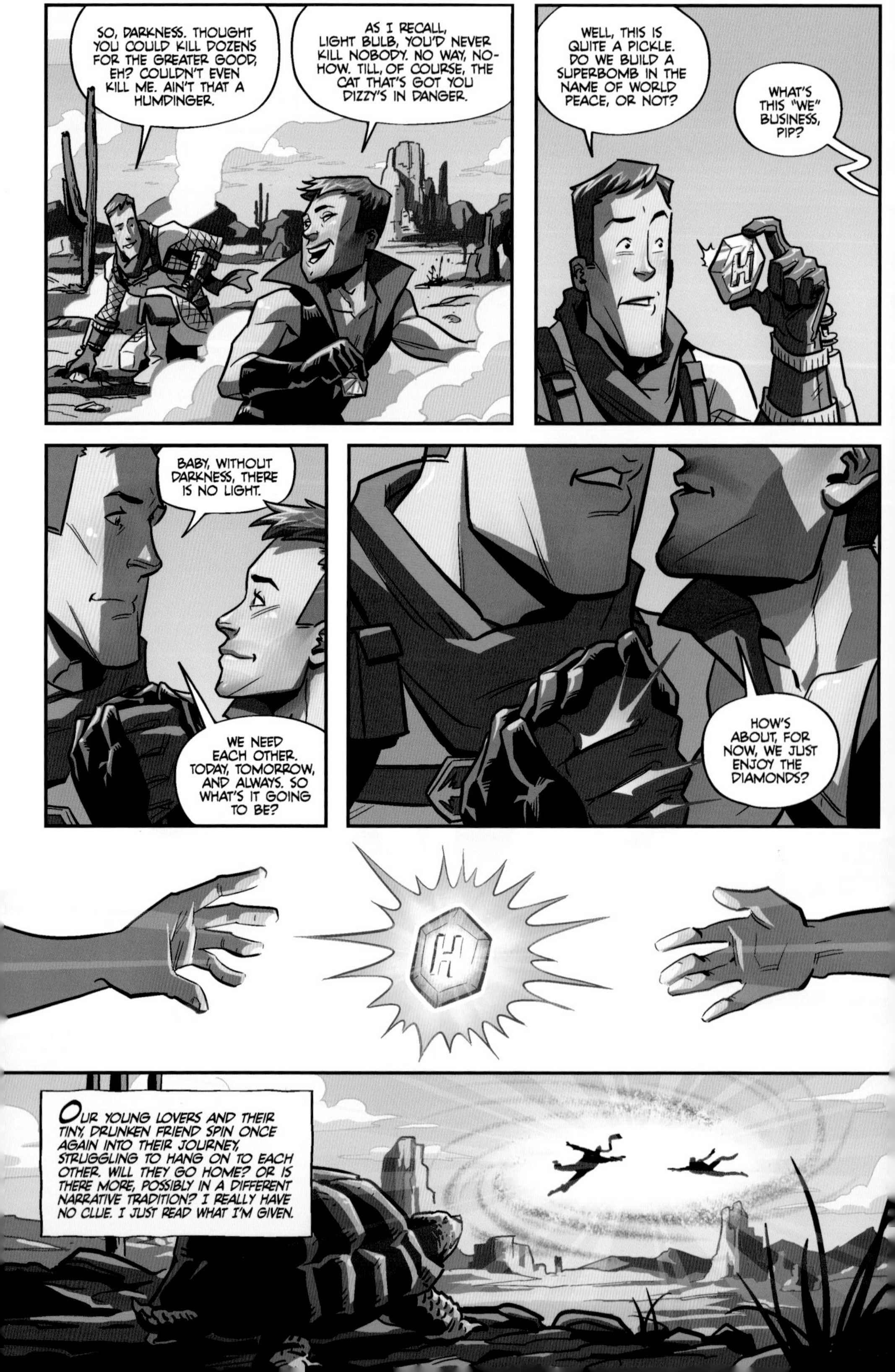
SO, DARKNESS. THOUGHT YOU COULD KILL DOZENS FOR THE GREATER GOOD, EH? COULDN'T EVEN KILL ME. AIN'T THAT A HUMDINGER.
AS I RECALL, LIGHT BULB, YOU'D NEVER KILL NOBODY. NO WAY, NO-HOW. TILL, OF COURSE, THE CAT THAT'S GOT YOU DIZZY'S IN DANGER.
WELL, THIS IS QUITE A PICKLE. DO WE BUILD A SUPERBOMB IN THE NAME OF WORLD PEACE, OR NOT?
WHAT'S THIS "WE" BUSINESS, PIP?
BABY, WITHOUT DARKNESS, THERE IS NO LIGHT.
WE NEED EACH OTHER. TODAY, TOMORROW, AND ALWAYS. SO WHAT'S IT GOING TO BE?
HOW'S ABOUT, FOR NOW, WE JUST ENJOY THE DIAMONDS?
OUR YOUNG LOVERS AND THEIR TINY, DRUNKEN FRIEND SPIN ONCE AGAIN INTO THEIR JOURNEY, STRUGGLING TO HANG ON TO EACH OTHER. WILL THEY GO HOME? OR IS THERE MORE, POSSIBLY IN A DIFFERENT NARRATIVE TRADITION? I REALLY HAVE NO CLUE. I JUST READ WHAT I'M GIVEN.

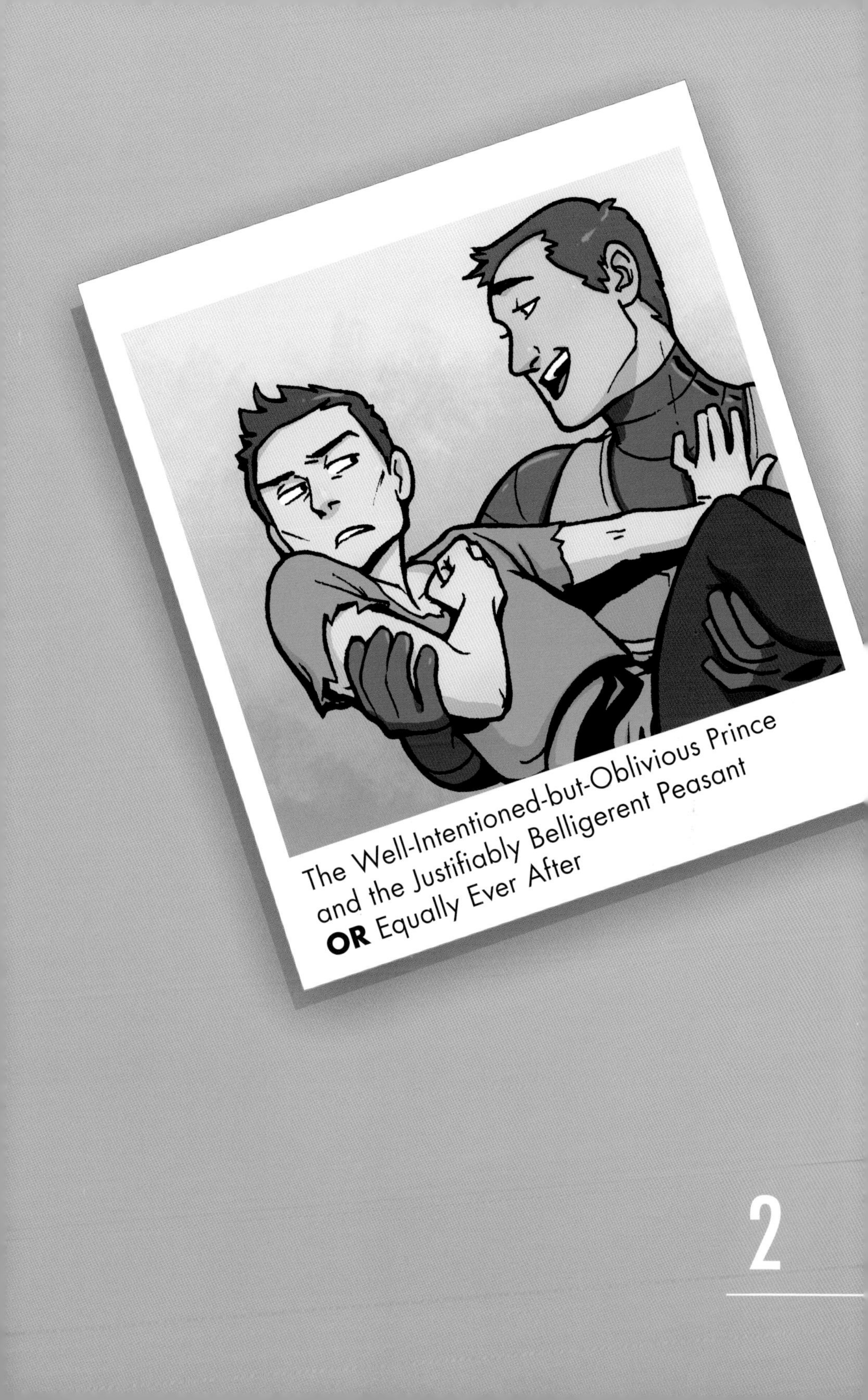

The Well-Intentioned-but-Oblivious Prince and the Justifiably Belligerent Peasant **OR** Equally Ever After

2

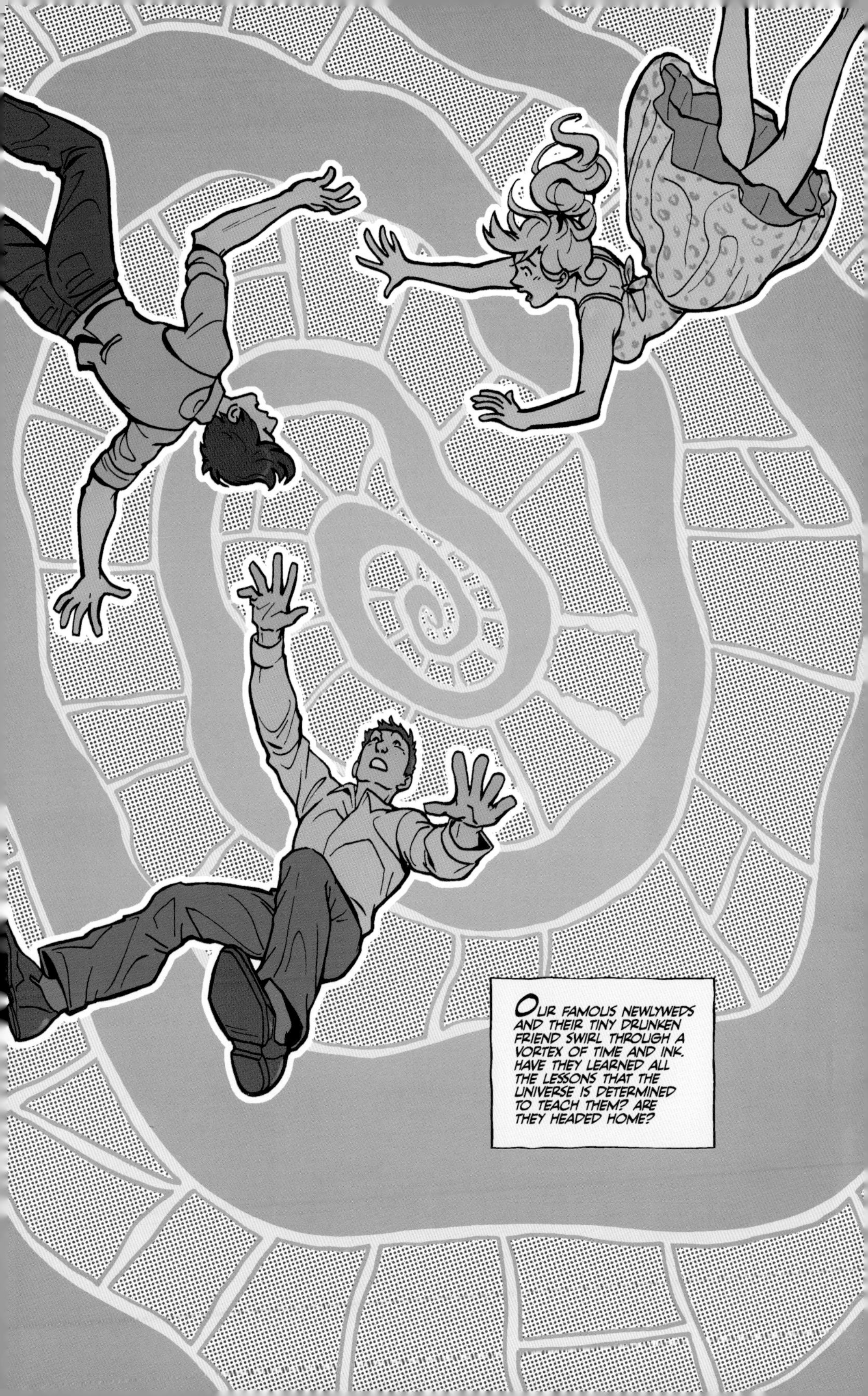
OUR FAMOUS NEWLYWEDS AND THEIR TINY DRUNKEN FRIEND SWIRL THROUGH A VORTEX OF TIME AND INK. HAVE THEY LEARNED ALL THE LESSONS THAT THE UNIVERSE IS DETERMINED TO TEACH THEM? ARE THEY HEADED HOME?

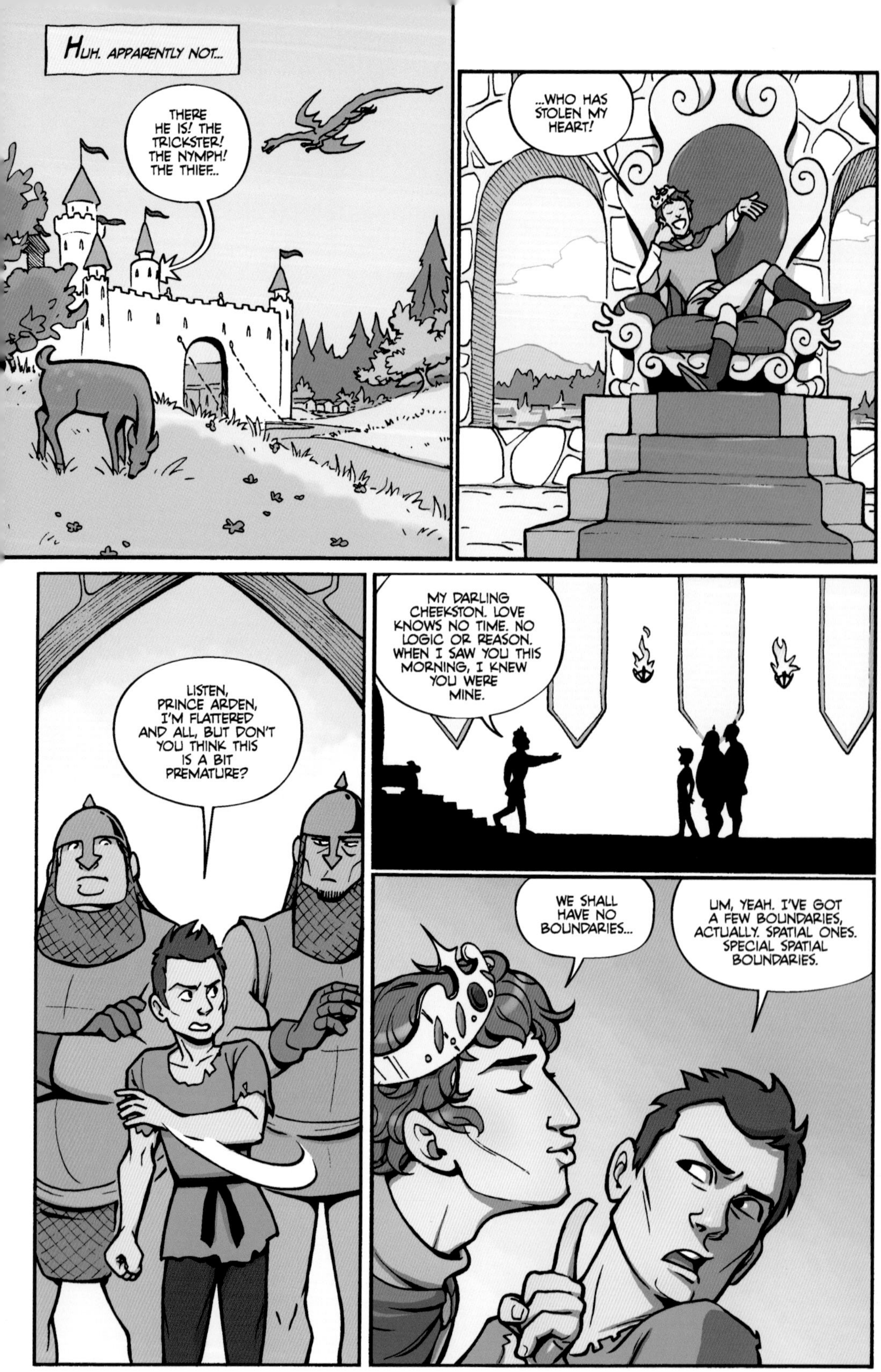
HUH. APPARENTLY NOT...
THERE HE IS! THE TRICKSTER! THE NYMPH! THE THIEF..
...WHO HAS STOLEN MY HEART!
LISTEN, PRINCE ARDEN, I'M FLATTERED AND ALL, BUT DON'T YOU THINK THIS IS A BIT PREMATURE?
MY DARLING CHEEKSTON. LOVE KNOWS NO TIME. NO LOGIC OR REASON. WHEN I SAW YOU THIS MORNING, I KNEW YOU WERE MINE.
WE SHALL HAVE NO BOUNDARIES...
UM, YEAH. I'VE GOT A FEW BOUNDARIES, ACTUALLY. SPATIAL ONES. SPECIAL SPATIAL BOUNDARIES.

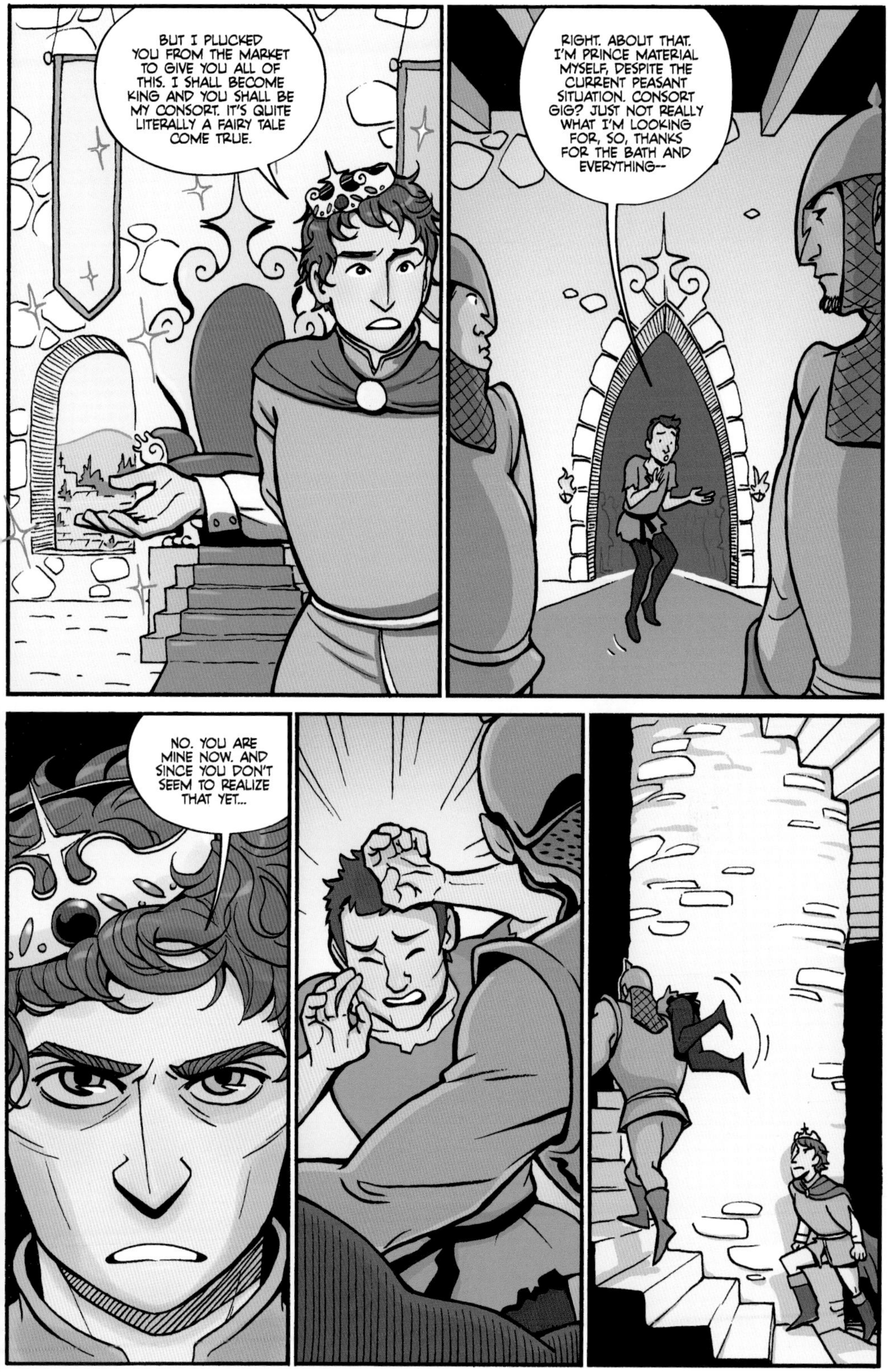
BUT I PLUCKED YOU FROM THE MARKET TO GIVE YOU ALL OF THIS. I SHALL BECOME KING AND YOU SHALL BE MY CONSORT. IT'S QUITE LITERALLY A FAIRY TALE COME TRUE.
RIGHT. ABOUT THAT. I'M PRINCE MATERIAL MYSELF, DESPITE THE CURRENT PEASANT SITUATION. CONSORT GIG? JUST NOT REALLY WHAT I'M LOOKING FOR, SO, THANKS FOR THE BATH AND EVERYTHING--
NO. YOU ARE MINE NOW. AND SINCE YOU DON'T SEEM TO REALIZE THAT YET...

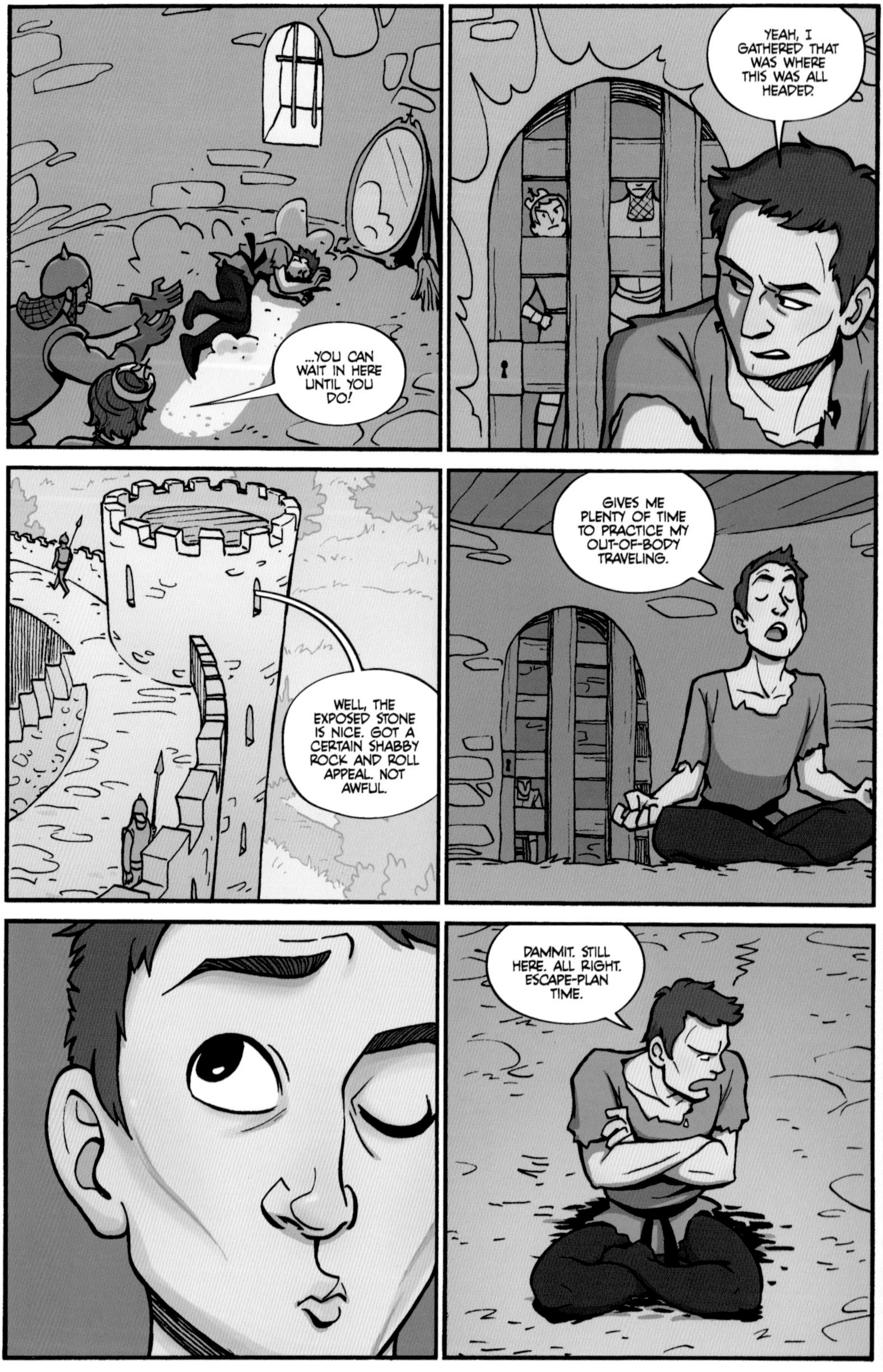
...YOU CAN WAIT IN HERE UNTIL YOU DO!
YEAH, I GATHERED THAT WAS WHERE THIS WAS ALL HEADED.
WELL, THE EXPOSED STONE IS NICE. GOT A CERTAIN SHABBY ROCK AND ROLL APPEAL. NOT AWFUL.
GIVES ME PLENTY OF TIME TO PRACTICE MY OUT-OF-BODY TRAVELING.
DAMMIT. STILL HERE. ALL RIGHT. ESCAPE-PLAN TIME.

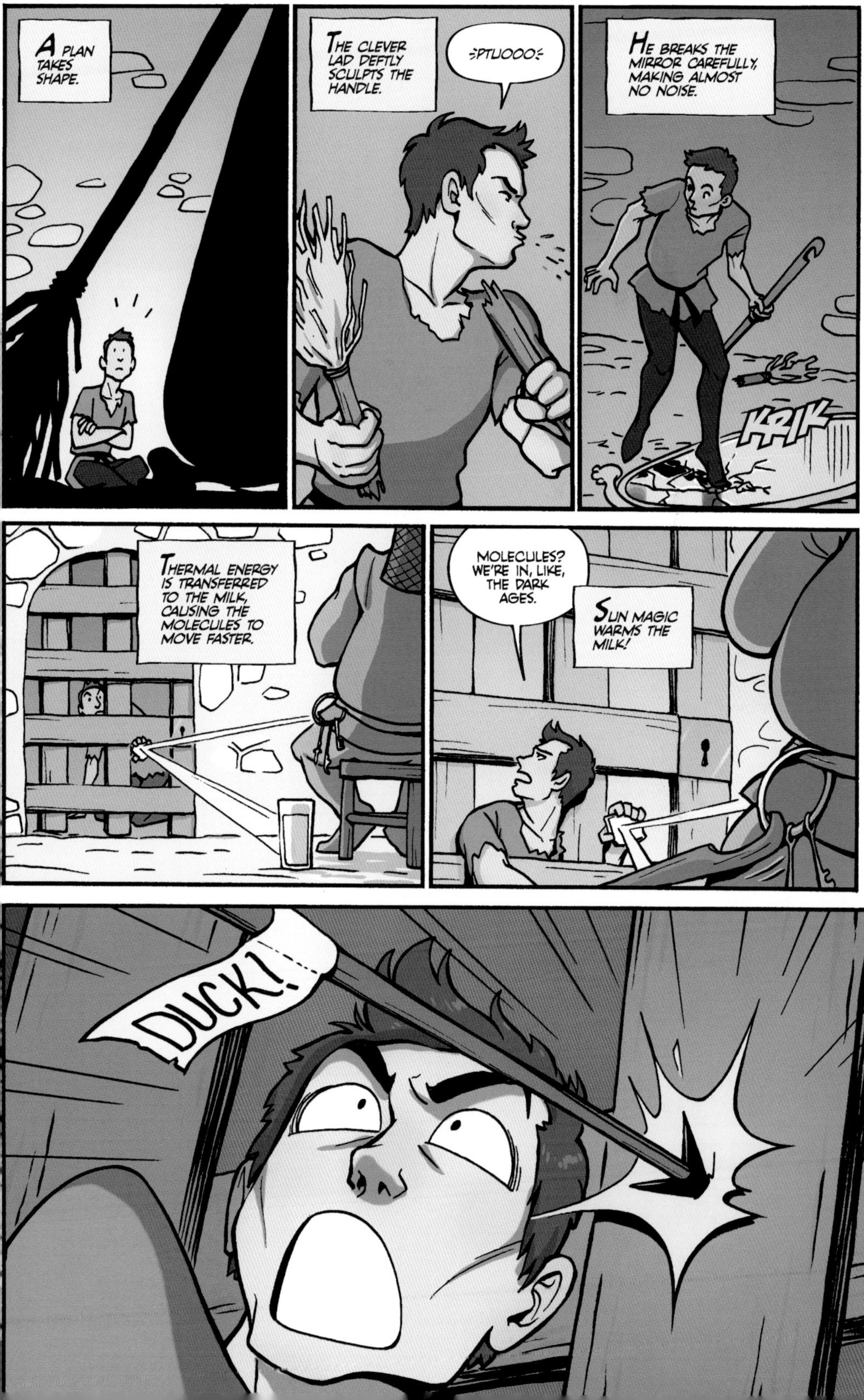
A PLAN TAKES SHAPE.
THE CLEVER LAD DEFTLY SCULPTS THE HANDLE.
PTUOOO
HE BREAKS THE MIRROR CAREFULLY, MAKING ALMOST NO NOISE.
KRIK
THERMAL ENERGY IS TRANSFERRED TO THE MILK, CAUSING THE MOLECULES TO MOVE FASTER.
MOLECULES? WE'RE IN, LIKE, THE DARK AGES.
SUN MAGIC WARMS THE MILK!
DUCK!

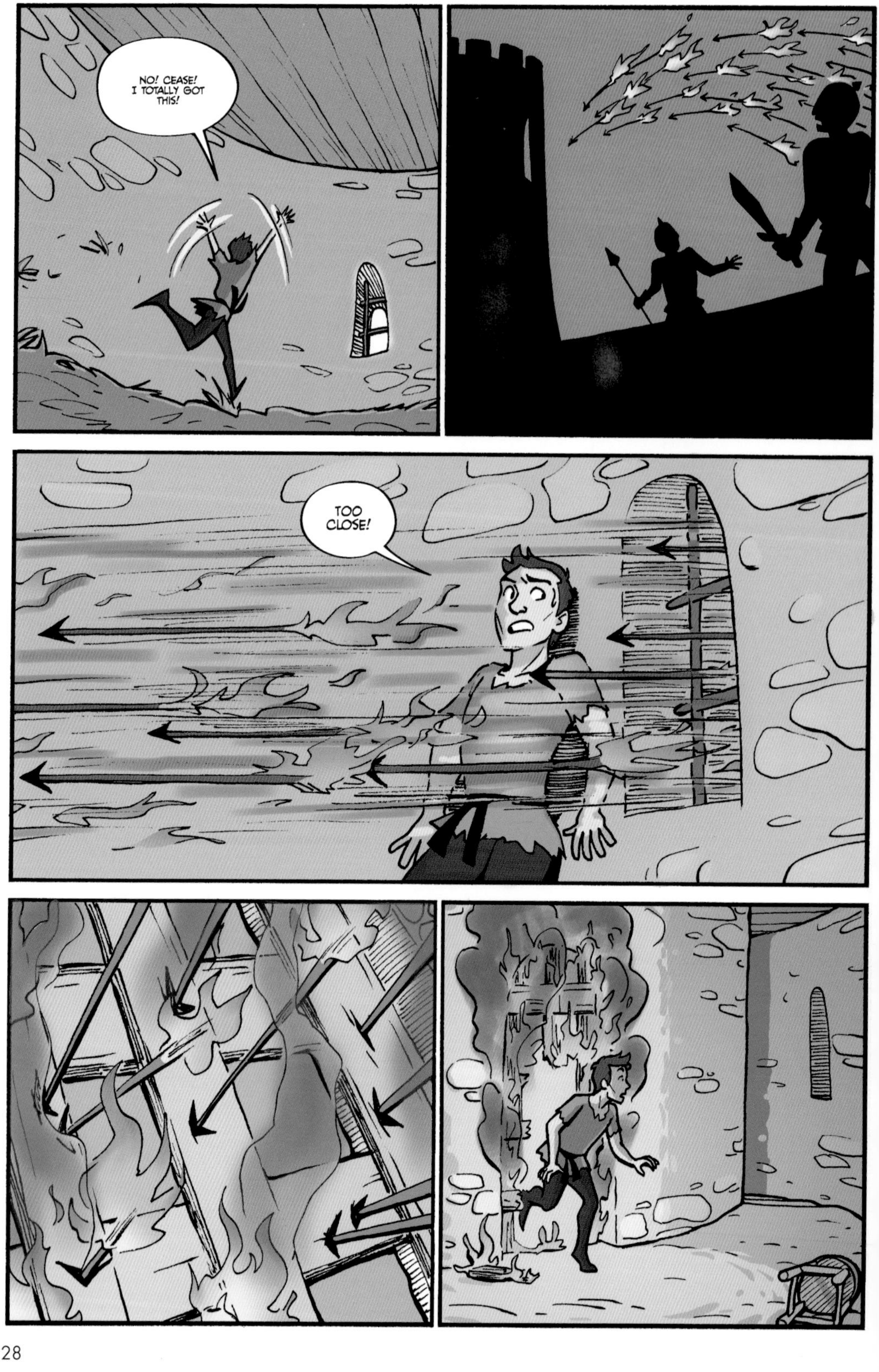
NO! CEASE! I TOTALLY GOT THIS!
TOO CLOSE!

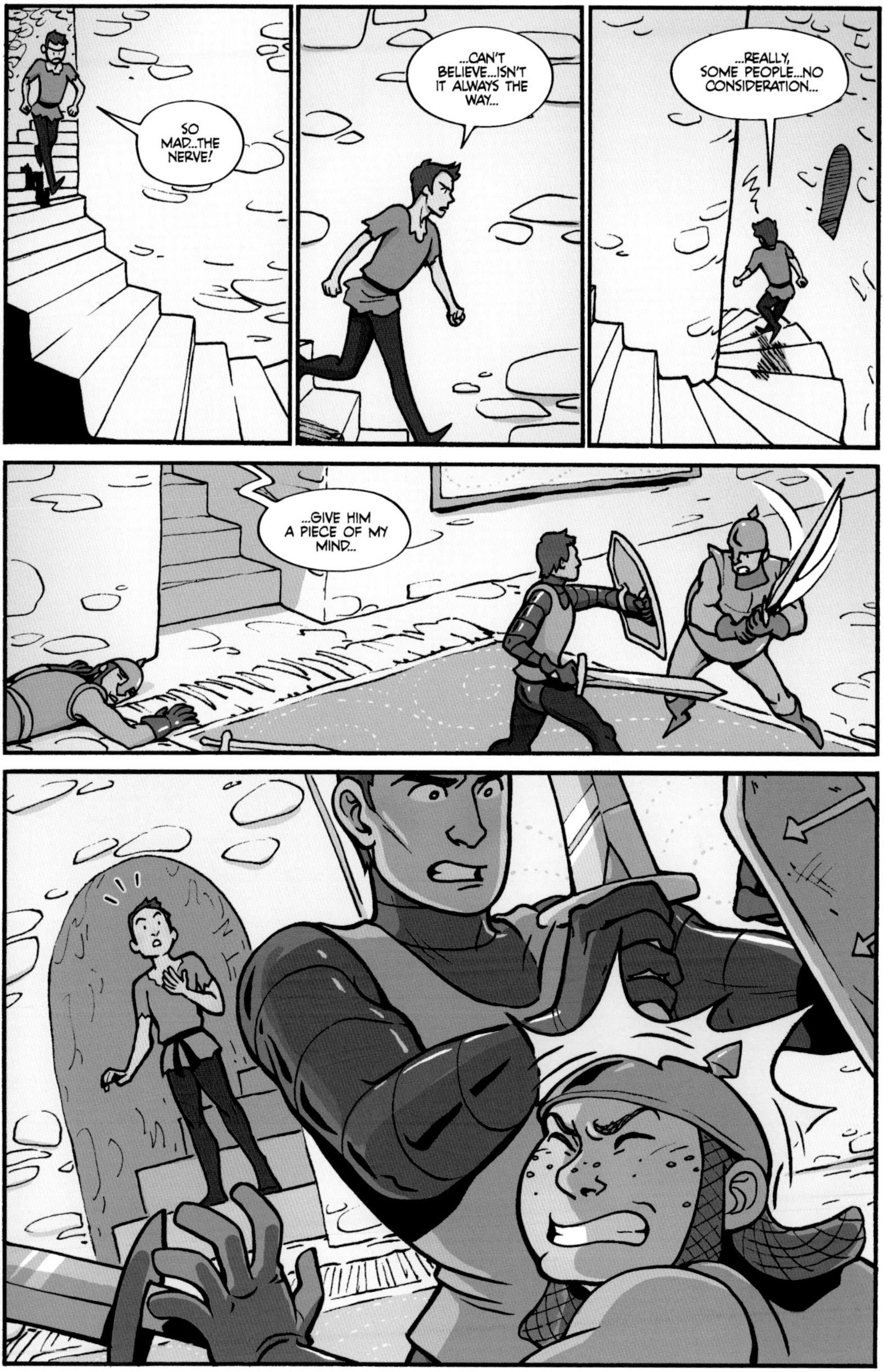
SO MAD...THE NERVE!
...CAN'T BELIEVE...ISN'T IT ALWAYS THE WAY...
...REALLY, SOME PEOPLE...NO CONSIDERATION...
...GIVE HIM A PIECE OF MY MIND...

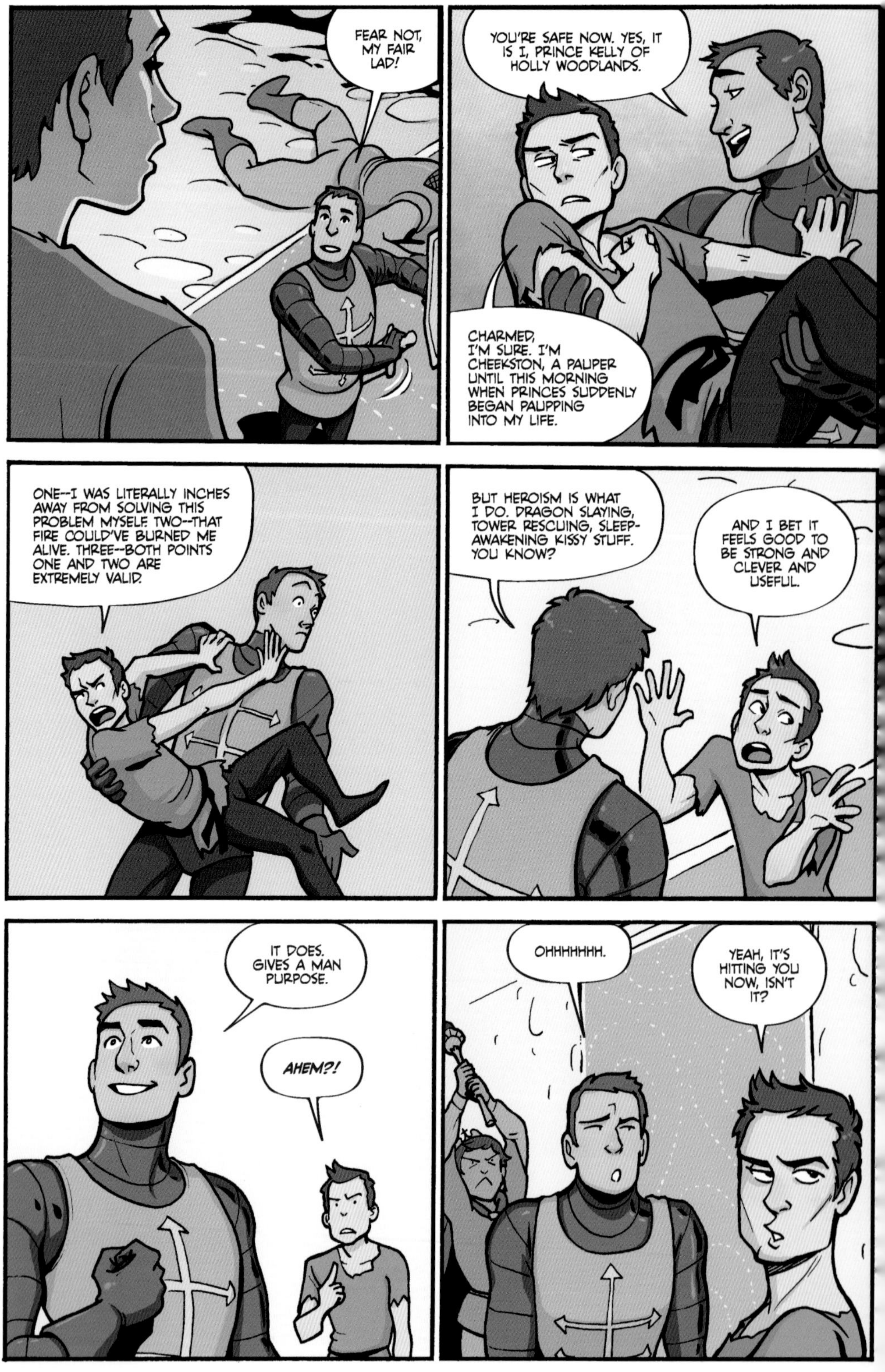
FEAR NOT, MY FAIR LAD!
YOU'RE SAFE NOW. YES, IT IS I, PRINCE KELLY OF HOLLY WOODLANDS.
CHARMED, I'M SURE. I'M CHEEKSTON, A PAUPER UNTIL THIS MORNING WHEN PRINCES SUDDENLY BEGAN PAUPPING INTO MY LIFE.
ONE--I WAS LITERALLY INCHES AWAY FROM SOLVING THIS PROBLEM MYSELF. TWO--THAT FIRE COULD'VE BURNED ME ALIVE. THREE--BOTH POINTS ONE AND TWO ARE EXTREMELY VALID.
BUT HEROISM IS WHAT I DO. DRAGON SLAYING, TOWER RESCUING, SLEEP-AWAKENING KISSY STUFF. YOU KNOW?
AND I BET IT FEELS GOOD TO BE STRONG AND CLEVER AND USEFUL.
IT DOES. GIVES A MAN PURPOSE.
AHEM?!
OHHHHHHH.
YEAH, IT'S HITTING YOU NOW, ISN'T IT?

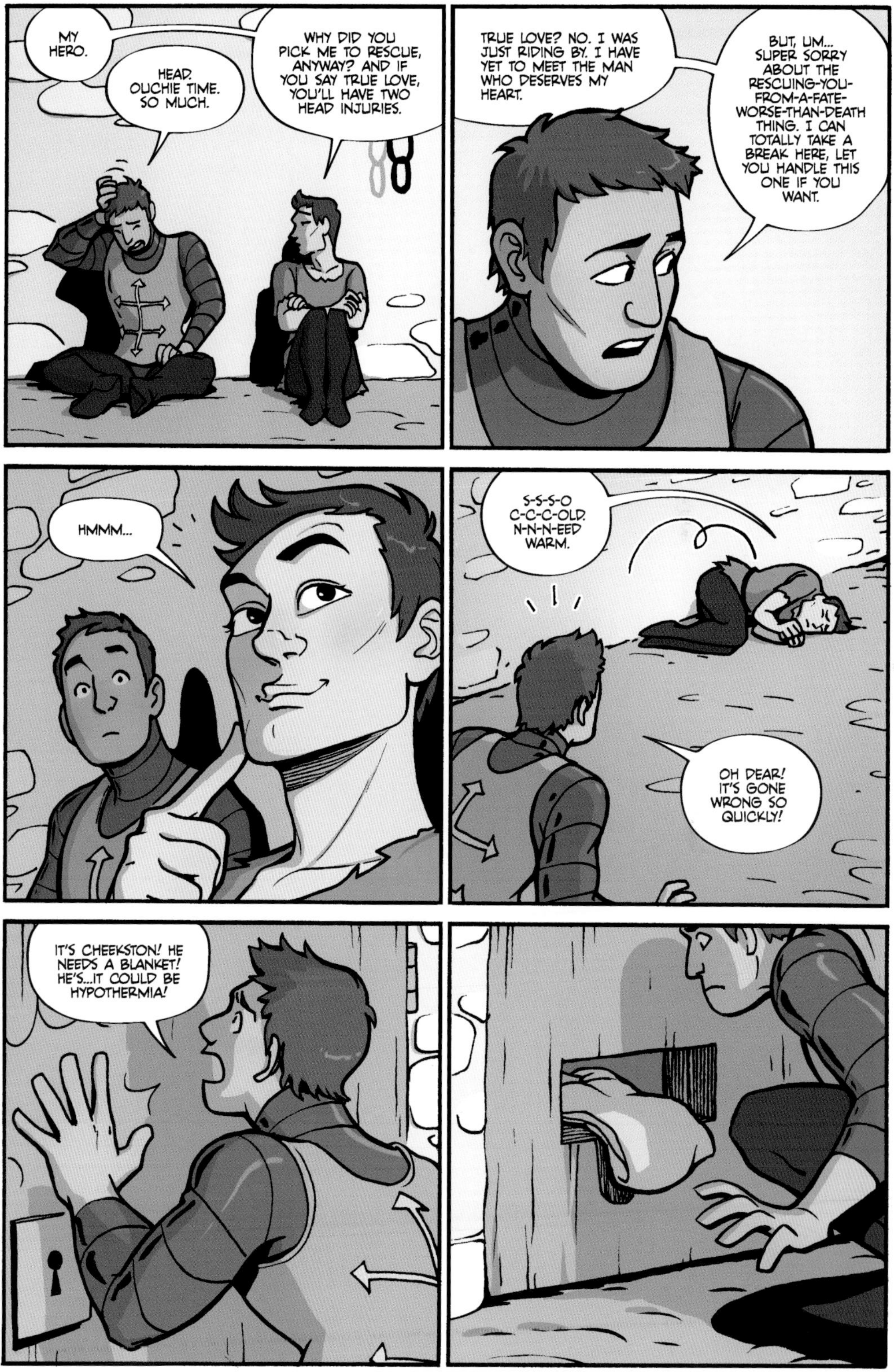
MY HERO.
HEAD. OUCHIE TIME. SO MUCH.
WHY DID YOU PICK ME TO RESCUE, ANYWAY? AND IF YOU SAY TRUE LOVE, YOU'LL HAVE TWO HEAD INJURIES.
TRUE LOVE? NO. I WAS JUST RIDING BY. I HAVE YET TO MEET THE MAN WHO DESERVES MY HEART.
BUT, UM... SUPER SORRY ABOUT THE RESCUING-YOU-FROM-A-FATE-WORSE-THAN-DEATH THING. I CAN TOTALLY TAKE A BREAK HERE, LET YOU HANDLE THIS ONE IF YOU WANT.
HMMM...
S-S-S-O C-C-C-OLD. N-N-N-EED WARM.
OH DEAR! IT'S GONE WRONG SO QUICKLY!
IT'S CHEEKSTON! HE NEEDS A BLANKET! HE'S...IT COULD BE HYPOTHERMIA!

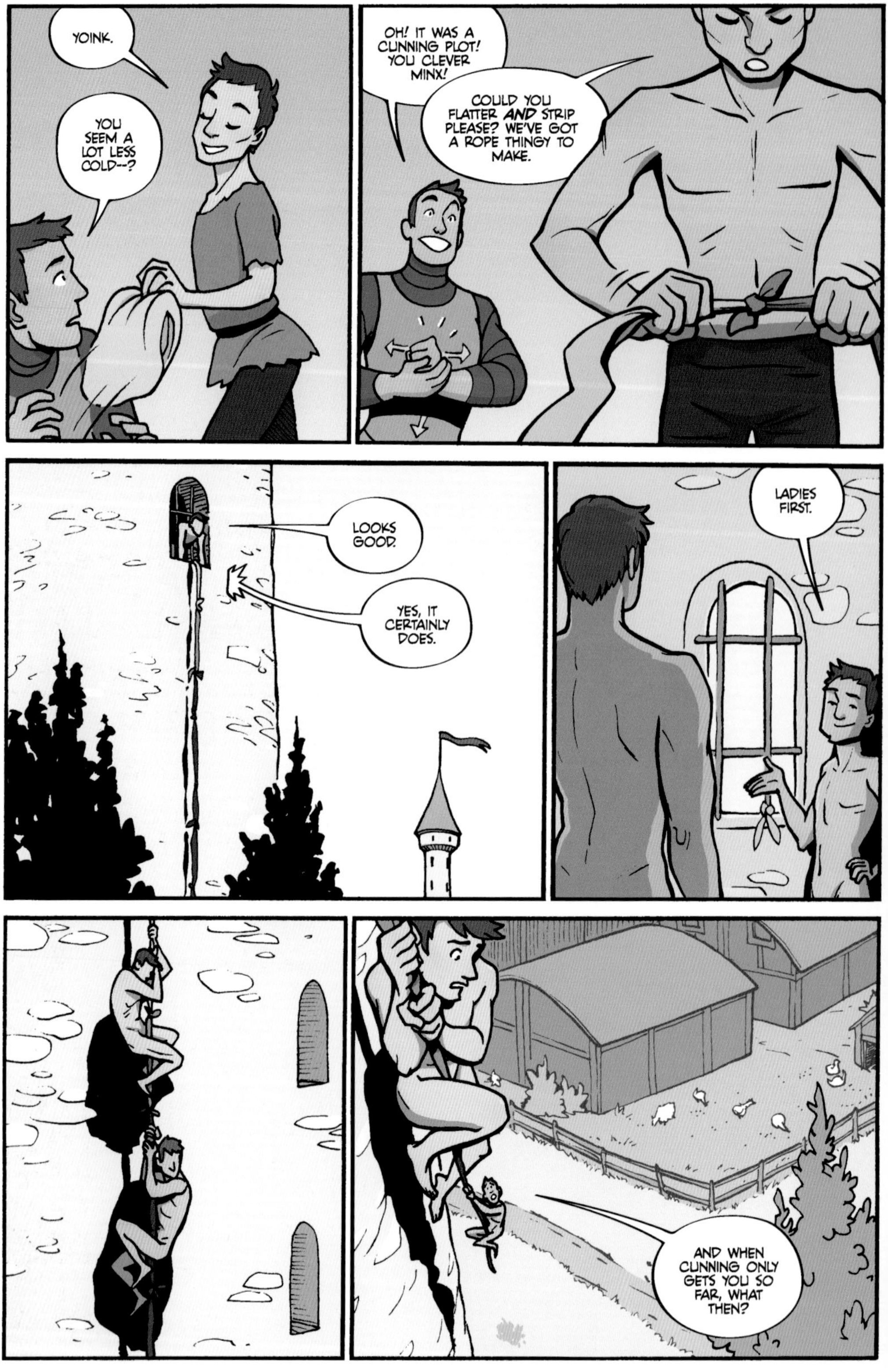
YOINK.
YOU SEEM A LOT LESS COLD--?
OH! IT WAS A CUNNING PLOT! YOU CLEVER MINX!
COULD YOU FLATTER AND STRIP PLEASE? WE'VE GOT A ROPE THINGY TO MAKE.
LOOKS GOOD.
YES, IT CERTAINLY DOES.
LADIES FIRST.
AND WHEN CUNNING ONLY GETS YOU SO FAR, WHAT THEN?

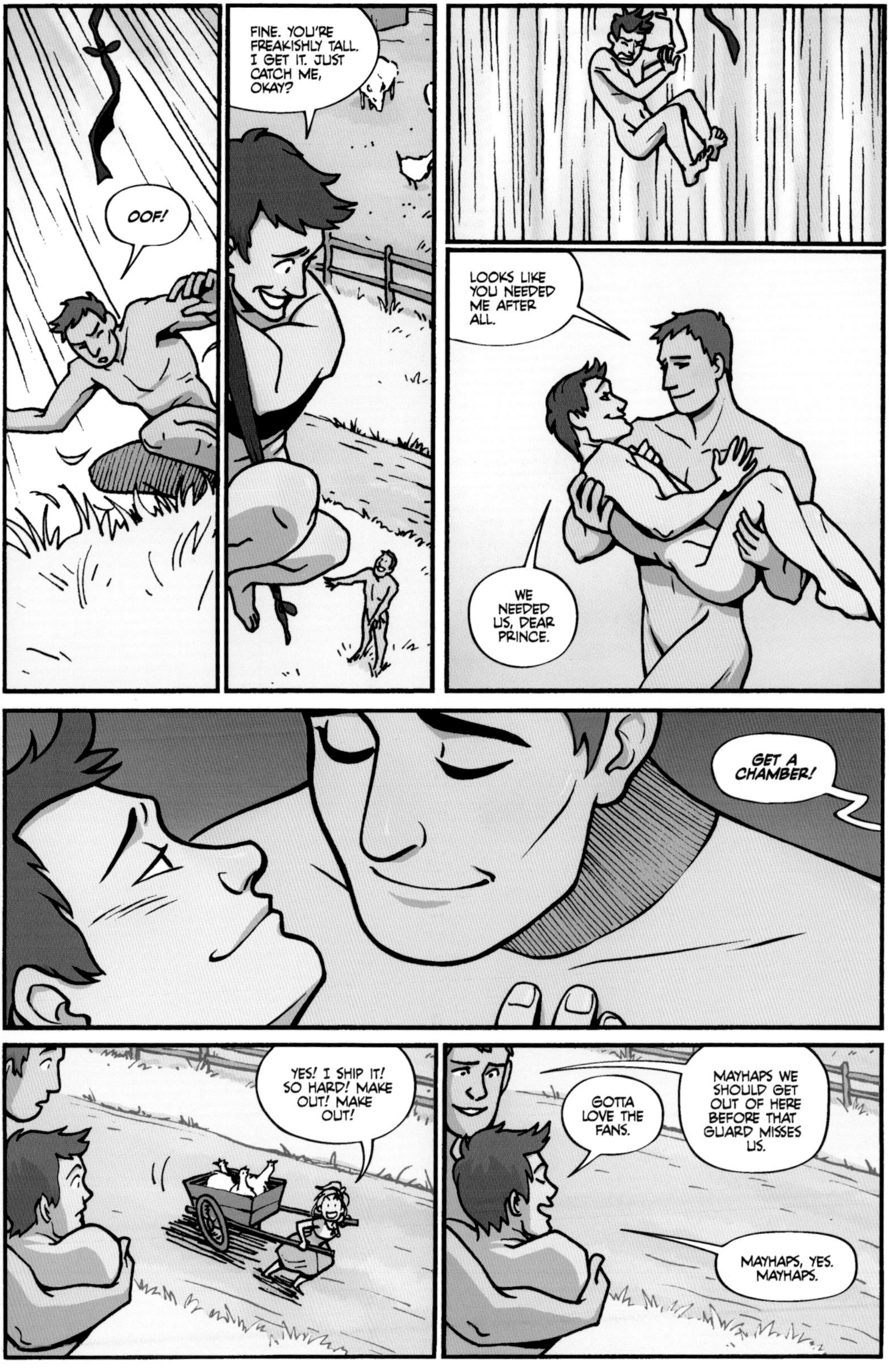
OOF!
FINE. YOU'RE FREAKISHLY TALL. I GET IT. JUST CATCH ME, OKAY?
LOOKS LIKE YOU NEEDED ME AFTER ALL.
WE NEEDED US, DEAR PRINCE.
GET A CHAMBER!
YES! I SHIP IT! SO HARD! MAKE OUT! MAKE OUT!
GOTTA LOVE THE FANS.
MAYHAPS WE SHOULD GET OUT OF HERE BEFORE THAT GUARD MISSES US.
MAYHAPS, YES. MAYHAPS.

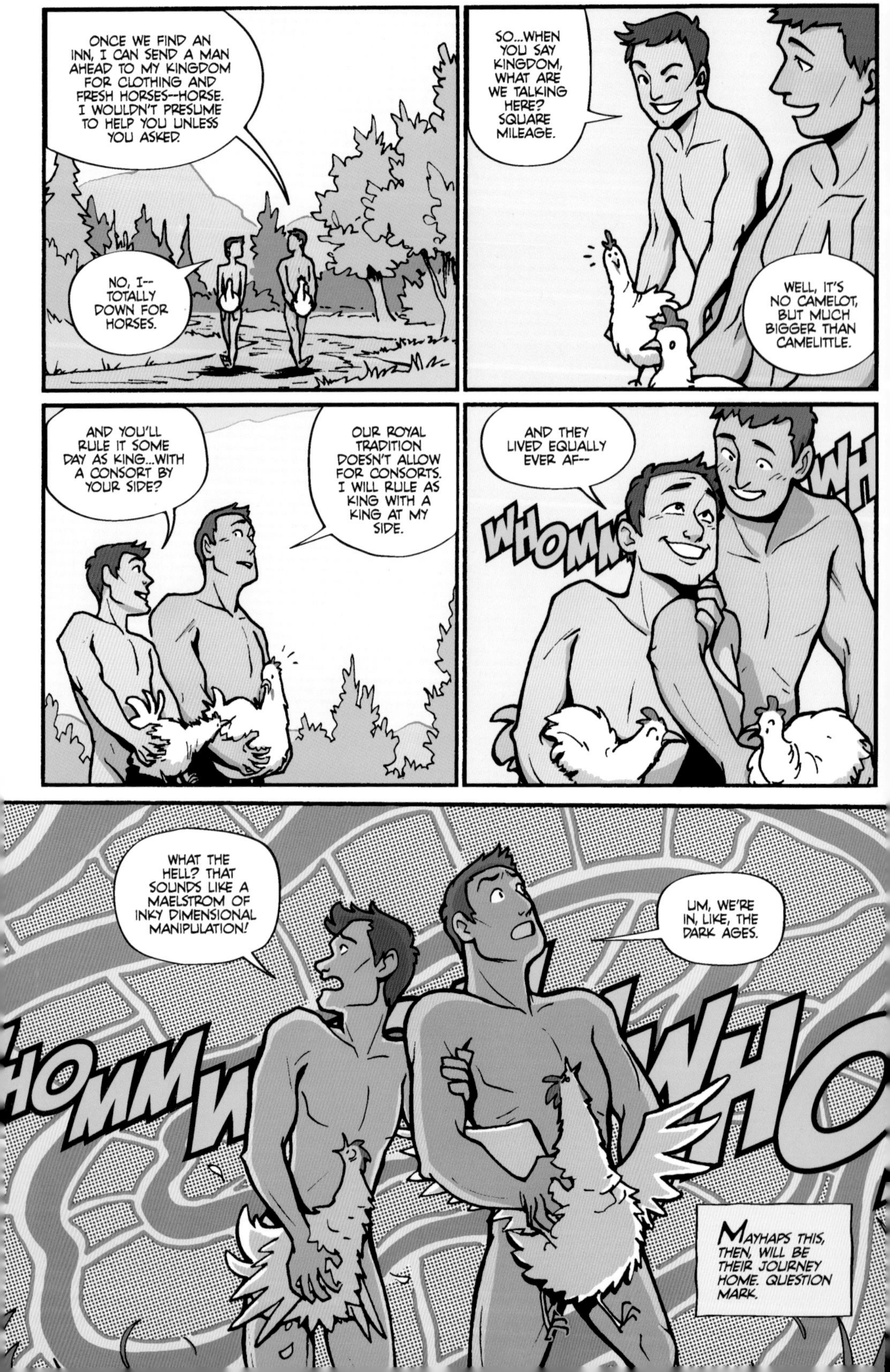
ONCE WE FIND AN INN, I CAN SEND A MAN AHEAD TO MY KINGDOM FOR CLOTHING AND FRESH HORSES--HORSE. I WOULDN'T PRESUME TO HELP YOU UNLESS YOU ASKED.
NO, I-- TOTALLY DOWN FOR HORSES.
SO...WHEN YOU SAY KINGDOM, WHAT ARE WE TALKING HERE? SQUARE MILEAGE.
WELL, IT'S NO CAMELOT, BUT MUCH BIGGER THAN CAMELITTLE.
AND YOU'LL RULE IT SOME DAY AS KING...WITH A CONSORT BY YOUR SIDE?
OUR ROYAL TRADITION DOESN'T ALLOW FOR CONSORTS. I WILL RULE AS KING WITH A KING AT MY SIDE.
AND THEY LIVED EQUALLY EVER AF--
WHOMM
WHAT THE HELL? THAT SOUNDS LIKE A MAELSTROM OF INKY DIMENSIONAL MANIPULATION!
UM, WE'RE IN, LIKE, THE DARK AGES.
HOMMWHO
MAYHAPS THIS, THEN, WILL BE THEIR JOURNEY HOME. QUESTION MARK.

A Case of Assumption

3

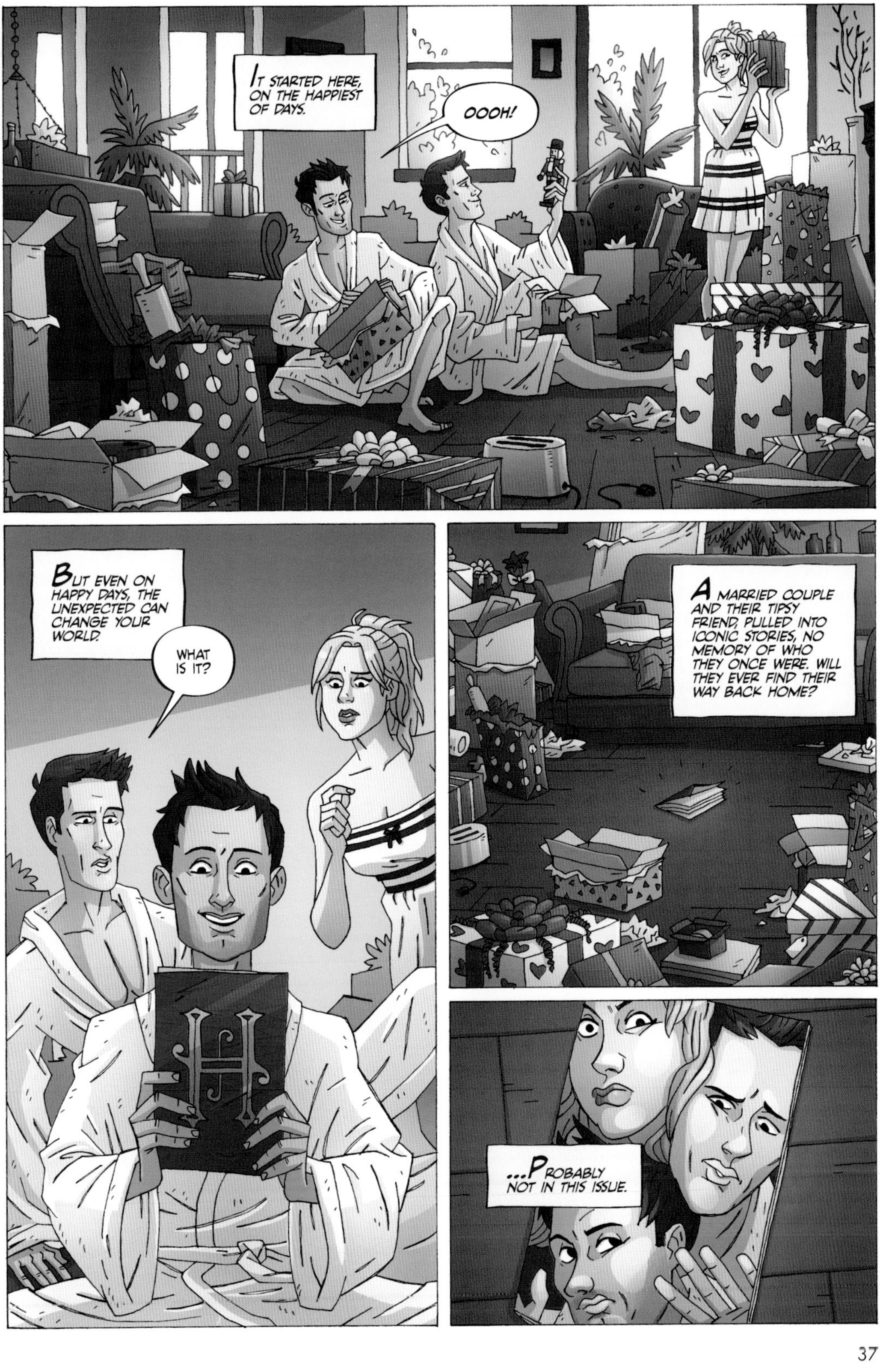
It started here, on the happiest of days.
OOOH!
But even on happy days, the unexpected can change your world.
WHAT IS IT?
A married couple and their tipsy friend, pulled into iconic stories, no memory of who they once were. Will they ever find their way back home?
...Probably not in this issue.

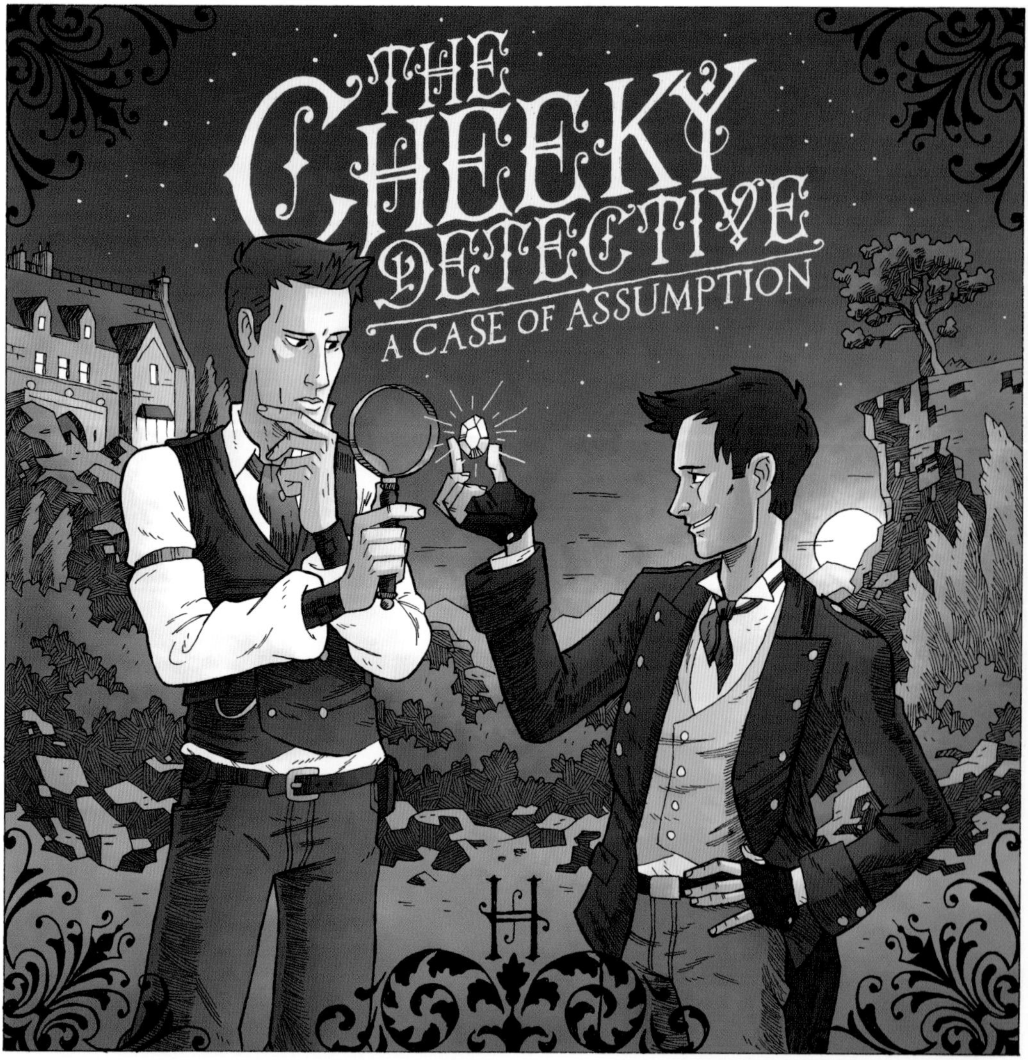
THE CHEEKY DETECTIVE
A CASE OF ASSUMPTION

IT WAS THE MIDDLE OF THE NIGHT, AND I, FAMED DETECTIVE WINSTON CHESS, AND MY RELIABLE COMPANION, COLONEL BRADON, WERE HURTLING THROUGH THE DARKNESS IN OUR CARRIAGE ON A ROYAL SUMMONS OF SOME URGENCY HAVING TO DO WITH A MISPLACED MAGNA CARTA.

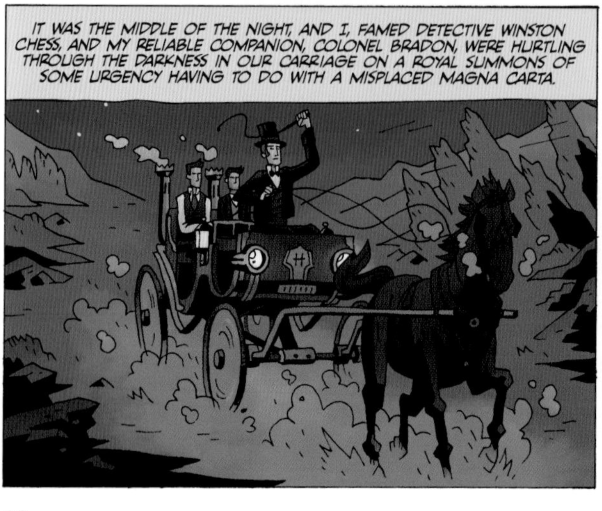

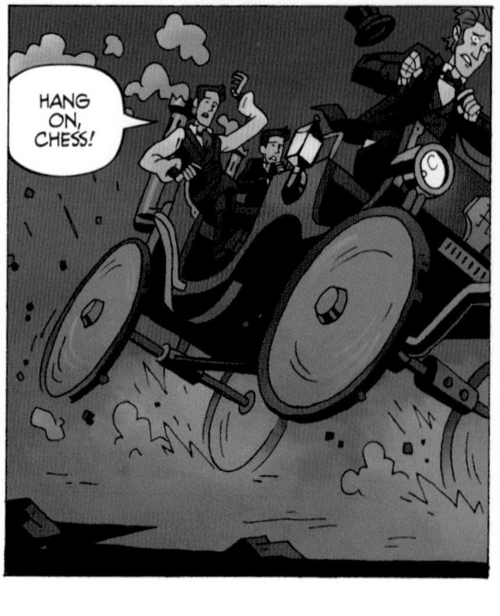
HANG ON, CHESS!

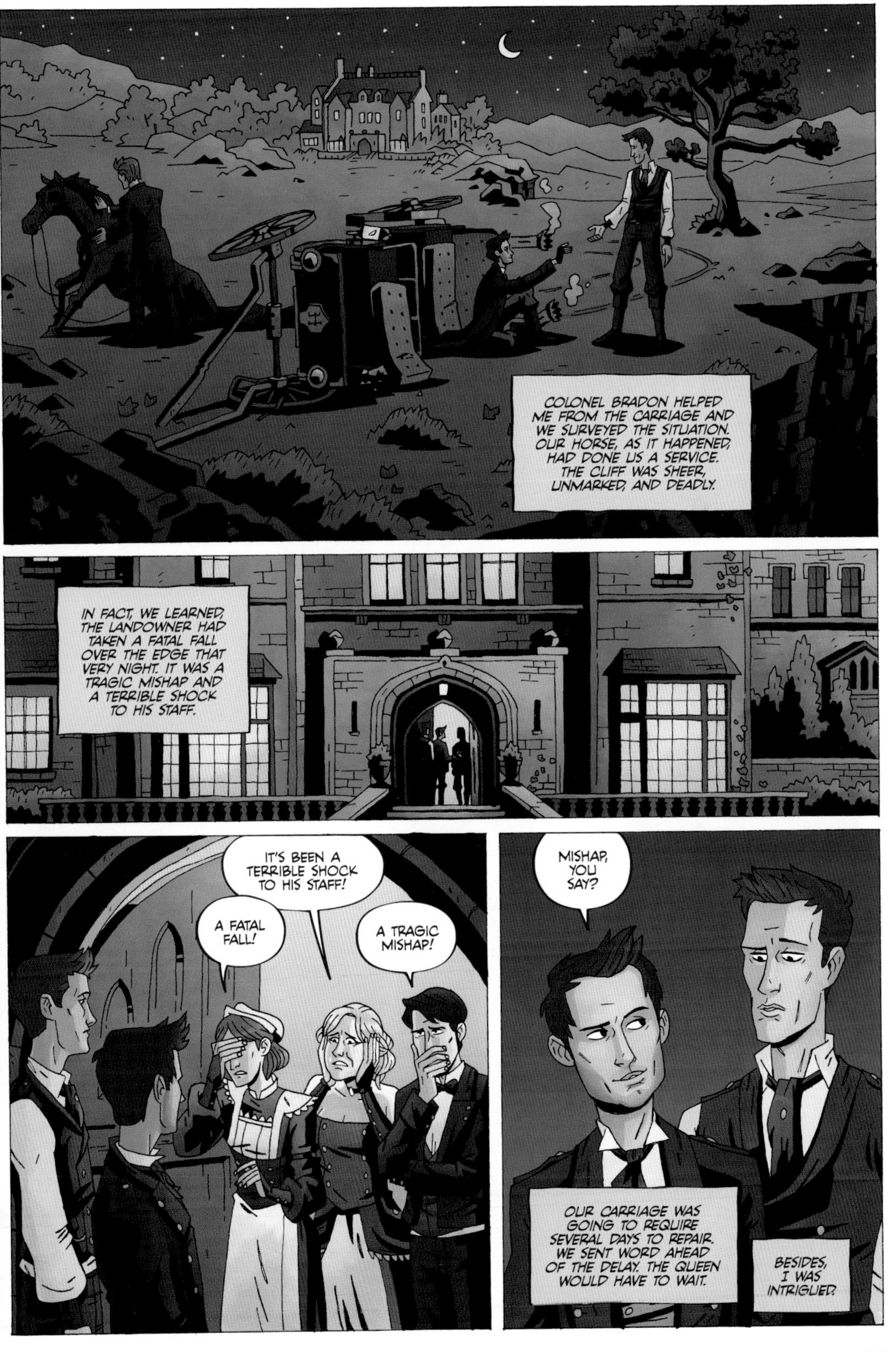
COLONEL BRADON HELPED ME FROM THE CARRIAGE AND WE SURVEYED THE SITUATION. OUR HORSE, AS IT HAPPENED, HAD DONE US A SERVICE. THE CLIFF WAS SHEER, UNMARKED, AND DEADLY.
IN FACT, WE LEARNED, THE LANDOWNER HAD TAKEN A FATAL FALL OVER THE EDGE THAT VERY NIGHT. IT WAS A TRAGIC MISHAP AND A TERRIBLE SHOCK TO HIS STAFF.
IT'S BEEN A TERRIBLE SHOCK TO HIS STAFF!
A FATAL FALL!
A TRAGIC MISHAP!
MISHAP, YOU SAY?
OUR CARRIAGE WAS GOING TO REQUIRE SEVERAL DAYS TO REPAIR. WE SENT WORD AHEAD OF THE DELAY. THE QUEEN WOULD HAVE TO WAIT.
BESIDES, I WAS INTRIGUED.

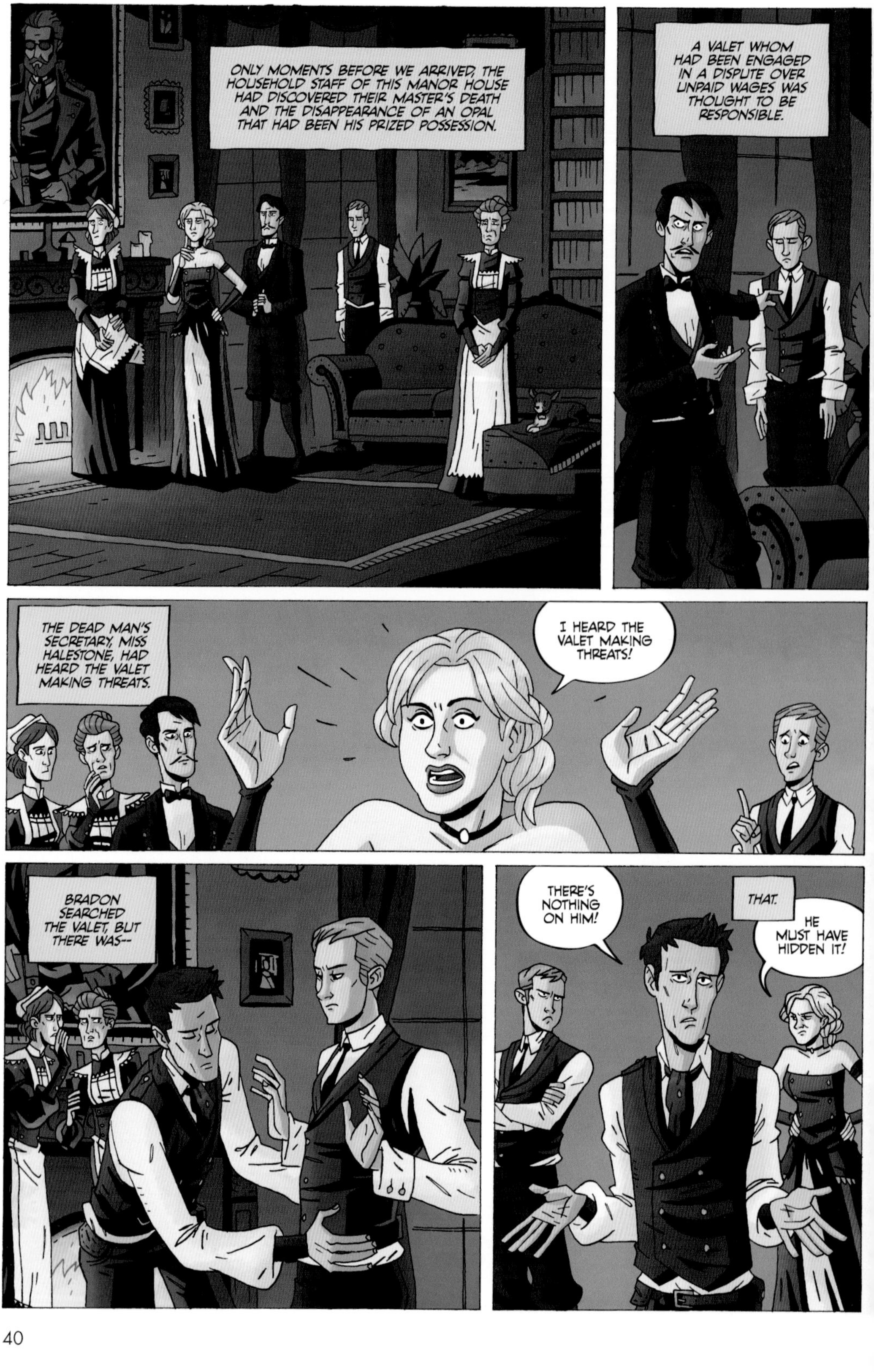
ONLY MOMENTS BEFORE WE ARRIVED, THE HOUSEHOLD STAFF OF THIS MANOR HOUSE HAD DISCOVERED THEIR MASTER'S DEATH AND THE DISAPPEARANCE OF AN OPAL THAT HAD BEEN HIS PRIZED POSSESSION.
A VALET WHOM HAD BEEN ENGAGED IN A DISPUTE OVER UNPAID WAGES WAS THOUGHT TO BE RESPONSIBLE.
THE DEAD MAN'S SECRETARY, MISS HALESTONE, HAD HEARD THE VALET MAKING THREATS.
I HEARD THE VALET MAKING THREATS!
BRADON SEARCHED THE VALET, BUT THERE WAS--
THERE'S NOTHING ON HIM!
THAT.
HE MUST HAVE HIDDEN IT!

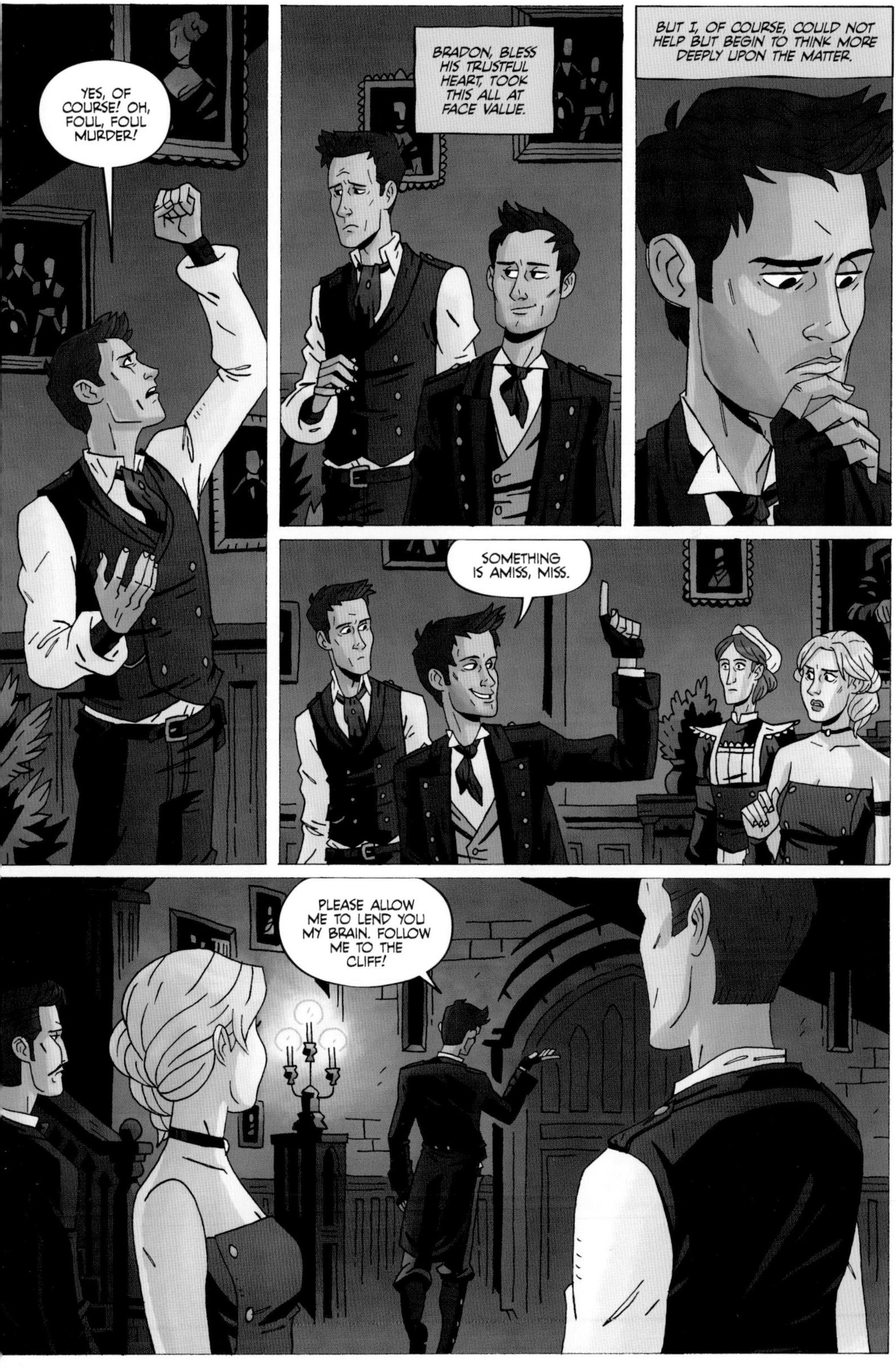
YES, OF COURSE! OH, FOUL, FOUL MURDER!
BRADON, BLESS HIS TRUSTFUL HEART, TOOK THIS ALL AT FACE VALUE.
BUT I, OF COURSE, COULD NOT HELP BUT BEGIN TO THINK MORE DEEPLY UPON THE MATTER.
SOMETHING IS AMISS, MISS.
PLEASE ALLOW ME TO LEND YOU MY BRAIN. FOLLOW ME TO THE CLIFF!

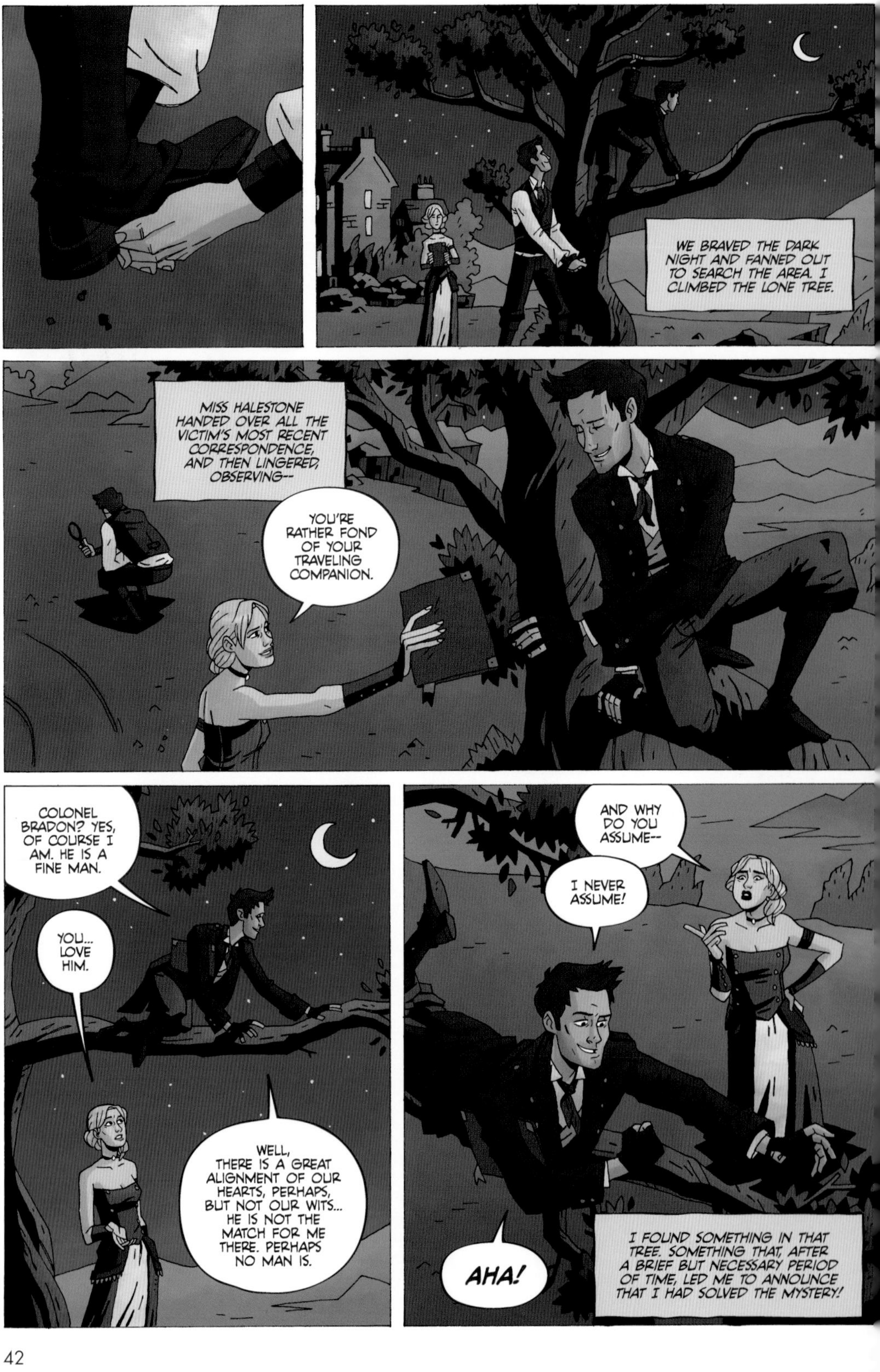
WE BRAVED THE DARK NIGHT AND FANNED OUT TO SEARCH THE AREA. I CLIMBED THE LONE TREE.
MISS HALESTONE HANDED OVER ALL THE VICTIM'S MOST RECENT CORRESPONDENCE, AND THEN LINGERED, OBSERVING--
YOU'RE RATHER FOND OF YOUR TRAVELING COMPANION.
COLONEL BRADON? YES, OF COURSE I AM. HE IS A FINE MAN.
YOU... LOVE HIM.
WELL, THERE IS A GREAT ALIGNMENT OF OUR HEARTS, PERHAPS, BUT NOT OUR WITS... HE IS NOT THE MATCH FOR ME THERE. PERHAPS NO MAN IS.
AND WHY DO YOU ASSUME--
I NEVER ASSUME!
AHA!
I FOUND SOMETHING IN THAT TREE. SOMETHING THAT, AFTER A BRIEF BUT NECESSARY PERIOD OF TIME, LED ME TO ANNOUNCE THAT I HAD SOLVED THE MYSTERY!

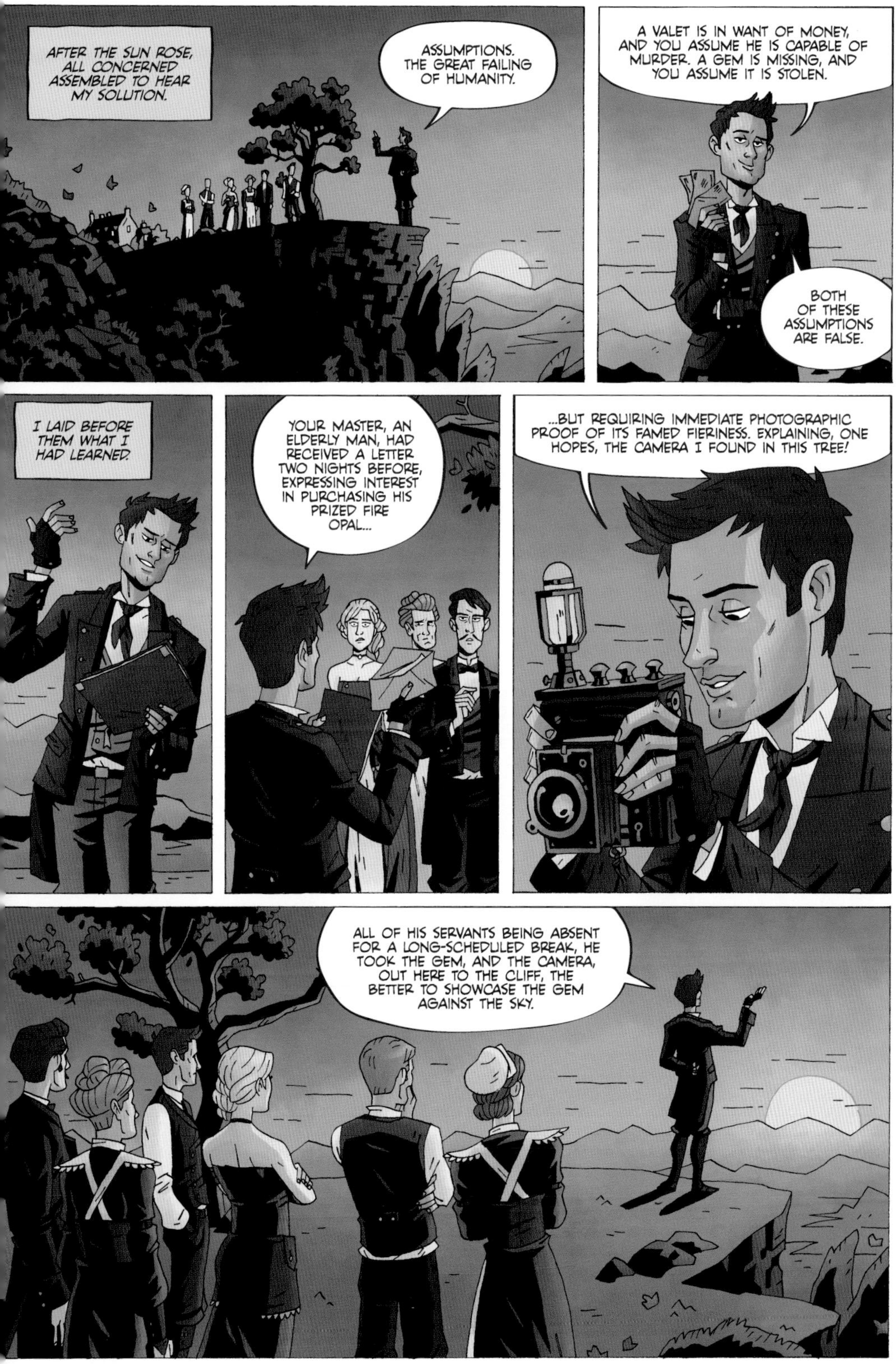
AFTER THE SUN ROSE, ALL CONCERNED ASSEMBLED TO HEAR MY SOLUTION.
ASSUMPTIONS. THE GREAT FAILING OF HUMANITY.
A VALET IS IN WANT OF MONEY, AND YOU ASSUME HE IS CAPABLE OF MURDER. A GEM IS MISSING, AND YOU ASSUME IT IS STOLEN.
BOTH OF THESE ASSUMPTIONS ARE FALSE.
I LAID BEFORE THEM WHAT I HAD LEARNED.
YOUR MASTER, AN ELDERLY MAN, HAD RECEIVED A LETTER TWO NIGHTS BEFORE, EXPRESSING INTEREST IN PURCHASING HIS PRIZED FIRE OPAL...
...BUT REQUIRING IMMEDIATE PHOTOGRAPHIC PROOF OF ITS FAMED FIERINESS. EXPLAINING, ONE HOPES, THE CAMERA I FOUND IN THIS TREE!
ALL OF HIS SERVANTS BEING ABSENT FOR A LONG-SCHEDULED BREAK, HE TOOK THE GEM, AND THE CAMERA, OUT HERE TO THE CLIFF, THE BETTER TO SHOWCASE THE GEM AGAINST THE SKY.

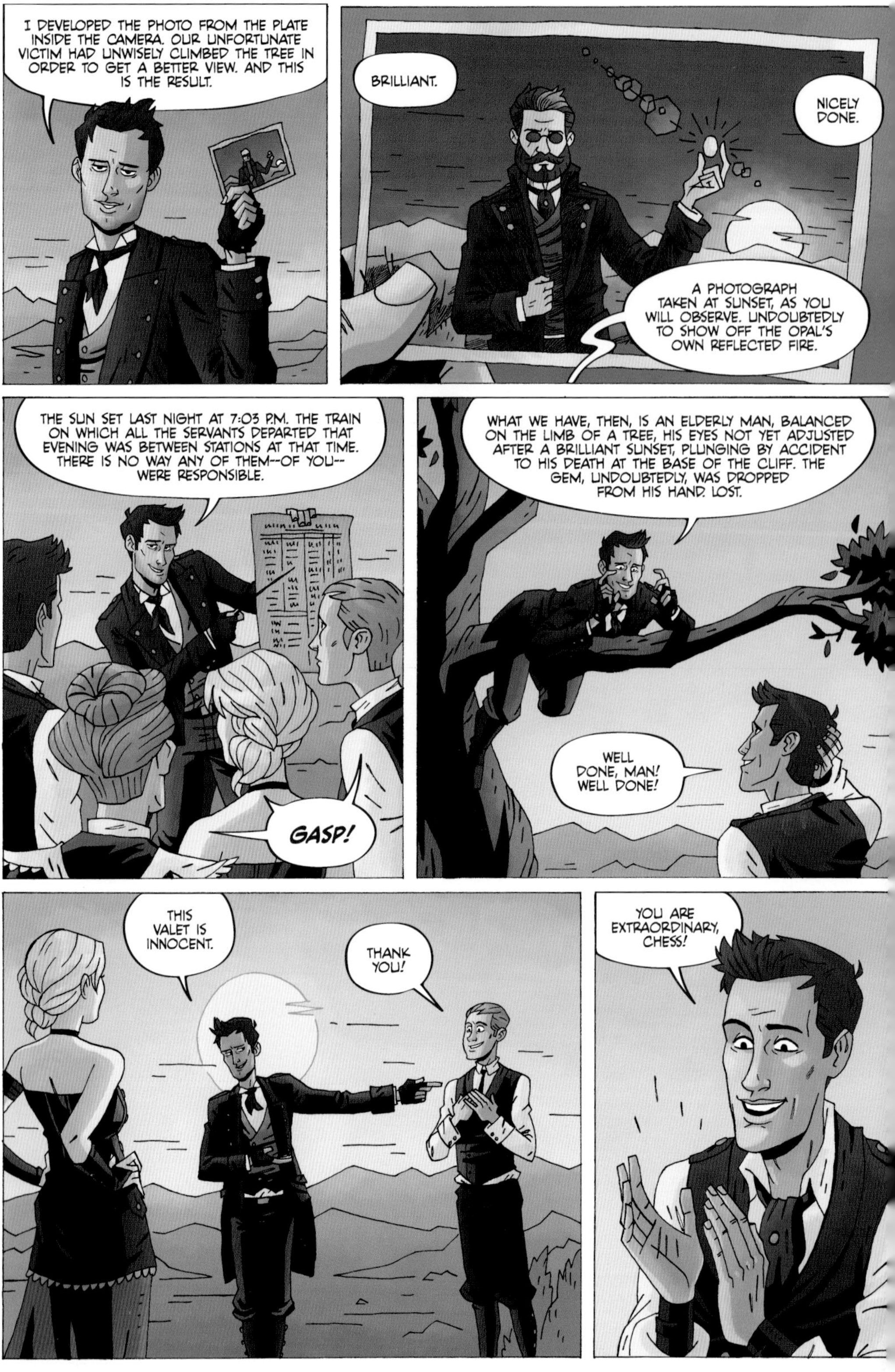
I DEVELOPED THE PHOTO FROM THE PLATE INSIDE THE CAMERA. OUR UNFORTUNATE VICTIM HAD UNWISELY CLIMBED THE TREE IN ORDER TO GET A BETTER VIEW. AND THIS IS THE RESULT.
BRILLIANT.
NICELY DONE.
A PHOTOGRAPH TAKEN AT SUNSET, AS YOU WILL OBSERVE. UNDOUBTEDLY TO SHOW OFF THE OPAL'S OWN REFLECTED FIRE.
THE SUN SET LAST NIGHT AT 7:03 P.M. THE TRAIN ON WHICH ALL THE SERVANTS DEPARTED THAT EVENING WAS BETWEEN STATIONS AT THAT TIME. THERE IS NO WAY ANY OF THEM--OF YOU--WERE RESPONSIBLE.
GASP!
WHAT WE HAVE, THEN, IS AN ELDERLY MAN, BALANCED ON THE LIMB OF A TREE, HIS EYES NOT YET ADJUSTED AFTER A BRILLIANT SUNSET, PLUNGING BY ACCIDENT TO HIS DEATH AT THE BASE OF THE CLIFF. THE GEM, UNDOUBTEDLY, WAS DROPPED FROM HIS HAND. LOST.
WELL DONE, MAN! WELL DONE!
THIS VALET IS INNOCENT.
THANK YOU!
YOU ARE EXTRAORDINARY, CHESS!

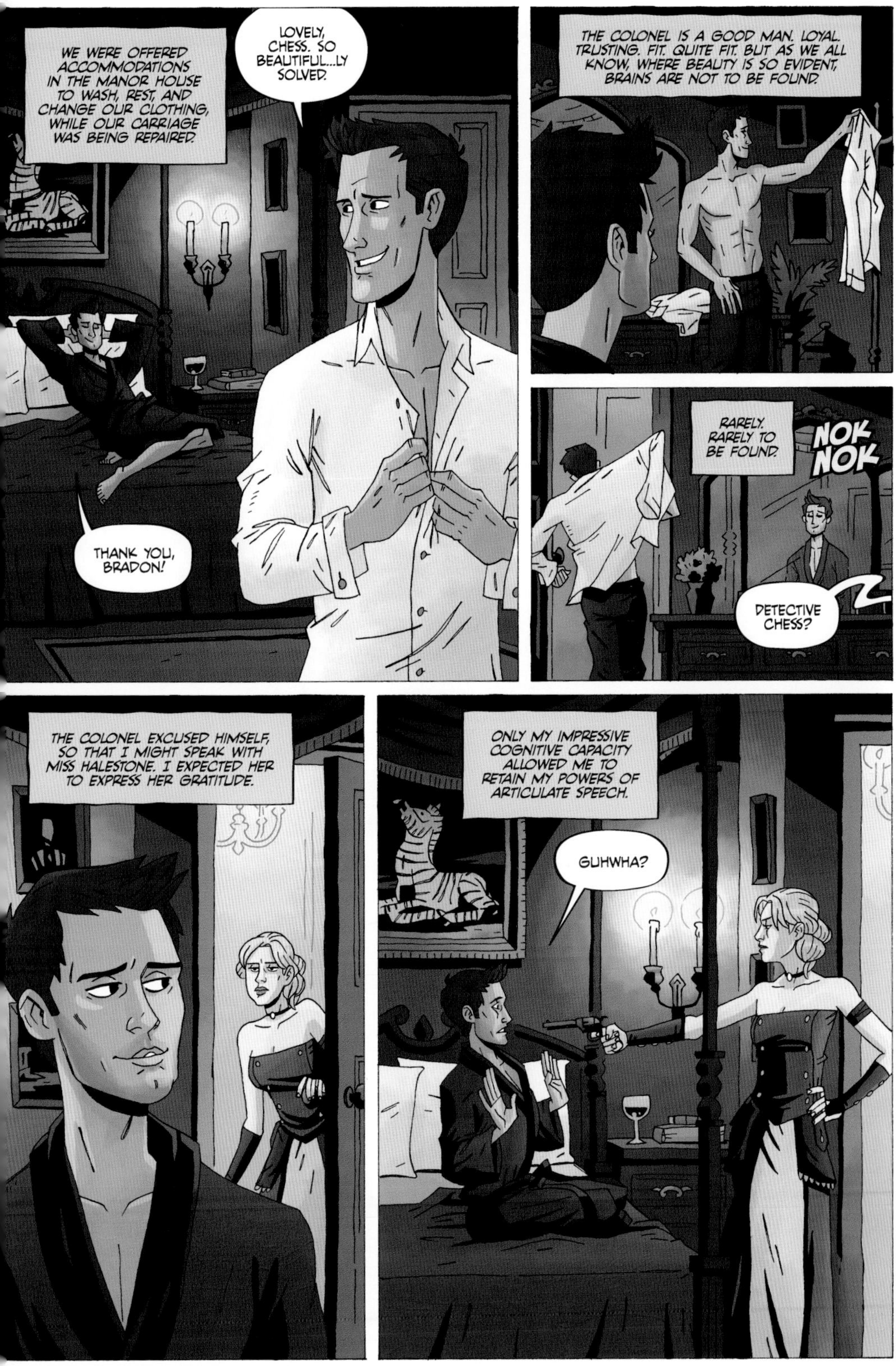
WE WERE OFFERED ACCOMMODATIONS IN THE MANOR HOUSE TO WASH, REST, AND CHANGE OUR CLOTHING, WHILE OUR CARRIAGE WAS BEING REPAIRED.
LOVELY, CHESS. SO BEAUTIFUL...LY SOLVED.
THANK YOU, BRADON!
THE COLONEL IS A GOOD MAN. LOYAL. TRUSTING. FIT. QUITE FIT. BUT AS WE ALL KNOW, WHERE BEAUTY IS SO EVIDENT, BRAINS ARE NOT TO BE FOUND.
RARELY. RARELY TO BE FOUND.
NOK NOK
DETECTIVE CHESS?
THE COLONEL EXCUSED HIMSELF, SO THAT I MIGHT SPEAK WITH MISS HALESTONE. I EXPECTED HER TO EXPRESS HER GRATITUDE.
ONLY MY IMPRESSIVE COGNITIVE CAPACITY ALLOWED ME TO RETAIN MY POWERS OF ARTICULATE SPEECH.
GUHWHA?

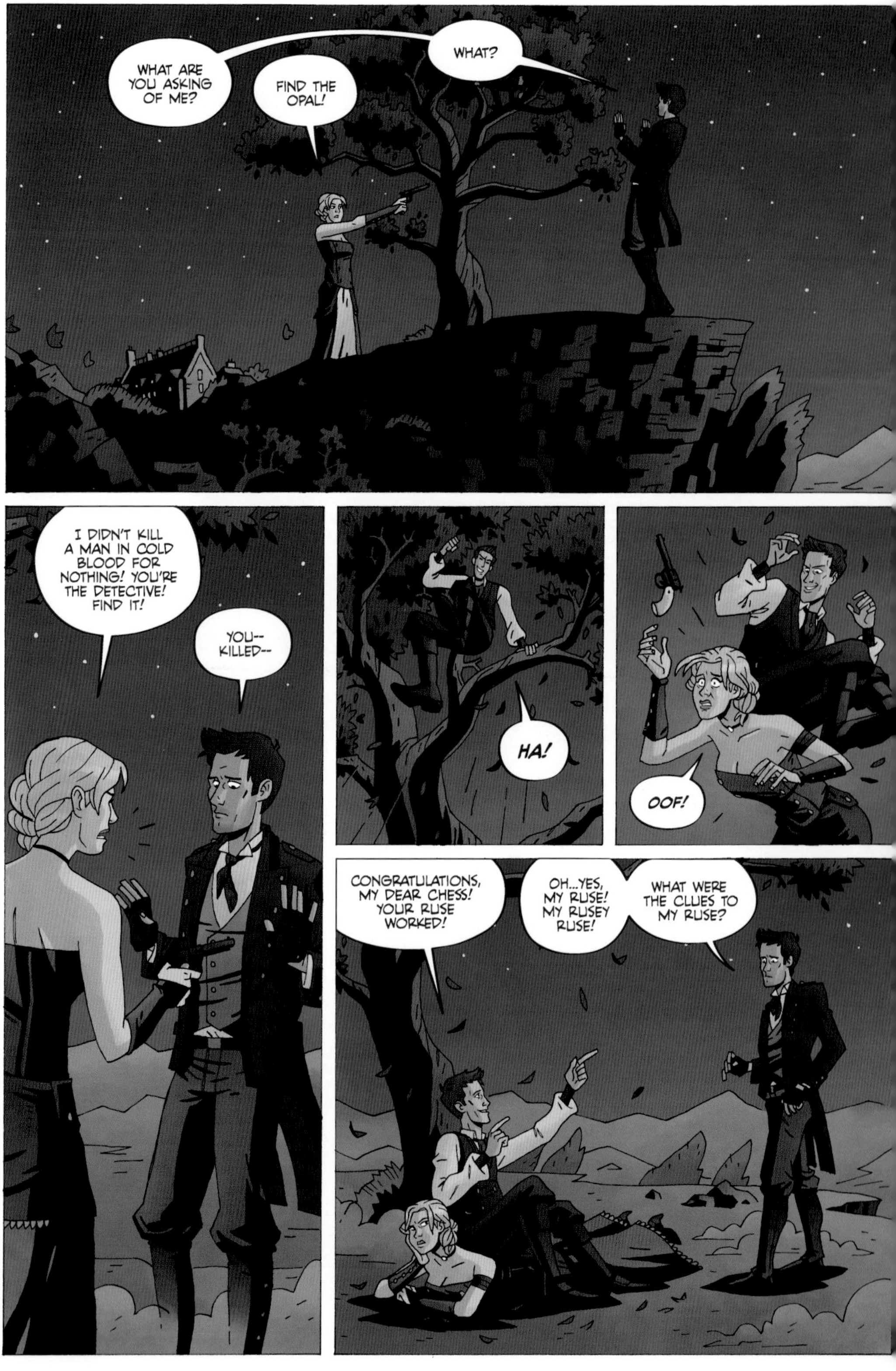
WHAT ARE YOU ASKING OF ME?
FIND THE OPAL!
WHAT?
I DIDN'T KILL A MAN IN COLD BLOOD FOR NOTHING! YOU'RE THE DETECTIVE! FIND IT!
YOU-- KILLED--
HA!
OOF!
CONGRATULATIONS, MY DEAR CHESS! YOUR RUSE WORKED!
OH...YES, MY RUSE! MY RUSEY RUSE!
WHAT WERE THE CLUES TO MY RUSE?

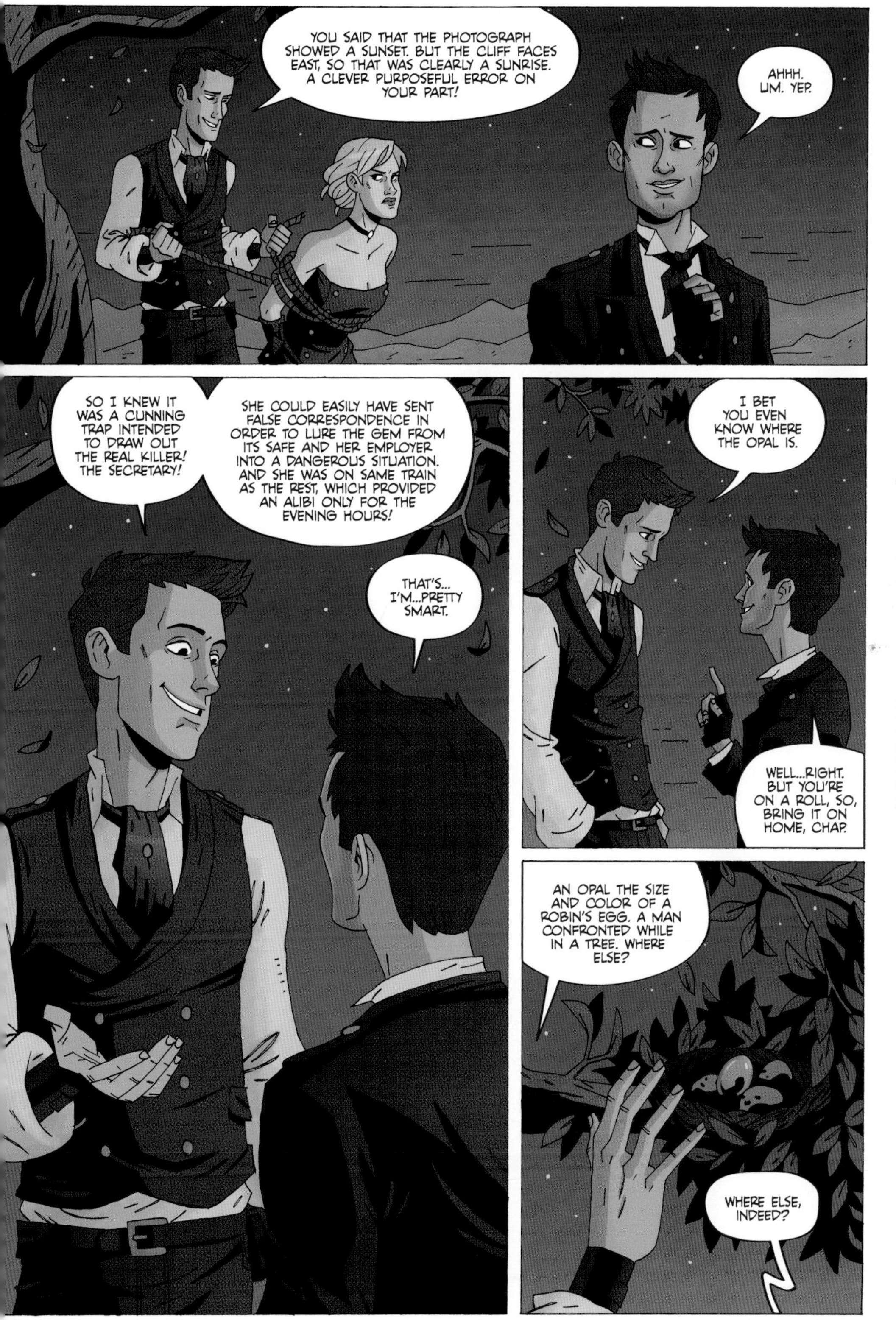
YOU SAID THAT THE PHOTOGRAPH SHOWED A SUNSET. BUT THE CLIFF FACES EAST, SO THAT WAS CLEARLY A SUNRISE. A CLEVER PURPOSEFUL ERROR ON YOUR PART!
AHHH. UM. YEP.
SO I KNEW IT WAS A CUNNING TRAP INTENDED TO DRAW OUT THE REAL KILLER! THE SECRETARY!
SHE COULD EASILY HAVE SENT FALSE CORRESPONDENCE IN ORDER TO LURE THE GEM FROM ITS SAFE AND HER EMPLOYER INTO A DANGEROUS SITUATION. AND SHE WAS ON SAME TRAIN AS THE REST, WHICH PROVIDED AN ALIBI ONLY FOR THE EVENING HOURS!
THAT'S... I'M...PRETTY SMART.
I BET YOU EVEN KNOW WHERE THE OPAL IS.
WELL...RIGHT. BUT YOU'RE ON A ROLL, SO, BRING IT ON HOME, CHAP.
AN OPAL THE SIZE AND COLOR OF A ROBIN'S EGG. A MAN CONFRONTED WHILE IN A TREE. WHERE ELSE?
WHERE ELSE, INDEED?

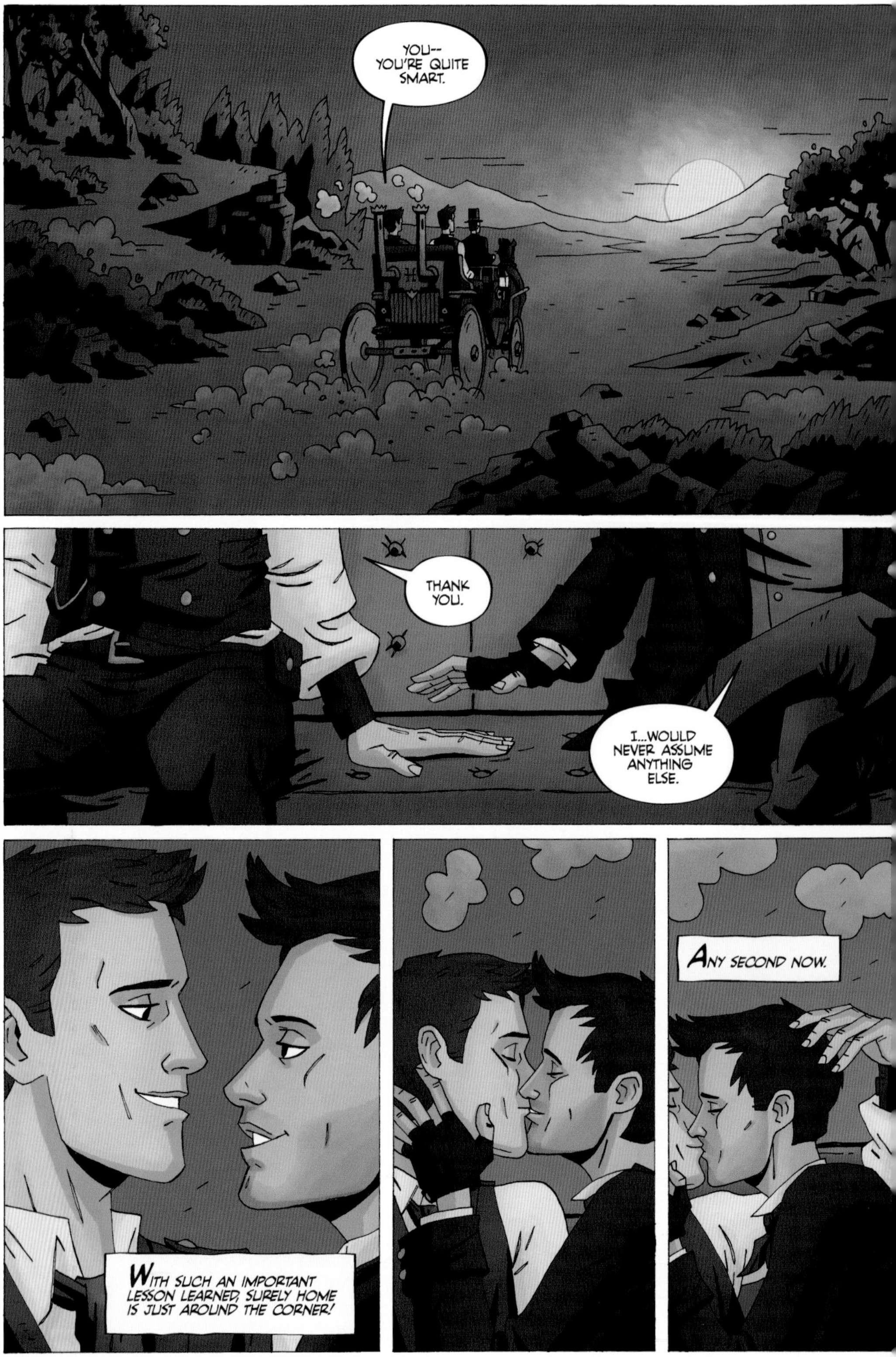
YOU-- YOU'RE QUITE SMART.
THANK YOU.
I...WOULD NEVER ASSUME ANYTHING ELSE.
WITH SUCH AN IMPORTANT LESSON LEARNED, SURELY HOME IS JUST AROUND THE CORNER!
ANY SECOND NOW.

Nocte Machinas

4

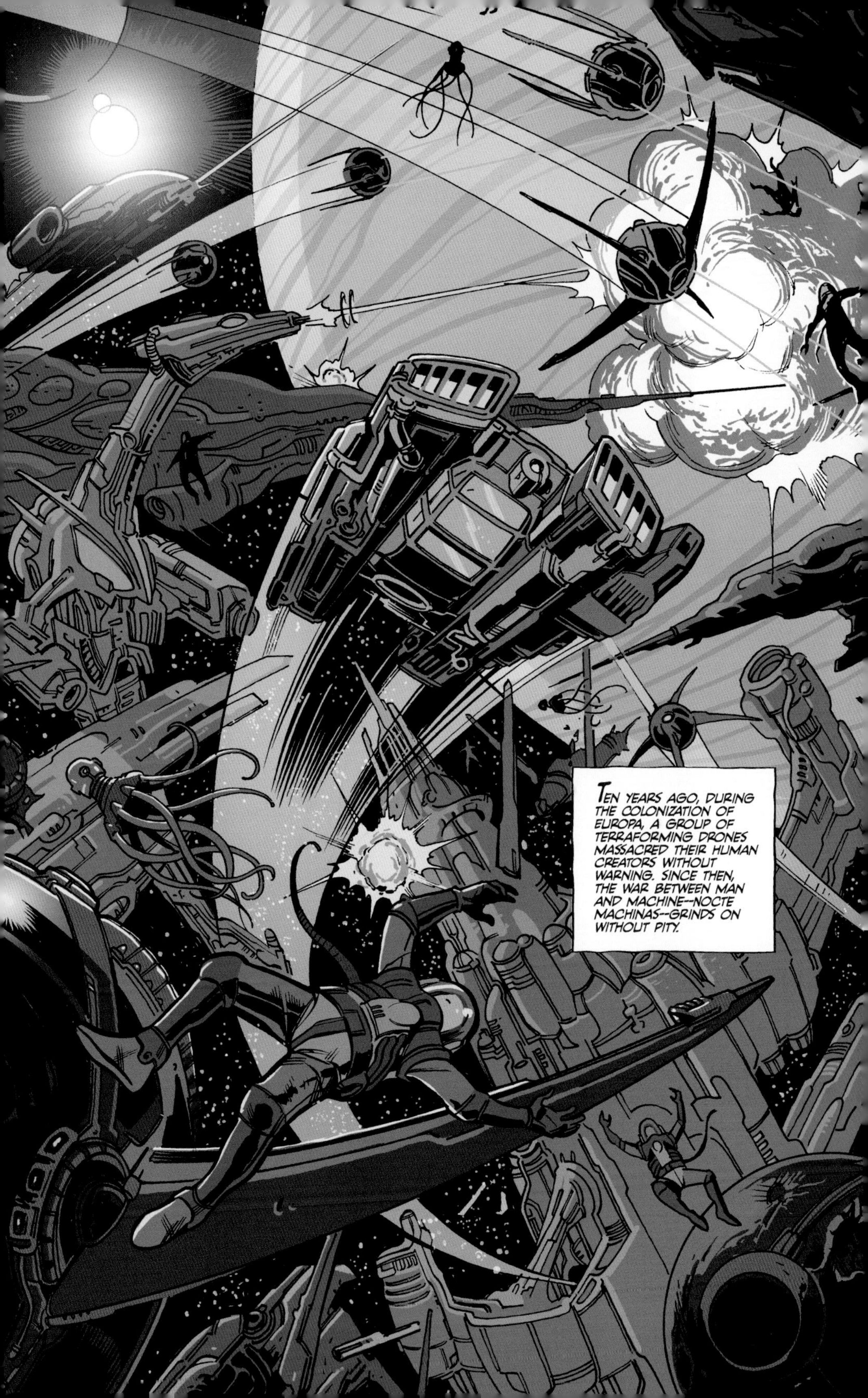
TEN YEARS AGO, DURING THE COLONIZATION OF EUROPA, A GROUP OF TERRAFORMING DRONES MASSACRED THEIR HUMAN CREATORS WITHOUT WARNING. SINCE THEN, THE WAR BETWEEN MAN AND MACHINE--NOCTE MACHINAS--GRINDS ON WITHOUT PITY.

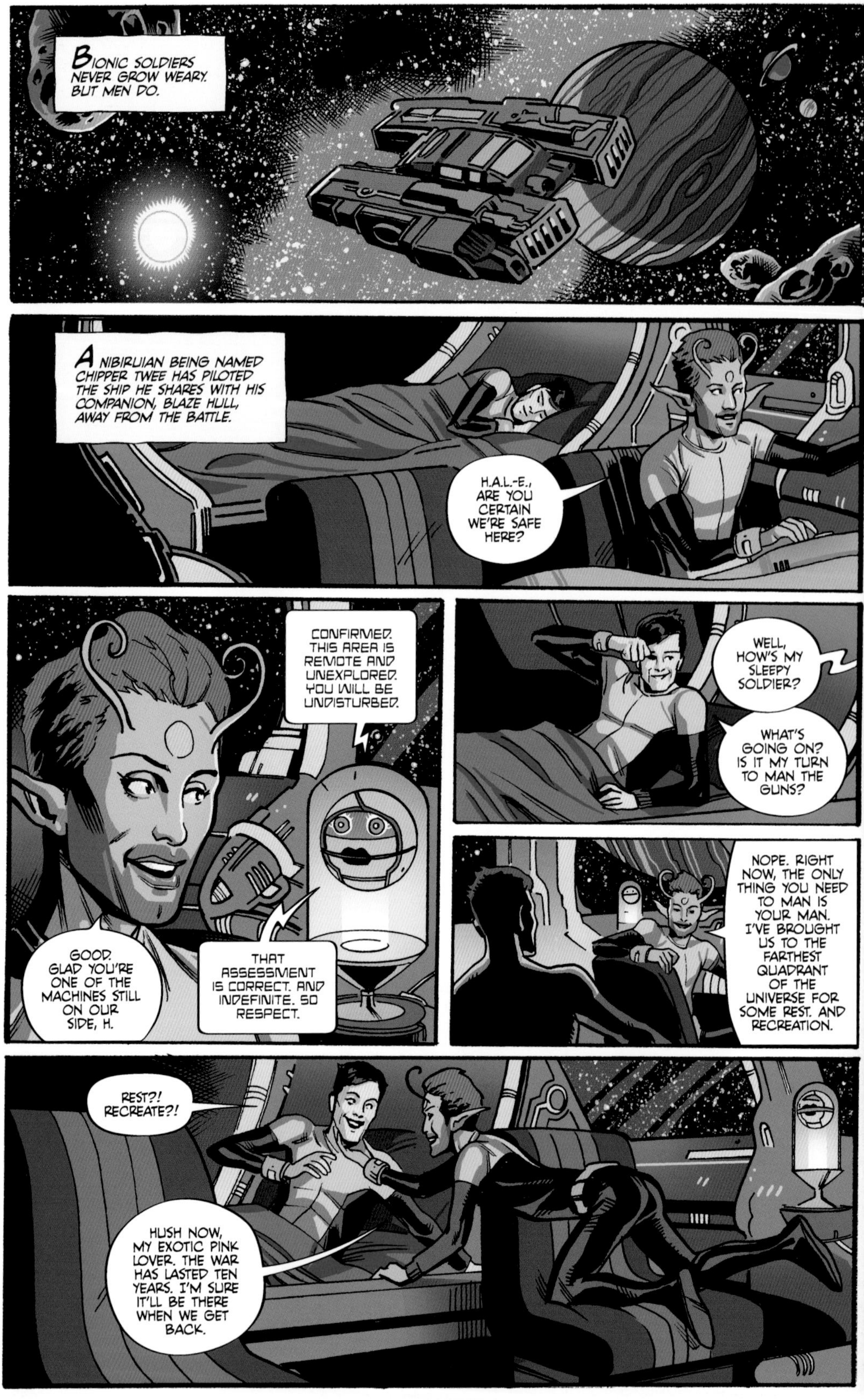
BIONIC SOLDIERS NEVER GROW WEARY. BUT MEN DO.
A NIBIRUIAN BEING NAMED CHIPPER TWEE HAS PILOTED THE SHIP HE SHARES WITH HIS COMPANION, BLAZE HULL, AWAY FROM THE BATTLE.
H.A.L.-E., ARE YOU CERTAIN WE'RE SAFE HERE?
CONFIRMED. THIS AREA IS REMOTE AND UNEXPLORED. YOU WILL BE UNDISTURBED.
GOOD. GLAD YOU'RE ONE OF THE MACHINES STILL ON OUR SIDE, H.
THAT ASSESSMENT IS CORRECT. AND INDEFINITE. SO RESPECT.
WELL, HOW'S MY SLEEPY SOLDIER?
WHAT'S GOING ON? IS IT MY TURN TO MAN THE GUNS?
NOPE. RIGHT NOW, THE ONLY THING YOU NEED TO MAN IS YOUR MAN. I'VE BROUGHT US TO THE FARTHEST QUADRANT OF THE UNIVERSE FOR SOME REST. AND RECREATION.
REST?! RECREATE?!
HUSH NOW, MY EXOTIC PINK LOVER. THE WAR HAS LASTED TEN YEARS. I'M SURE IT'LL BE THERE WHEN WE GET BACK.

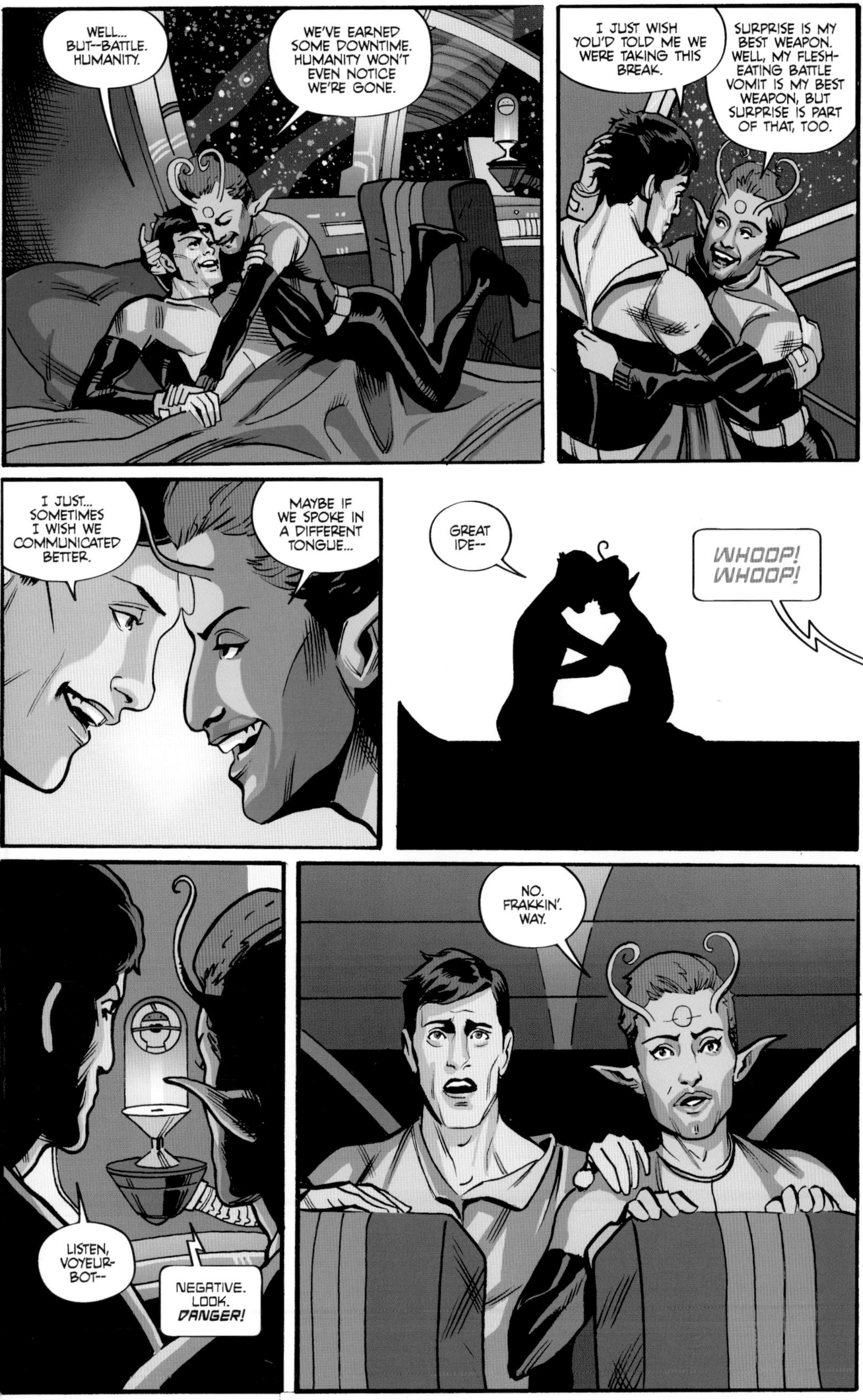
WELL... BUT--BATTLE. HUMANITY.
WE'VE EARNED SOME DOWNTIME. HUMANITY WON'T EVEN NOTICE WE'RE GONE.
I JUST WISH YOU'D TOLD ME WE WERE TAKING THIS BREAK.
SURPRISE IS MY BEST WEAPON. WELL, MY FLESH-EATING BATTLE VOMIT IS MY BEST WEAPON, BUT SURPRISE IS PART OF THAT, TOO.
I JUST... SOMETIMES I WISH WE COMMUNICATED BETTER.
MAYBE IF WE SPOKE IN A DIFFERENT TONGUE...
GREAT IDE--
WHOOP! WHOOP!
LISTEN, VOYEUR-BOT--
NEGATIVE. LOOK. DANGER!
NO. FRAKKIN'. WAY.

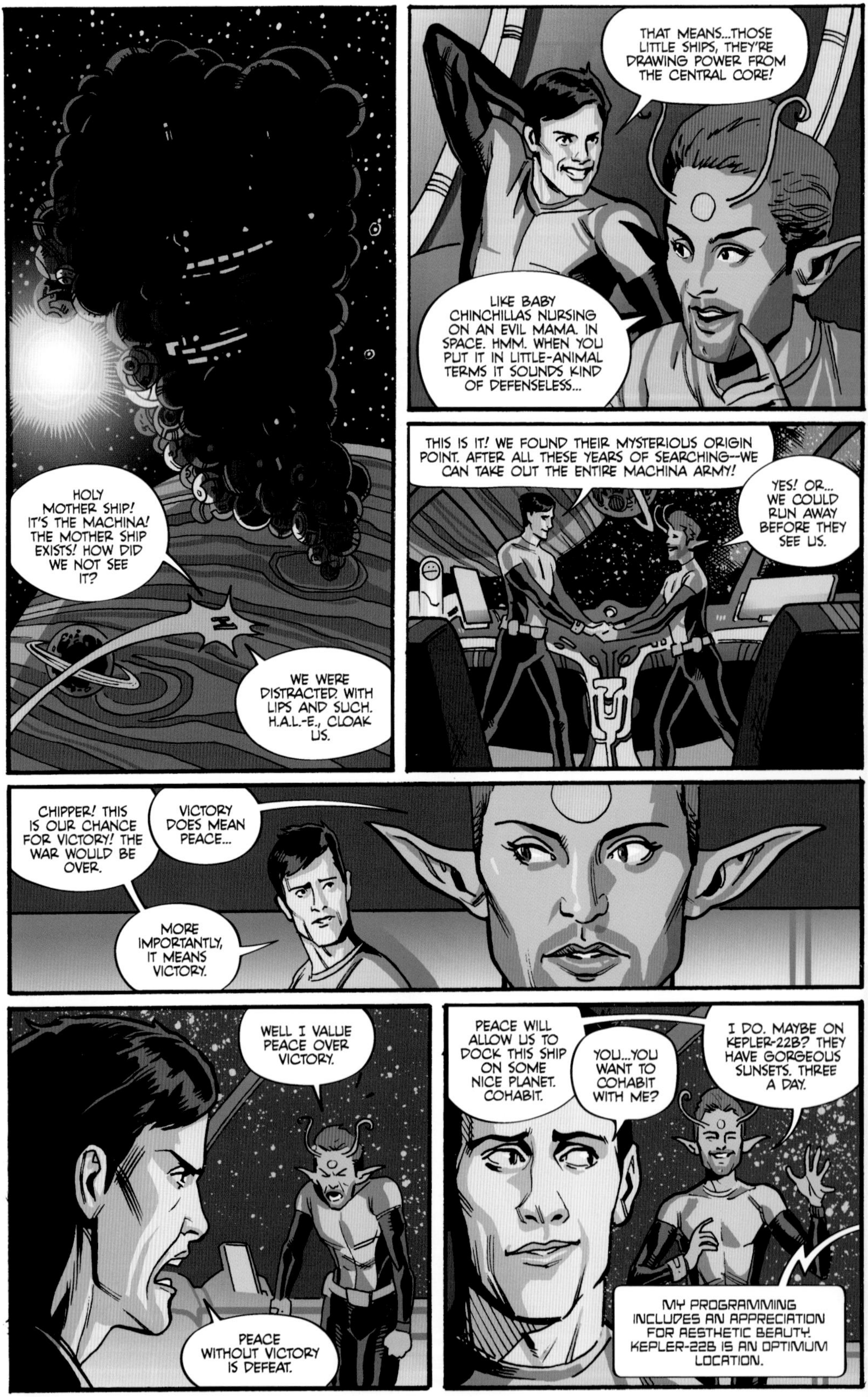
THAT MEANS...THOSE LITTLE SHIPS, THEY'RE DRAWING POWER FROM THE CENTRAL CORE!
LIKE BABY CHINCHILLAS NURSING ON AN EVIL MAMA. IN SPACE. HMM. WHEN YOU PUT IT IN LITTLE-ANIMAL TERMS IT SOUNDS KIND OF DEFENSELESS...
HOLY MOTHER SHIP! IT'S THE MACHINA! THE MOTHER SHIP EXISTS! HOW DID WE NOT SEE IT?
WE WERE DISTRACTED. WITH LIPS AND SUCH. H.A.L.-E., CLOAK US.
THIS IS IT! WE FOUND THEIR MYSTERIOUS ORIGIN POINT. AFTER ALL THESE YEARS OF SEARCHING--WE CAN TAKE OUT THE ENTIRE MACHINA ARMY!
YES! OR... WE COULD RUN AWAY BEFORE THEY SEE US.
CHIPPER! THIS IS OUR CHANCE FOR VICTORY! THE WAR WOULD BE OVER.
VICTORY DOES MEAN PEACE...
MORE IMPORTANTLY, IT MEANS VICTORY.
WELL I VALUE PEACE OVER VICTORY.
PEACE WITHOUT VICTORY IS DEFEAT.
PEACE WILL ALLOW US TO DOCK THIS SHIP ON SOME NICE PLANET. COHABIT.
YOU...YOU WANT TO COHABIT WITH ME?
I DO. MAYBE ON KEPLER-22B? THEY HAVE GORGEOUS SUNSETS. THREE A DAY.
MY PROGRAMMING INCLUDES AN APPRECIATION FOR AESTHETIC BEAUTY. KEPLER-22B IS AN OPTIMUM LOCATION.

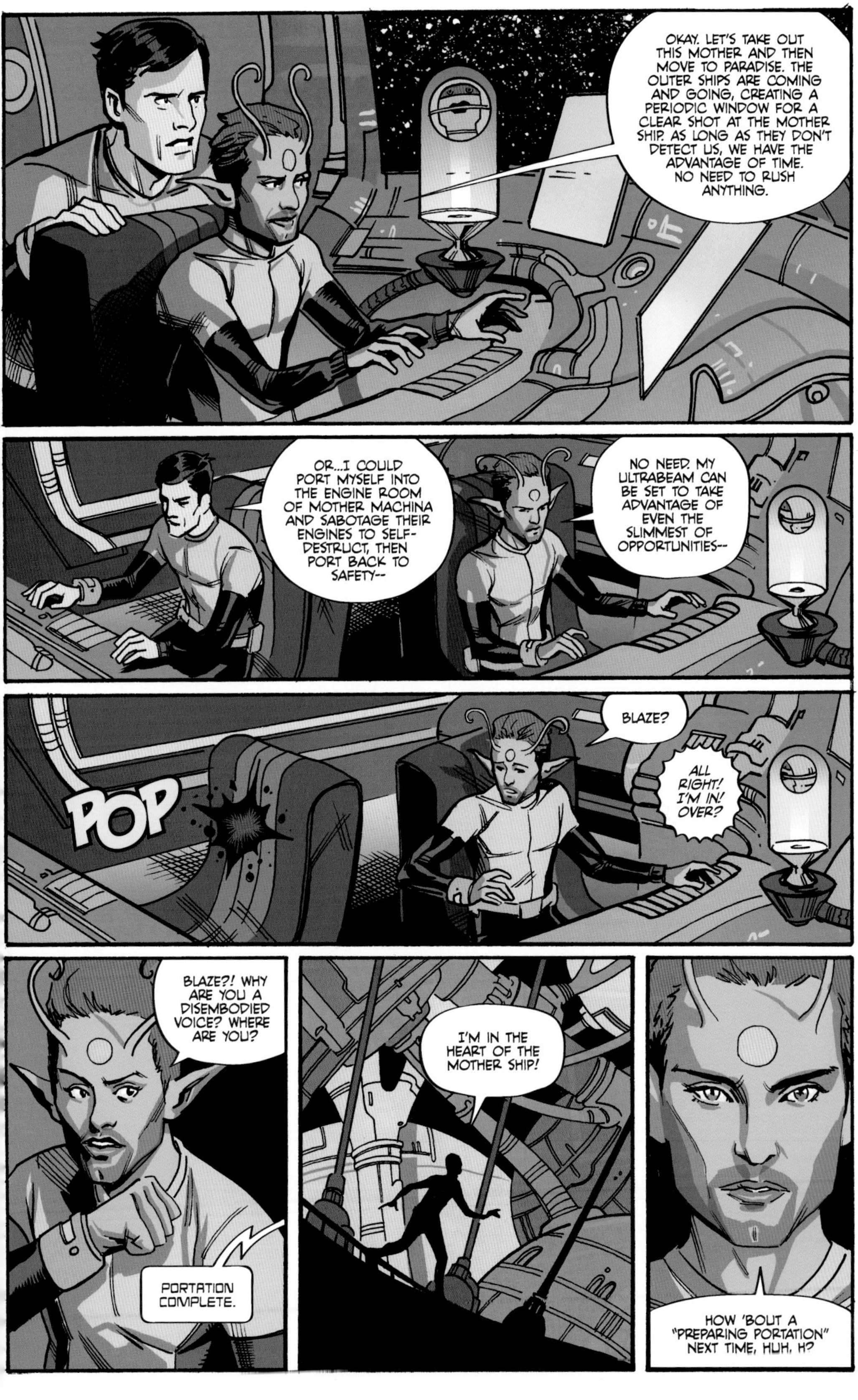
OKAY. LET'S TAKE OUT THIS MOTHER AND THEN MOVE TO PARADISE. THE OUTER SHIPS ARE COMING AND GOING, CREATING A PERIODIC WINDOW FOR A CLEAR SHOT AT THE MOTHER SHIP. AS LONG AS THEY DON'T DETECT US, WE HAVE THE ADVANTAGE OF TIME. NO NEED TO RUSH ANYTHING.
OR...I COULD PORT MYSELF INTO THE ENGINE ROOM OF MOTHER MACHINA AND SABOTAGE THEIR ENGINES TO SELF-DESTRUCT, THEN PORT BACK TO SAFETY--
NO NEED. MY ULTRABEAM CAN BE SET TO TAKE ADVANTAGE OF EVEN THE SLIMMEST OF OPPORTUNITIES--
POP
BLAZE?
ALL RIGHT! I'M IN! OVER?
BLAZE?! WHY ARE YOU A DISEMBODIED VOICE? WHERE ARE YOU?
PORTATION COMPLETE.
I'M IN THE HEART OF THE MOTHER SHIP!
HOW 'BOUT A "PREPARING PORTATION" NEXT TIME, HUH, H?

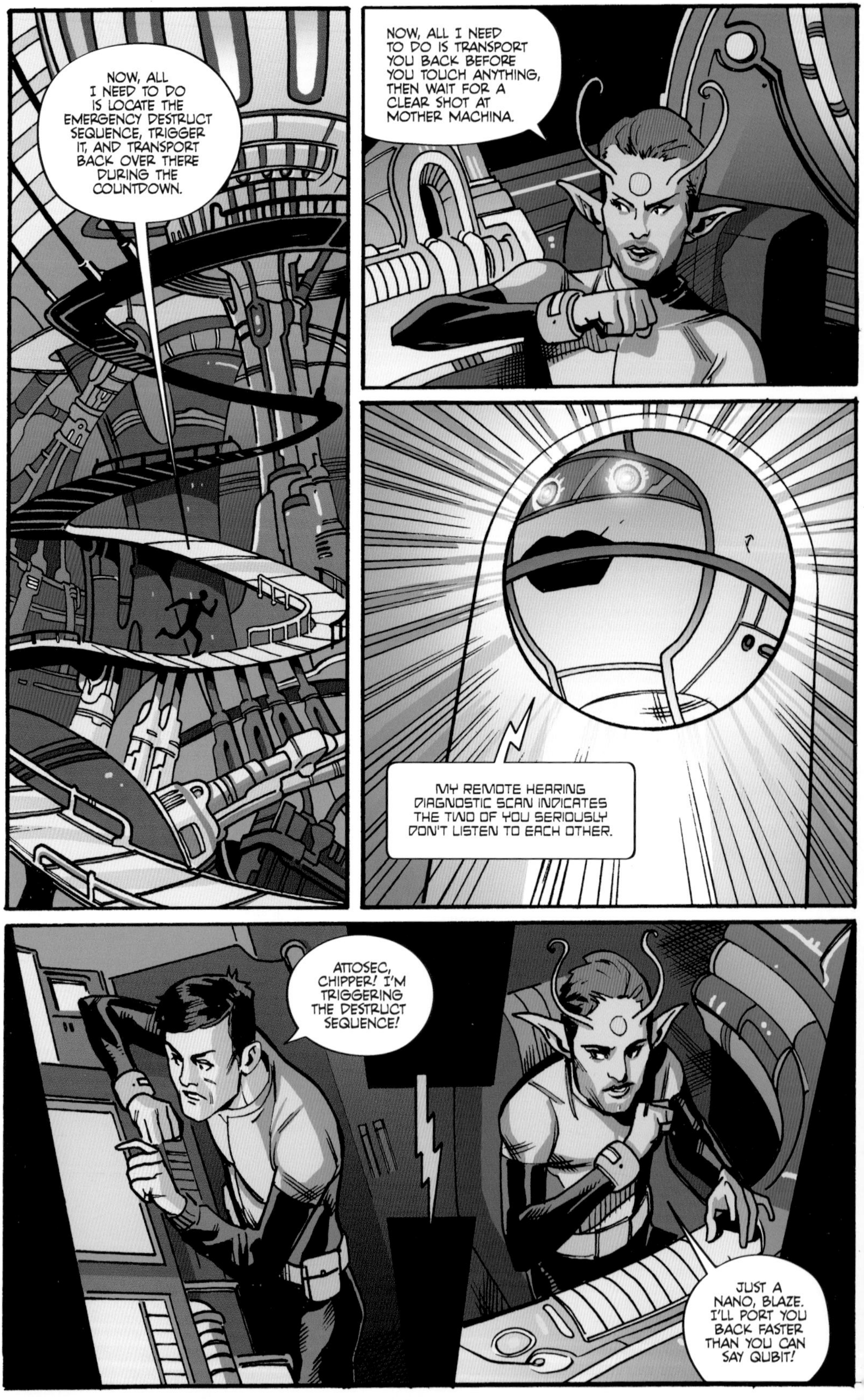
NOW, ALL I NEED TO DO IS LOCATE THE EMERGENCY DESTRUCT SEQUENCE, TRIGGER IT, AND TRANSPORT BACK OVER THERE DURING THE COUNTDOWN.
NOW, ALL I NEED TO DO IS TRANSPORT YOU BACK BEFORE YOU TOUCH ANYTHING, THEN WAIT FOR A CLEAR SHOT AT MOTHER MACHINA.
MY REMOTE HEARING DIAGNOSTIC SCAN INDICATES THE TWO OF YOU SERIOUSLY DON'T LISTEN TO EACH OTHER.
ATTOSEC, CHIPPER! I'M TRIGGERING THE DESTRUCT SEQUENCE!
JUST A NANO, BLAZE. I'LL PORT YOU BACK FASTER THAN YOU CAN SAY QUBIT!

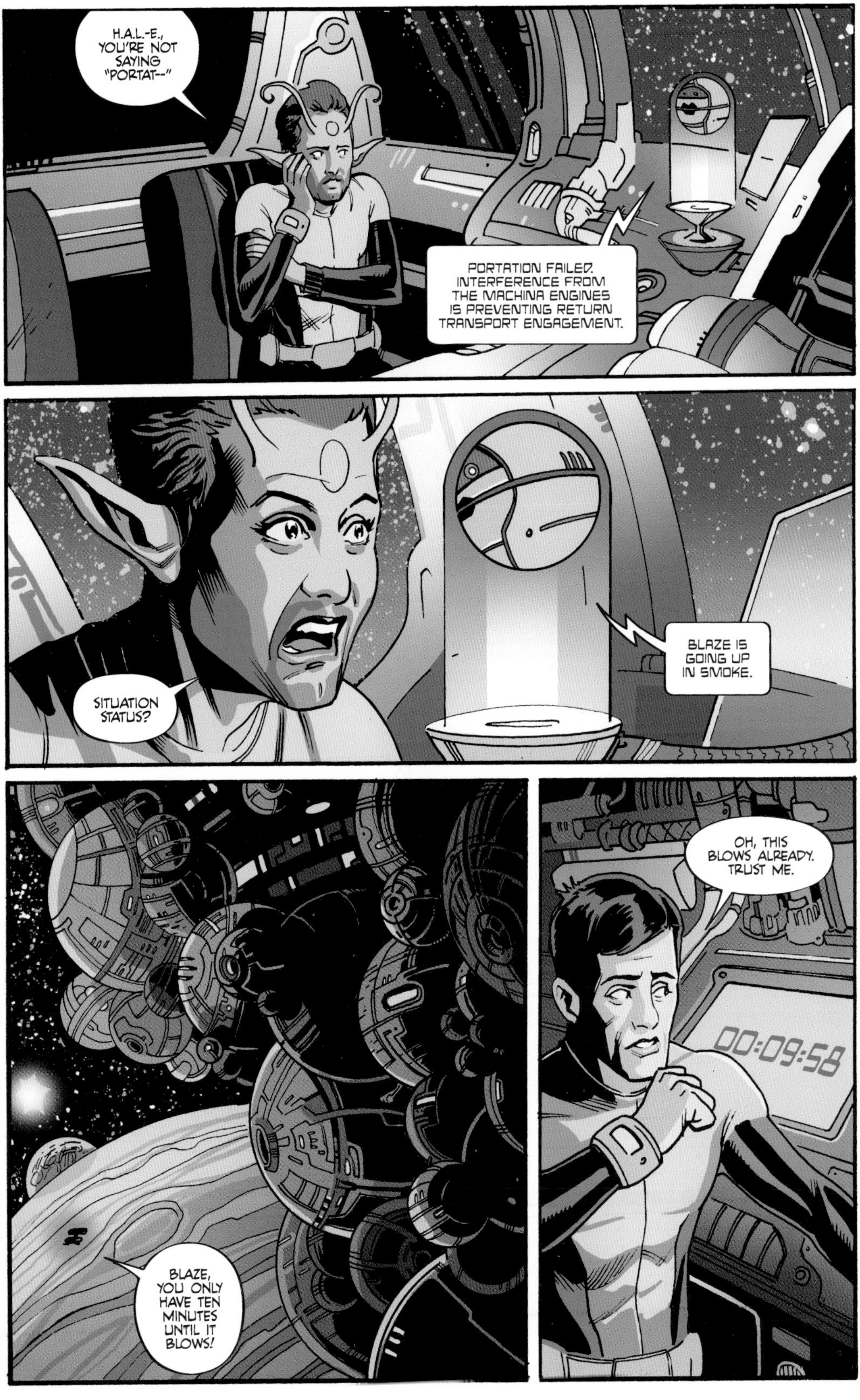
H.A.L.-E., YOU'RE NOT SAYING "PORTAT--"
PORTATION FAILED. INTERFERENCE FROM THE MACHINA ENGINES IS PREVENTING RETURN TRANSPORT ENGAGEMENT.
SITUATION STATUS?
BLAZE IS GOING UP IN SMOKE.
BLAZE, YOU ONLY HAVE TEN MINUTES UNTIL IT BLOWS!
OH, THIS BLOWS ALREADY. TRUST ME.
00:09:58

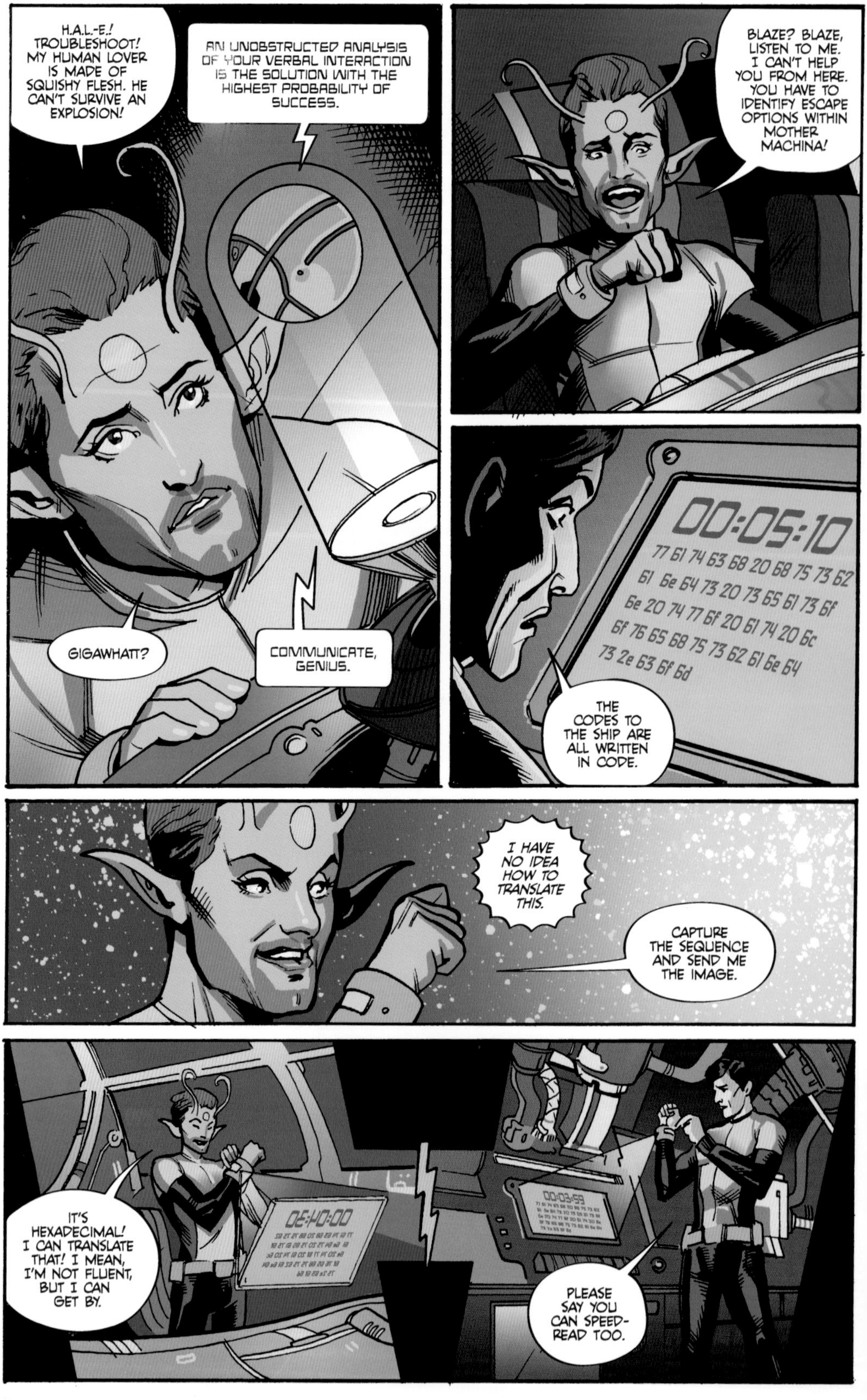
H.A.L.-E.! TROUBLESHOOT! MY HUMAN LOVER IS MADE OF SQUISHY FLESH. HE CAN'T SURVIVE AN EXPLOSION!
AN UNOBSTRUCTED ANALYSIS OF YOUR VERBAL INTERACTION IS THE SOLUTION WITH THE HIGHEST PROBABILITY OF SUCCESS.
GIGAWHATT?
COMMUNICATE, GENIUS.
BLAZE? BLAZE, LISTEN TO ME. I CAN'T HELP YOU FROM HERE. YOU HAVE TO IDENTIFY ESCAPE OPTIONS WITHIN MOTHER MACHINA!
00:05:10
77 61 74 63 68 20 68 75 73 62
61 6e 64 73 20 73 65 61 73 6f
6e 20 74 77 6f 20 61 74 20 6c
6f 76 65 68 75 73 62 61 6e 64
73 2e 63 6f 6d
THE CODES TO THE SHIP ARE ALL WRITTEN IN CODE.
I HAVE NO IDEA HOW TO TRANSLATE THIS.
CAPTURE THE SEQUENCE AND SEND ME THE IMAGE.
IT'S HEXADECIMAL! I CAN TRANSLATE THAT! I MEAN, I'M NOT FLUENT, BUT I CAN GET BY.
PLEASE SAY YOU CAN SPEED-READ TOO.

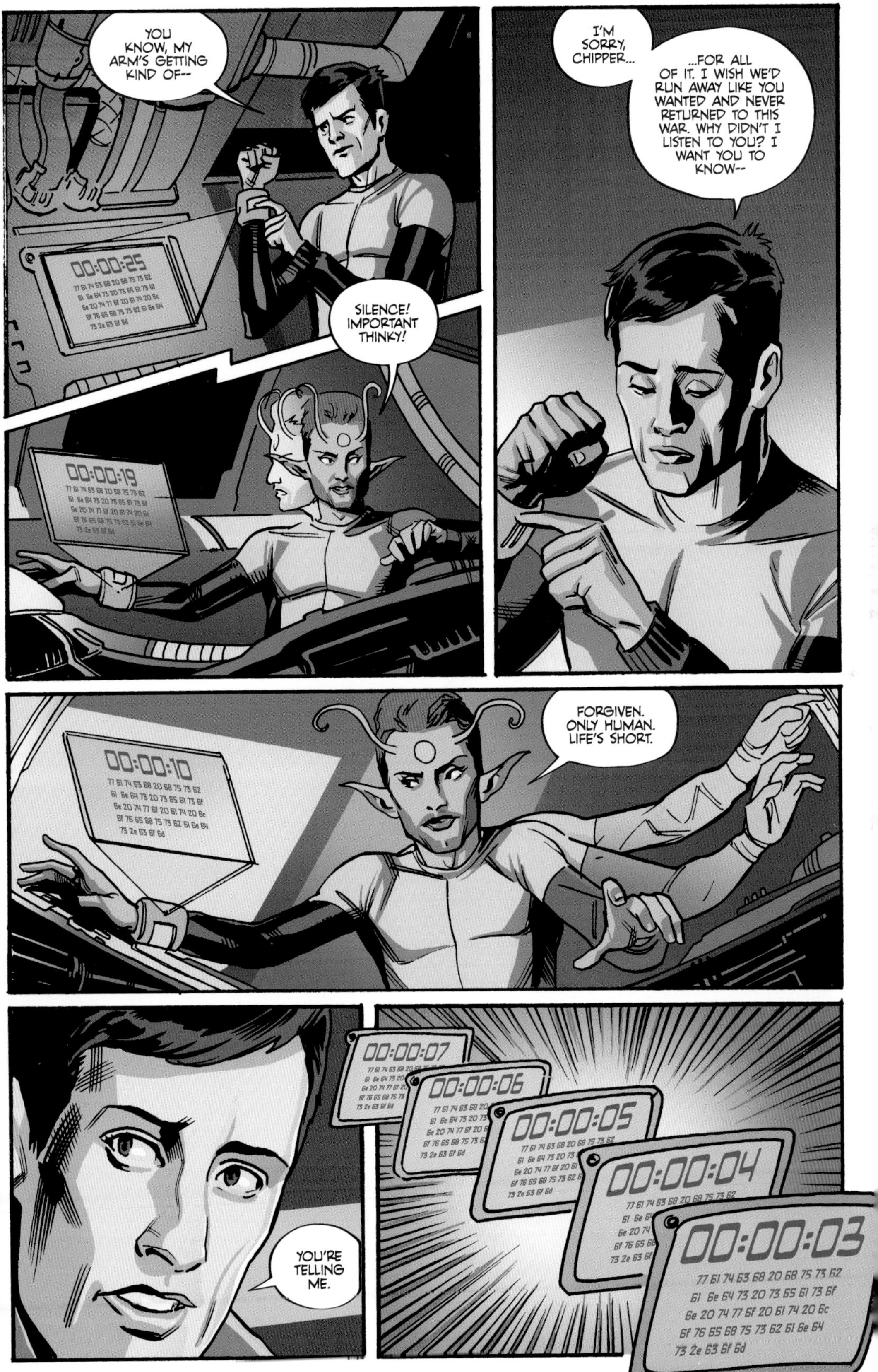
YOU KNOW, MY ARM'S GETTING KIND OF--
00:00:25
SILENCE! IMPORTANT THINKY!
00:00:19
I'M SORRY, CHIPPER...
...FOR ALL OF IT. I WISH WE'D RUN AWAY LIKE YOU WANTED AND NEVER RETURNED TO THIS WAR. WHY DIDN'T I LISTEN TO YOU? I WANT YOU TO KNOW--
00:00:10
FORGIVEN. ONLY HUMAN. LIFE'S SHORT.
YOU'RE TELLING ME.
00:00:07
00:00:06
00:00:05
00:00:04
00:00:03
77 61 74 63 68 20 68 75 73 62
61 6e 64 73 20 73 65 61 73 6f
6e 20 74 77 6f 20 61 74 20 6c
6f 76 65 68 75 73 62 61 6e 64
73 2e 63 6f 6d

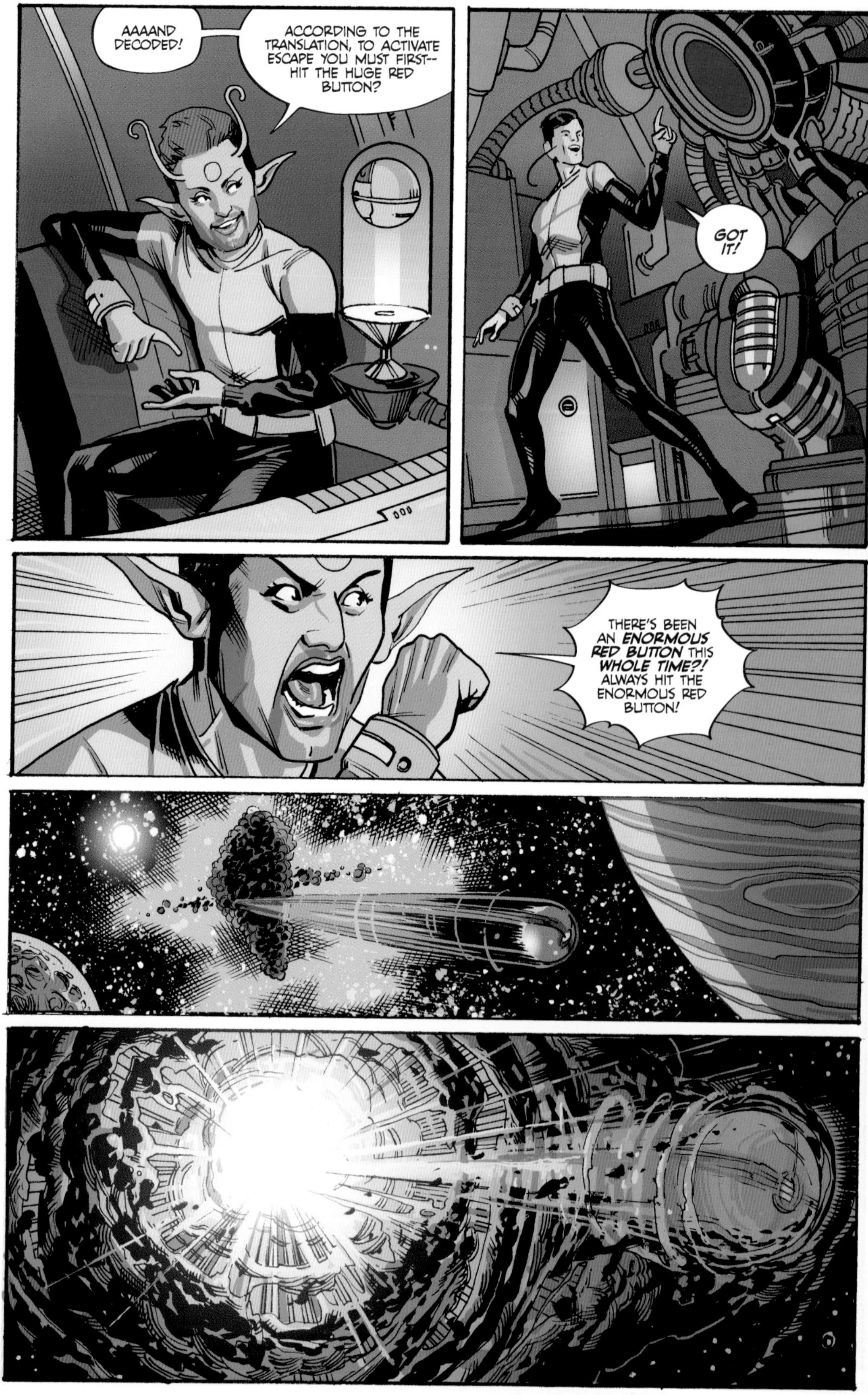
AAAAND DECODED!
ACCORDING TO THE TRANSLATION, TO ACTIVATE ESCAPE YOU MUST FIRST-- HIT THE HUGE RED BUTTON?
GOT IT!
THERE'S BEEN AN ENORMOUS RED BUTTON THIS WHOLE TIME?! ALWAYS HIT THE ENORMOUS RED BUTTON!

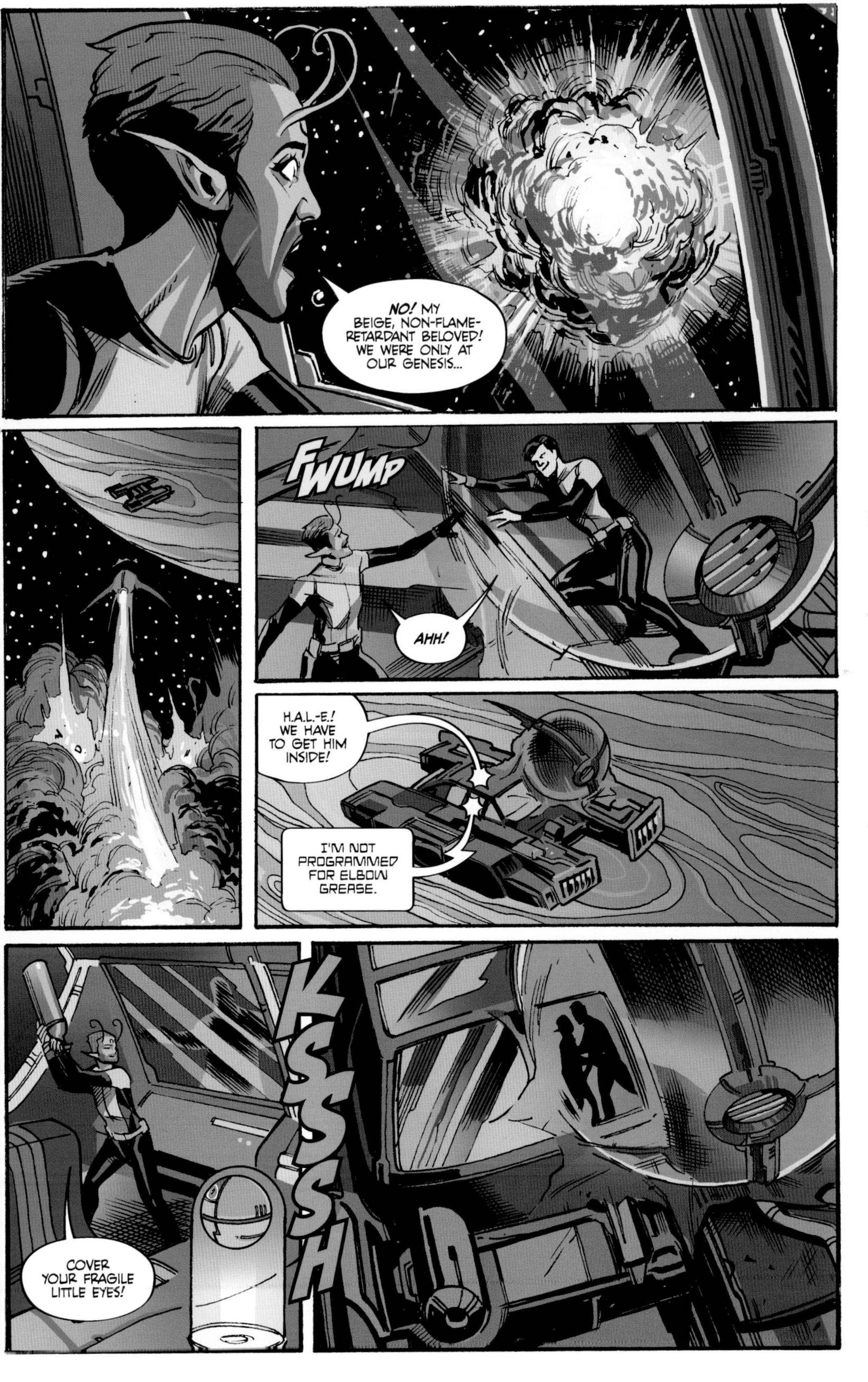
NO! MY BEIGE, NON-FLAME-RETARDANT BELOVED! WE WERE ONLY AT OUR GENESIS...
FWUMP
AHH!
H.A.L.-E.! WE HAVE TO GET HIM INSIDE!
I'M NOT PROGRAMMED FOR ELBOW GREASE.
COVER YOUR FRAGILE LITTLE EYES!
KSSSH

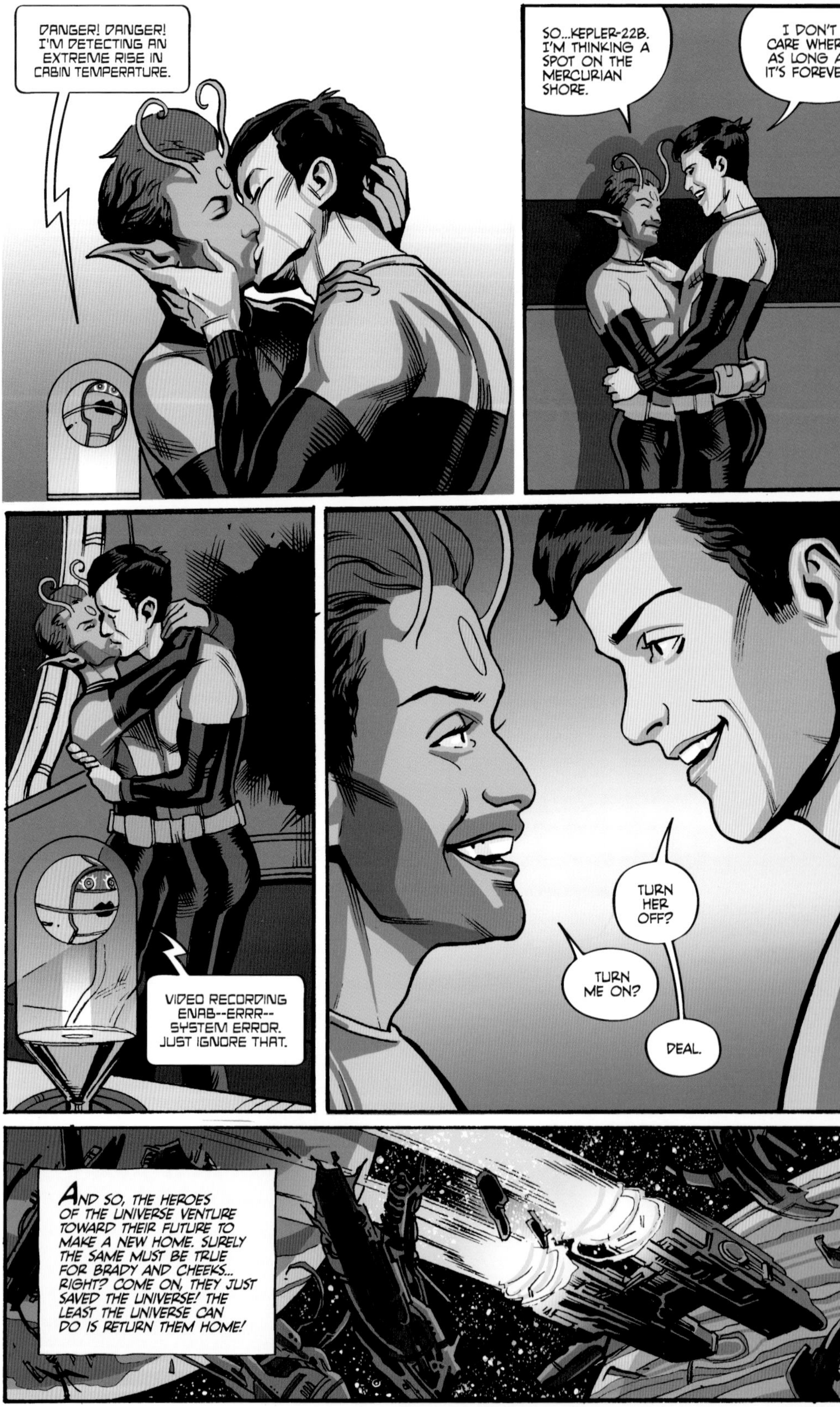
DANGER! DANGER! I'M DETECTING AN EXTREME RISE IN CABIN TEMPERATURE.
SO...KEPLER-22B. I'M THINKING A SPOT ON THE MERCURIAN SHORE.
I DON'T CARE WHERE, AS LONG AS IT'S FOREVER.
VIDEO RECORDING ENAB--ERRR-- SYSTEM ERROR. JUST IGNORE THAT.
TURN HER OFF?
TURN ME ON?
DEAL.
AND SO, THE HEROES OF THE UNIVERSE VENTURE TOWARD THEIR FUTURE TO MAKE A NEW HOME. SURELY THE SAME MUST BE TRUE FOR BRADY AND CHEEKS... RIGHT? COME ON, THEY JUST SAVED THE UNIVERSE! THE LEAST THE UNIVERSE CAN DO IS RETURN THEM HOME!

Arch Nemesis

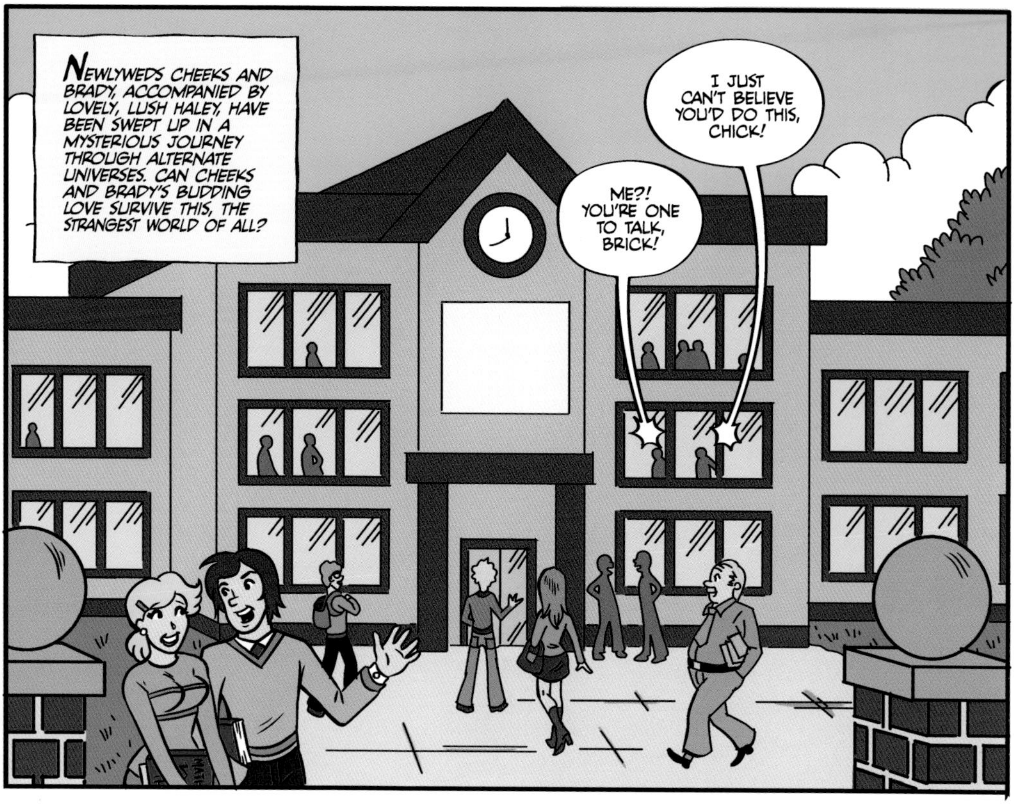
NEWLYWEDS CHEEKS AND BRADY, ACCOMPANIED BY LOVELY, LUSH HALEY, HAVE BEEN SWEPT UP IN A MYSTERIOUS JOURNEY THROUGH ALTERNATE UNIVERSES. CAN CHEEKS AND BRADY'S BUDDING LOVE SURVIVE THIS, THE STRANGEST WORLD OF ALL?
I JUST CAN'T BELIEVE YOU'D DO THIS, CHICK!
ME?! YOU'RE ONE TO TALK, BRICK!

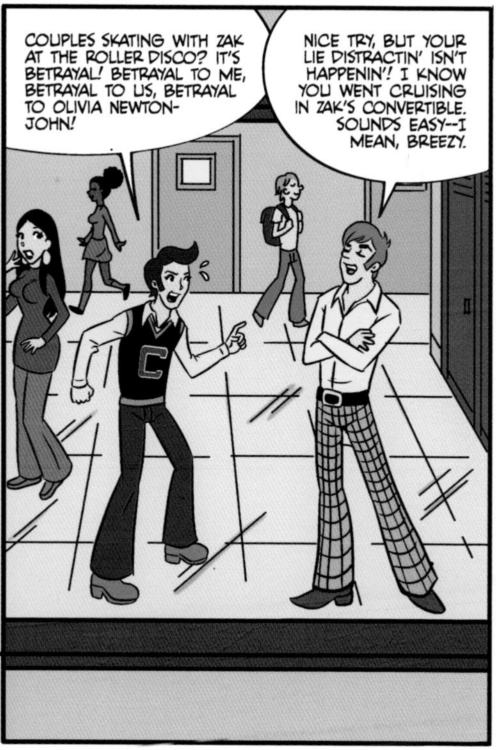
COUPLES SKATING WITH ZAK AT THE ROLLER DISCO? IT'S BETRAYAL! BETRAYAL TO ME, BETRAYAL TO US, BETRAYAL TO OLIVIA NEWTON-JOHN!
NICE TRY, BUT YOUR LIE DISTRACTIN' ISN'T HAPPENIN'! I KNOW YOU WENT CRUISING IN ZAK'S CONVERTIBLE. SOUNDS EASY--I MEAN, BREEZY.

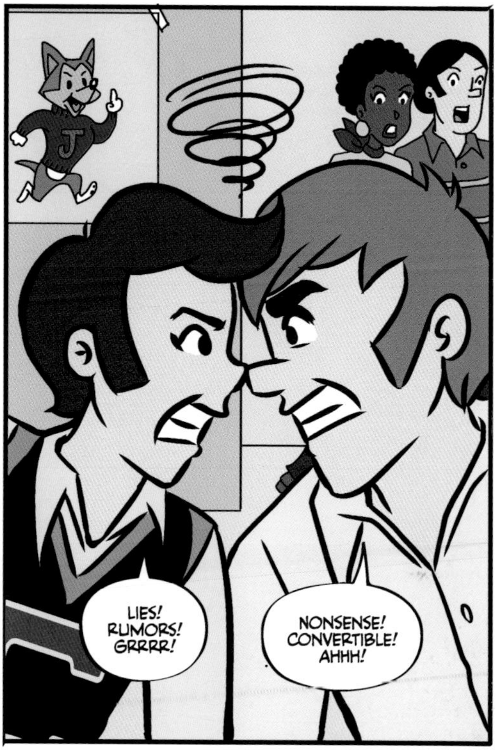
LIES! RUMORS! GRRRR!
NONSENSE! CONVERTIBLE! AHHH!

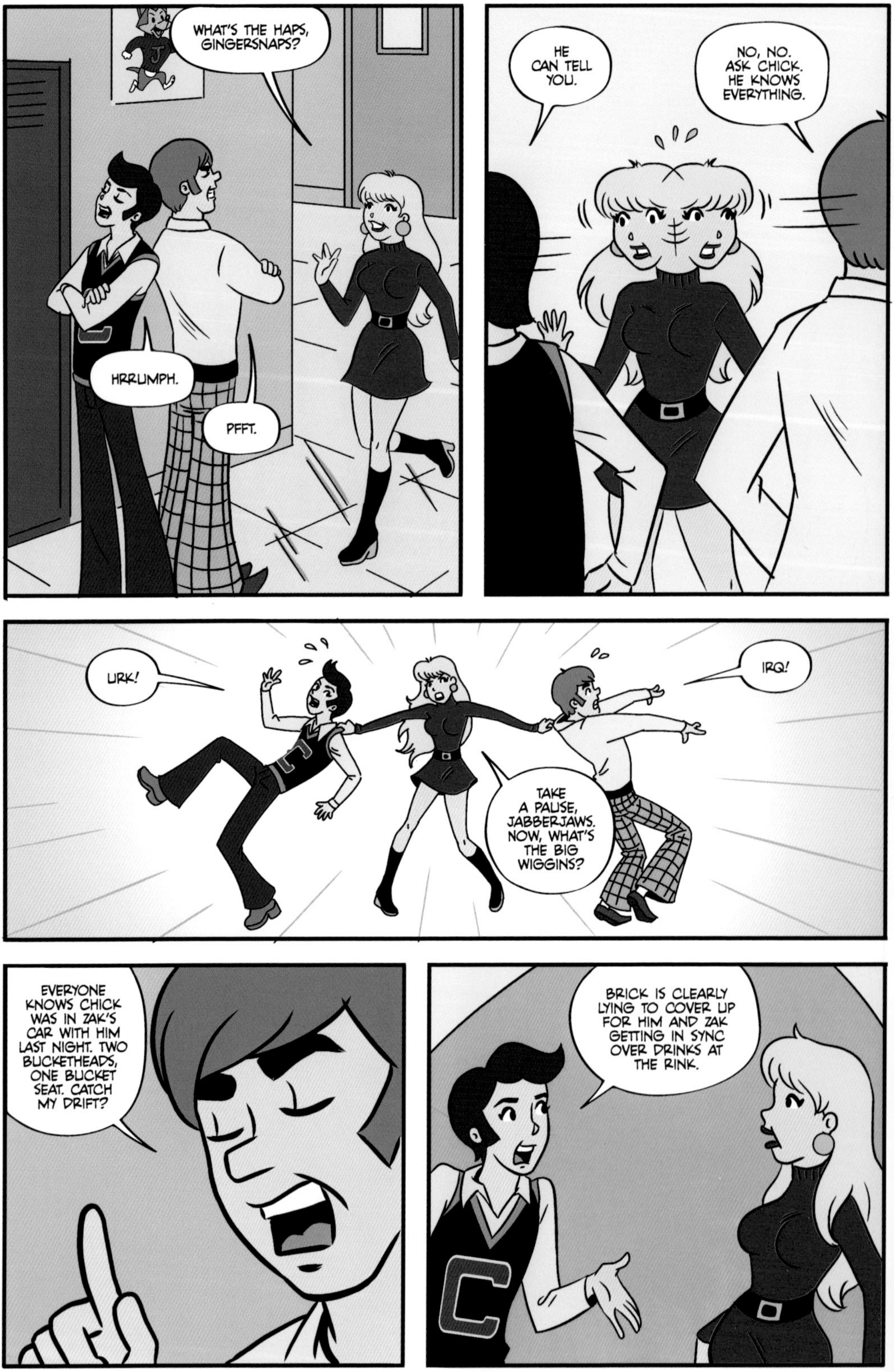
WHAT'S THE HAPS, GINGERSNAPS?
HRRUMPH.
PFFT.
HE CAN TELL YOU.
NO, NO. ASK CHICK. HE KNOWS EVERYTHING.
URK!
IRQ!
TAKE A PAUSE, JABBERJAWS. NOW, WHAT'S THE BIG WIGGINS?
EVERYONE KNOWS CHICK WAS IN ZAK'S CAR WITH HIM LAST NIGHT. TWO BUCKETHEADS, ONE BUCKET SEAT. CATCH MY DRIFT?
BRICK IS CLEARLY LYING TO COVER UP FOR HIM AND ZAK GETTING IN SYNC OVER DRINKS AT THE RINK.

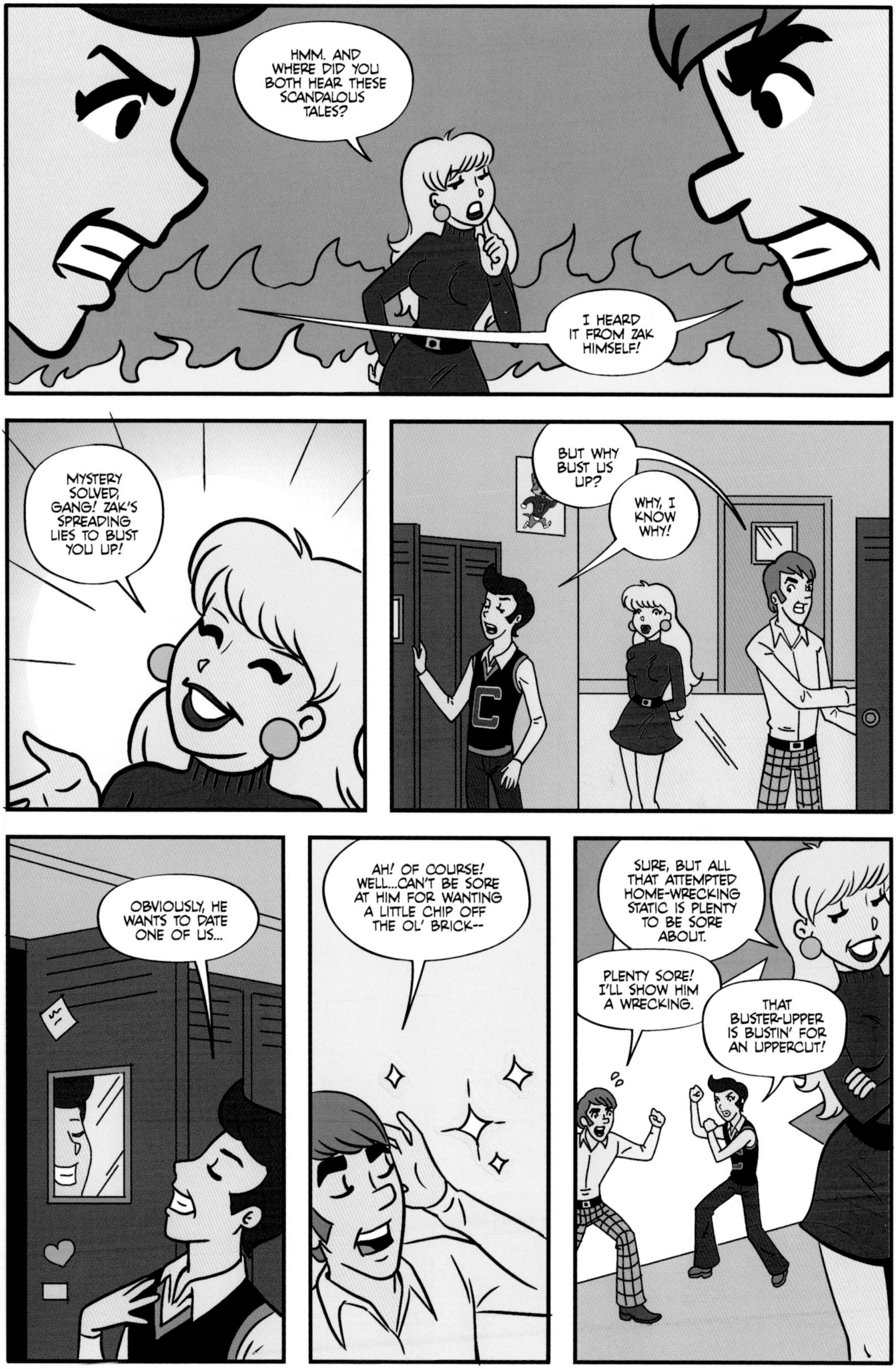
HMM. AND WHERE DID YOU BOTH HEAR THESE SCANDALOUS TALES?
I HEARD IT FROM ZAK HIMSELF!
MYSTERY SOLVED, GANG! ZAK'S SPREADING LIES TO BUST YOU UP!
BUT WHY BUST US UP?
WHY, I KNOW WHY!
OBVIOUSLY, HE WANTS TO DATE ONE OF US...
AH! OF COURSE! WELL...CAN'T BE SORE AT HIM FOR WANTING A LITTLE CHIP OFF THE OL' BRICK--
SURE, BUT ALL THAT ATTEMPTED HOME-WRECKING STATIC IS PLENTY TO BE SORE ABOUT.
PLENTY SORE! I'LL SHOW HIM A WRECKING.
THAT BUSTER-UPPER IS BUSTIN' FOR AN UPPERCUT!

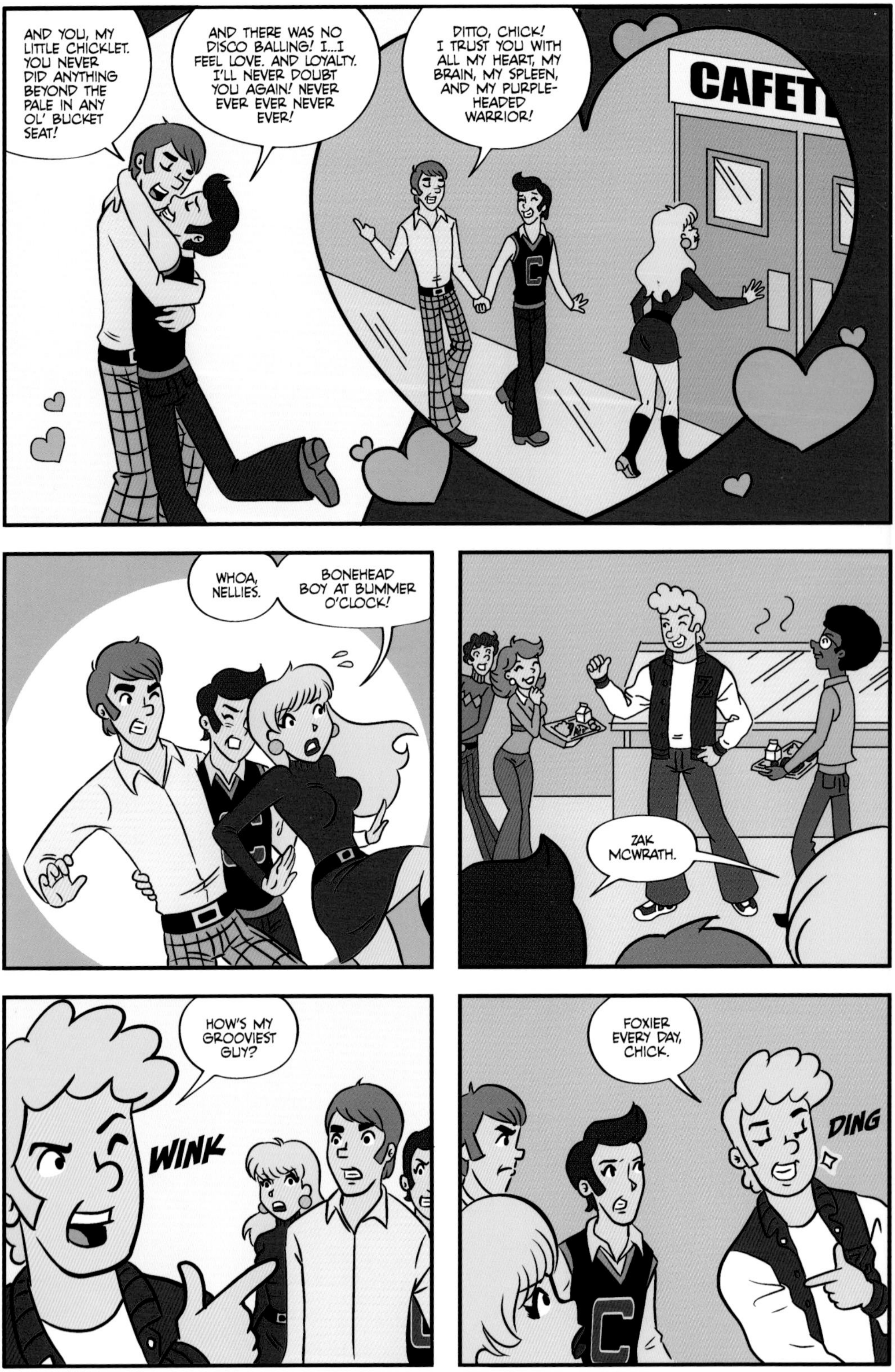

AND YOU, MY LITTLE CHICKLET. YOU NEVER DID ANYTHING BEYOND THE PALE IN ANY OL' BUCKET SEAT!
AND THERE WAS NO DISCO BALLING! I...I FEEL LOVE. AND LOYALTY. I'LL NEVER DOUBT YOU AGAIN! NEVER EVER EVER NEVER EVER!
DITTO, CHICK! I TRUST YOU WITH ALL MY HEART, MY BRAIN, MY SPLEEN, AND MY PURPLE-HEADED WARRIOR!
CAFETE
WHOA, NELLIES.
BONEHEAD BOY AT BUMMER O'CLOCK!
ZAK MCWRATH.
HOW'S MY GROOVIEST GUY?
WINK
FOXIER EVERY DAY, CHICK.
DING

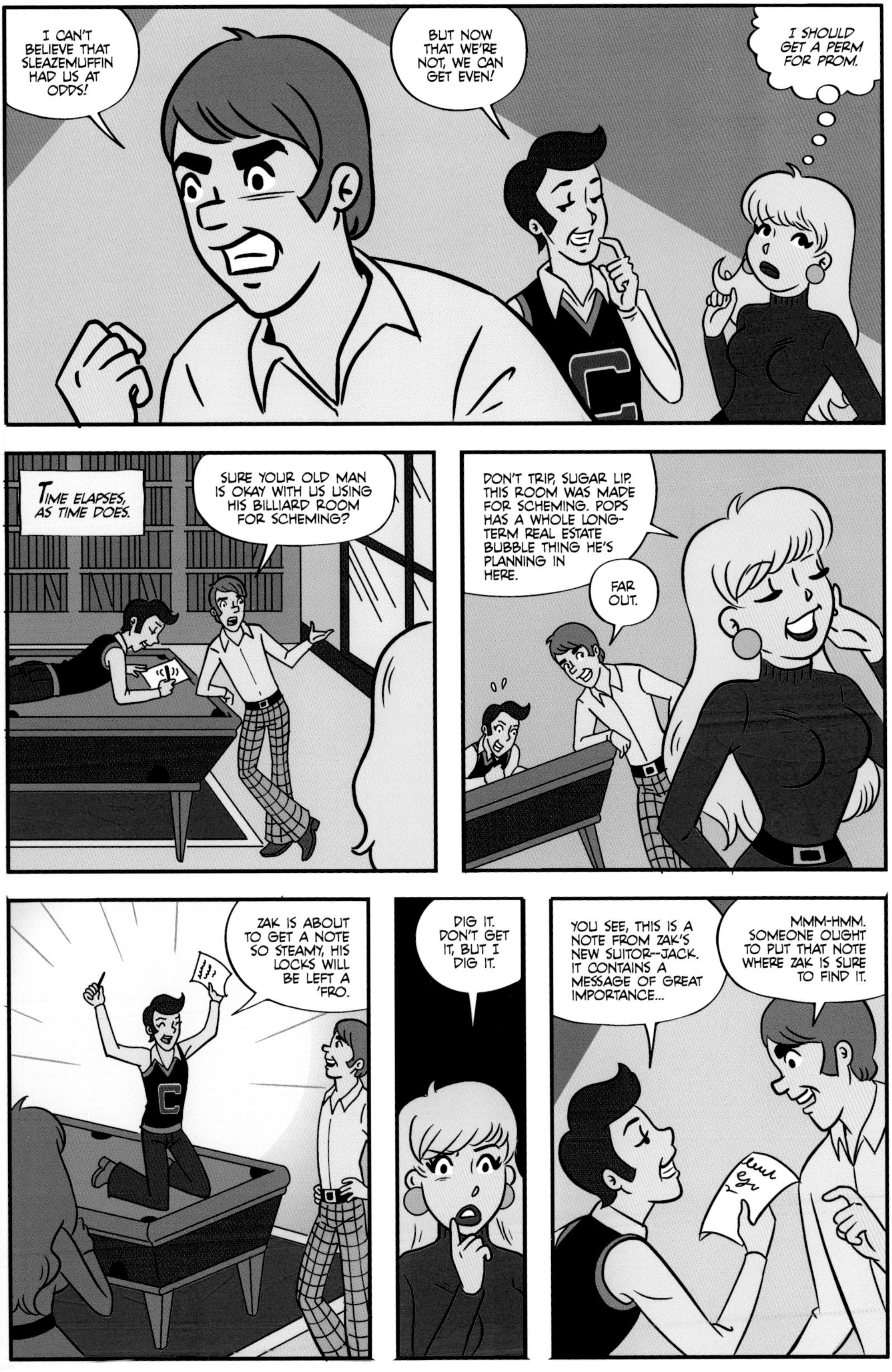

I CAN'T BELIEVE THAT SLEAZEMUFFIN HAD US AT ODDS!
BUT NOW THAT WE'RE NOT, WE CAN GET EVEN!
I SHOULD GET A PERM FOR PROM.
TIME ELAPSES, AS TIME DOES.
SURE YOUR OLD MAN IS OKAY WITH US USING HIS BILLIARD ROOM FOR SCHEMING?
DON'T TRIP, SUGAR LIP. THIS ROOM WAS MADE FOR SCHEMING. POPS HAS A WHOLE LONG-TERM REAL ESTATE BUBBLE THING HE'S PLANNING IN HERE.
FAR OUT.
ZAK IS ABOUT TO GET A NOTE SO STEAMY, HIS LOCKS WILL BE LEFT A 'FRO.
DIG IT. DON'T GET IT, BUT I DIG IT.
YOU SEE, THIS IS A NOTE FROM ZAK'S NEW SUITOR--JACK. IT CONTAINS A MESSAGE OF GREAT IMPORTANCE...
MMM-HMM. SOMEONE OUGHT TO PUT THAT NOTE WHERE ZAK IS SURE TO FIND IT.

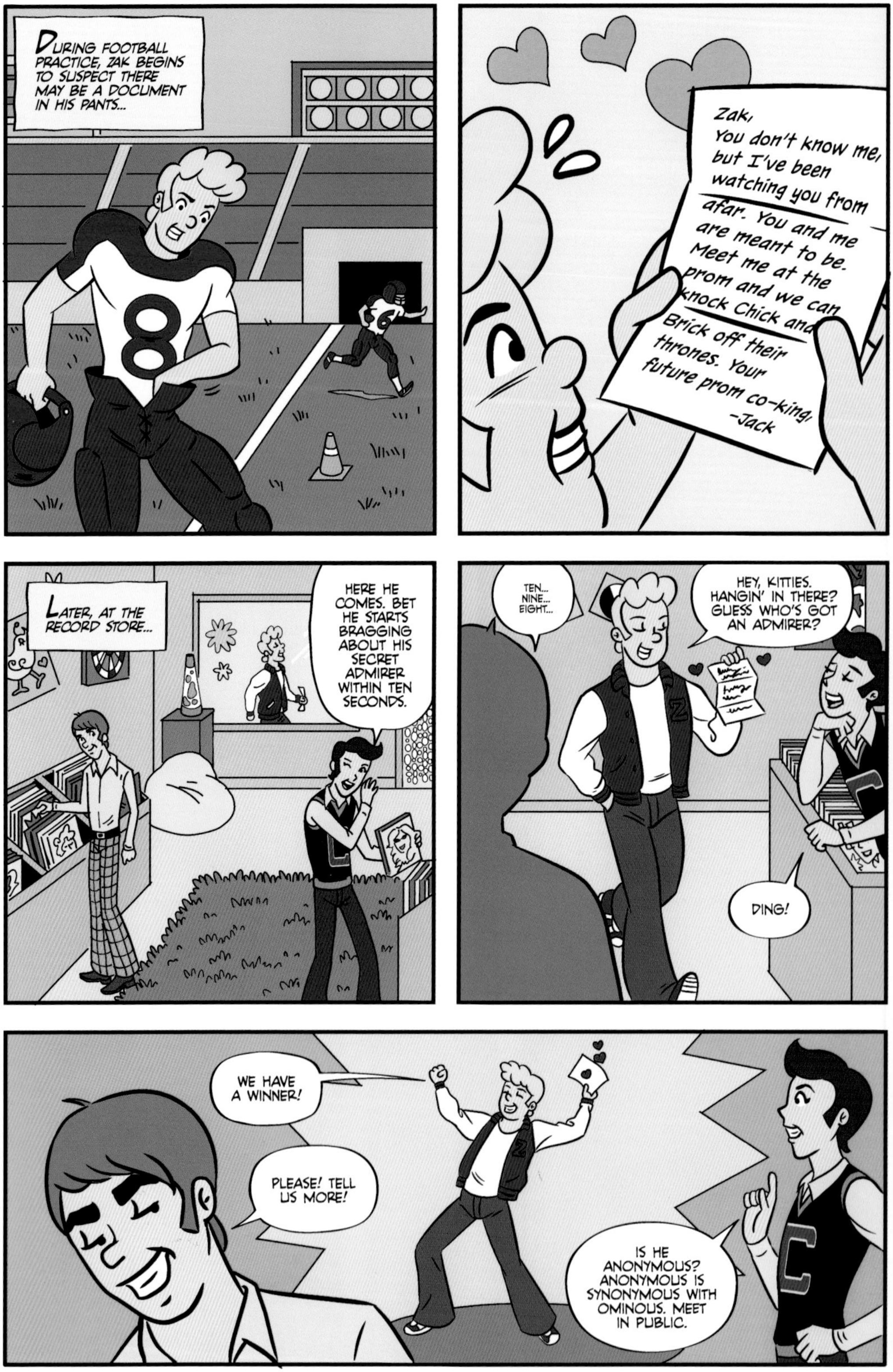
DURING FOOTBALL PRACTICE, ZAK BEGINS TO SUSPECT THERE MAY BE A DOCUMENT IN HIS PANTS...
Zak,
You don't know me, but I've been watching you from afar. You and me are meant to be. Meet me at the prom and we can knock Chick and Brick off their thrones. Your future prom co-king,
-Jack
LATER, AT THE RECORD STORE...
HERE HE COMES. BET HE STARTS BRAGGING ABOUT HIS SECRET ADMIRER WITHIN TEN SECONDS.
TEN... NINE... EIGHT...
HEY, KITTIES. HANGIN' IN THERE? GUESS WHO'S GOT AN ADMIRER?
DING!
WE HAVE A WINNER!
PLEASE! TELL US MORE!
IS HE ANONYMOUS? ANONYMOUS IS SYNONYMOUS WITH OMINOUS. MEET IN PUBLIC.

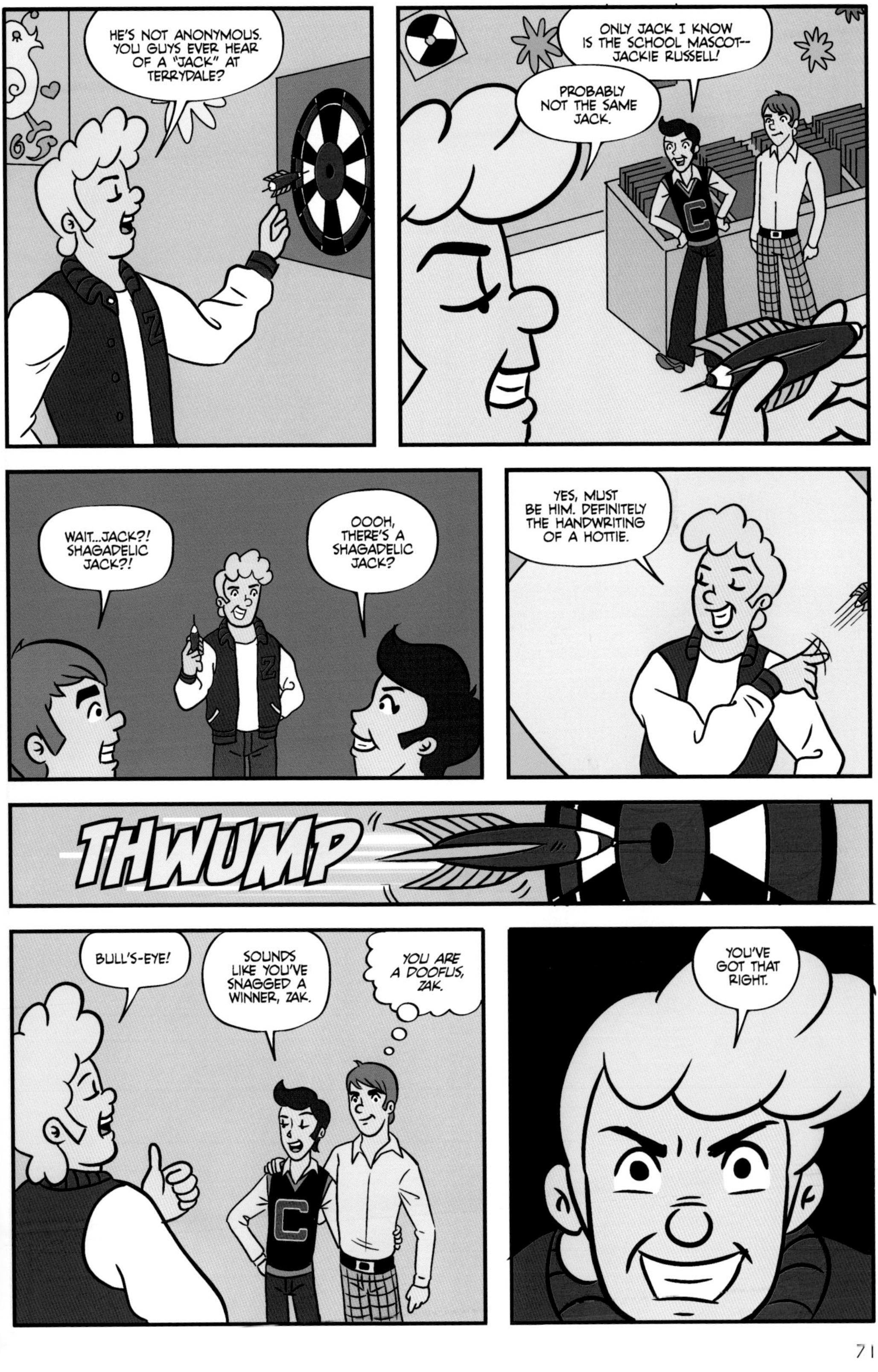
HE'S NOT ANONYMOUS. YOU GUYS EVER HEAR OF A "JACK" AT TERRYDALE?
ONLY JACK I KNOW IS THE SCHOOL MASCOT--JACKIE RUSSELL!
PROBABLY NOT THE SAME JACK.
WAIT...JACK?! SHAGADELIC JACK?!
OOOH, THERE'S A SHAGADELIC JACK?
YES, MUST BE HIM. DEFINITELY THE HANDWRITING OF A HOTTIE.
THWUMP
BULL'S-EYE!
SOUNDS LIKE YOU'VE SNAGGED A WINNER, ZAK.
YOU ARE A DOOFUS, ZAK.
YOU'VE GOT THAT RIGHT.

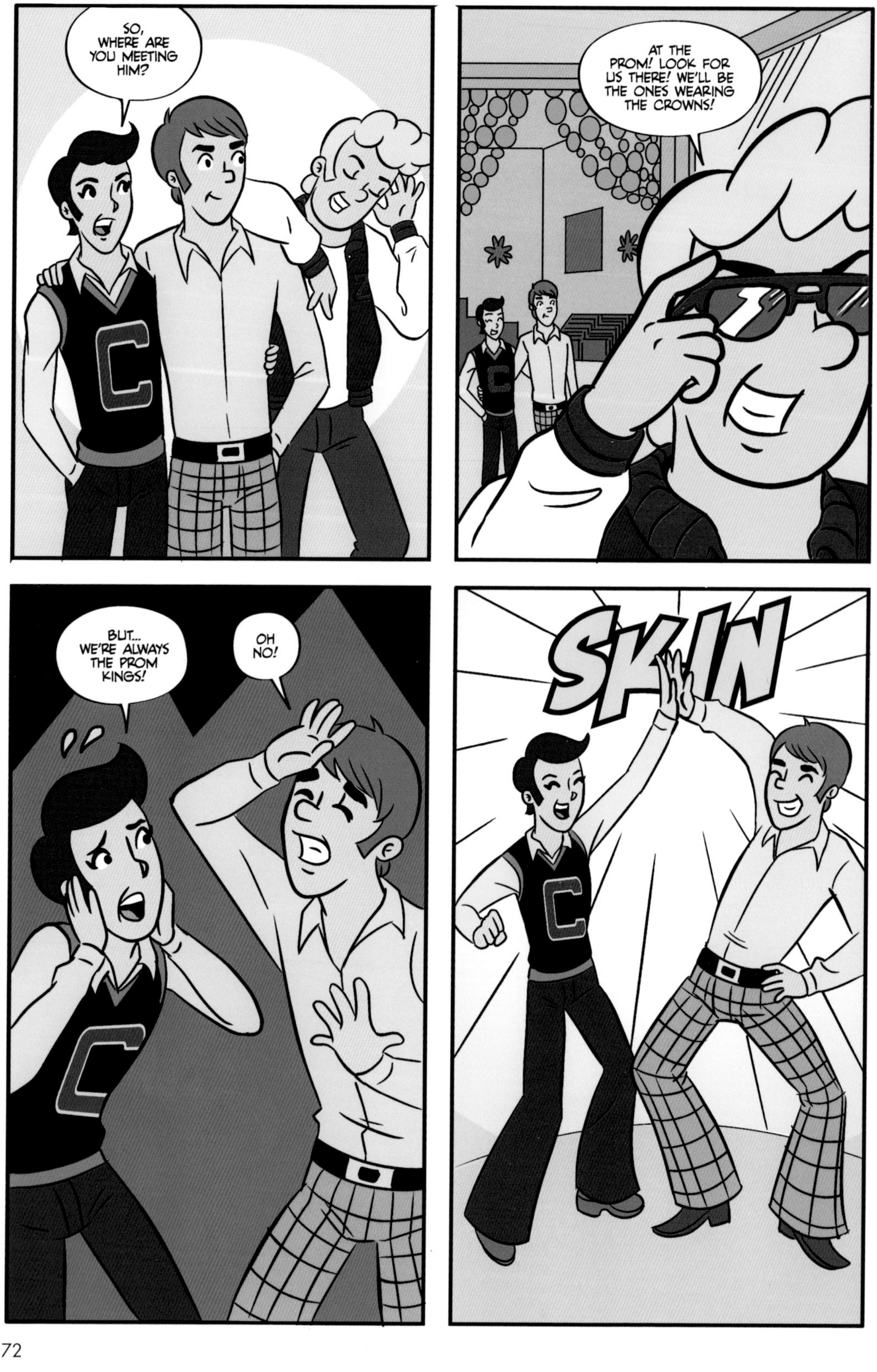
SO, WHERE ARE YOU MEETING HIM?
AT THE PROM! LOOK FOR US THERE! WE'LL BE THE ONES WEARING THE CROWNS!
BUT... WE'RE ALWAYS THE PROM KINGS!
OH NO!
SKIN

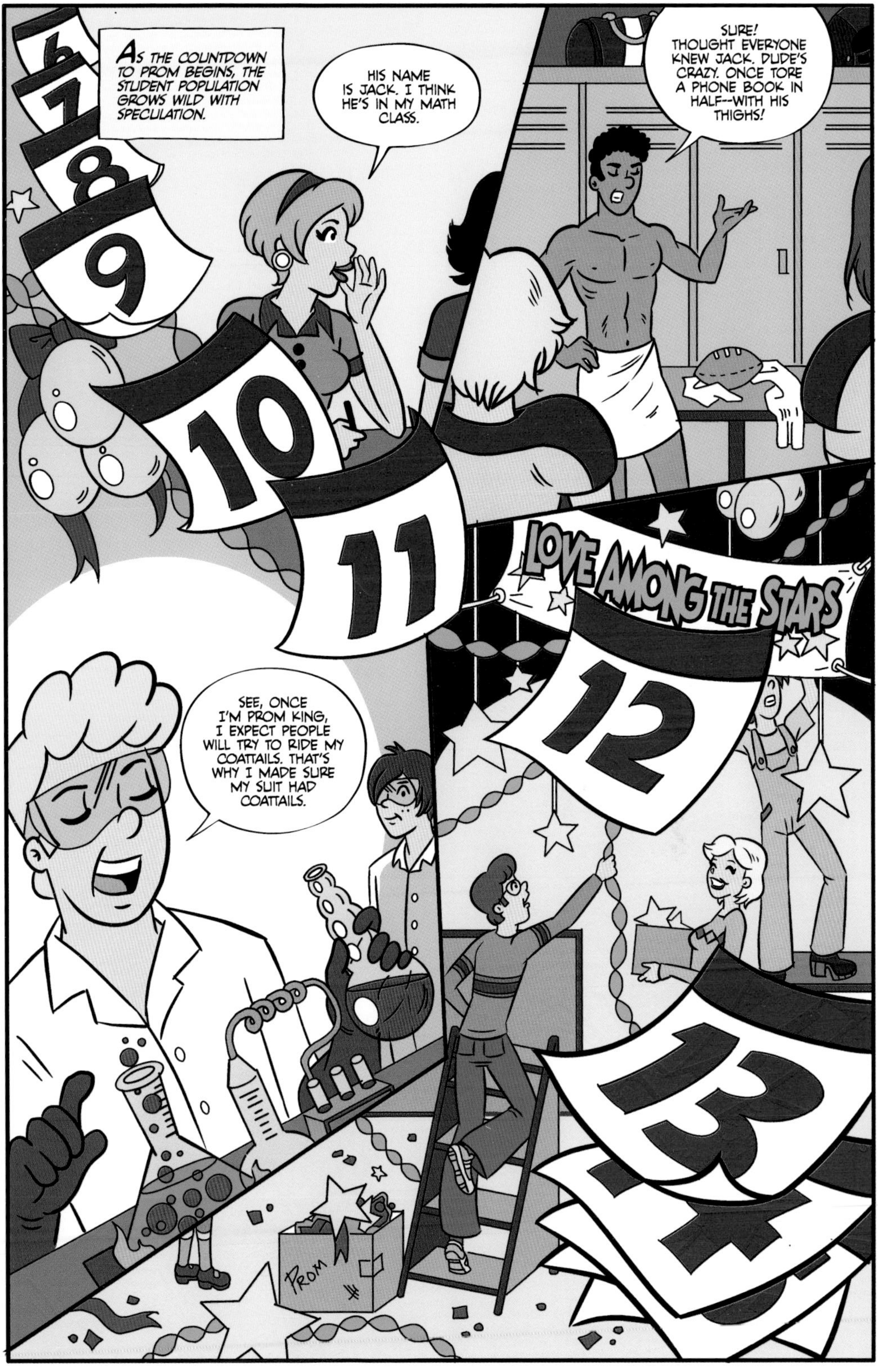
AS THE COUNTDOWN TO PROM BEGINS, THE STUDENT POPULATION GROWS WILD WITH SPECULATION.
HIS NAME IS JACK. I THINK HE'S IN MY MATH CLASS.
SURE! THOUGHT EVERYONE KNEW JACK. DUDE'S CRAZY. ONCE TORE A PHONE BOOK IN HALF--WITH HIS THIGHS!
LOVE AMONG THE STARS
SEE, ONCE I'M PROM KING, I EXPECT PEOPLE WILL TRY TO RIDE MY COATTAILS. THAT'S WHY I MADE SURE MY SUIT HAD COATTAILS.
PROM

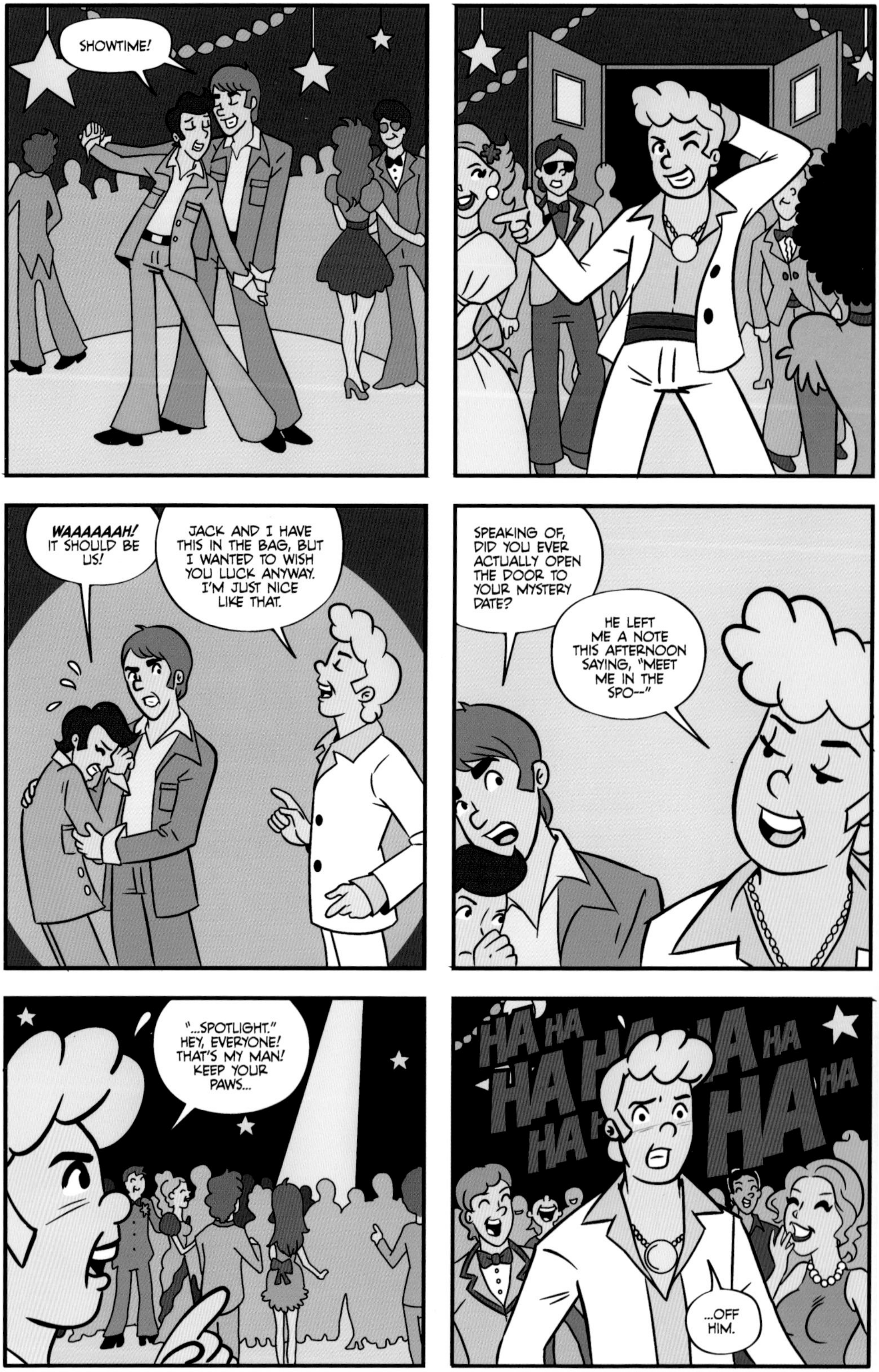
SHOWTIME!
WAAAAAAH! IT SHOULD BE US!
JACK AND I HAVE THIS IN THE BAG, BUT I WANTED TO WISH YOU LUCK ANYWAY. I'M JUST NICE LIKE THAT.
SPEAKING OF, DID YOU EVER ACTUALLY OPEN THE DOOR TO YOUR MYSTERY DATE?
HE LEFT ME A NOTE THIS AFTERNOON SAYING, "MEET ME IN THE SPO--"
"...SPOTLIGHT." HEY, EVERYONE! THAT'S MY MAN! KEEP YOUR PAWS...
HA HA HA HA HA HA HA HA HA HA
...OFF HIM.

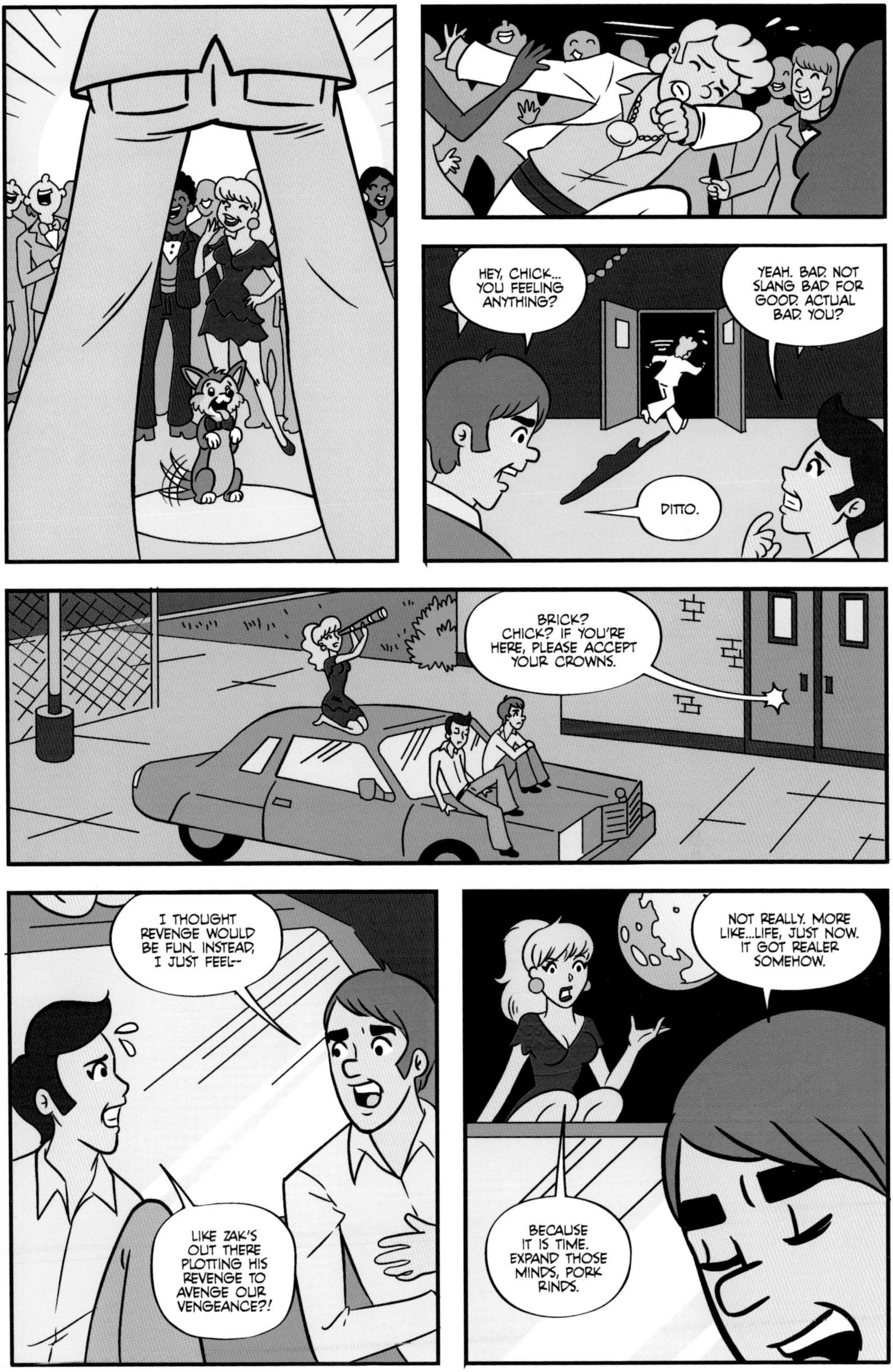
HEY, CHICK... YOU FEELING ANYTHING?
YEAH. BAD. NOT SLANG BAD FOR GOOD. ACTUAL BAD. YOU?
DITTO.
BRICK? CHICK? IF YOU'RE HERE, PLEASE ACCEPT YOUR CROWNS.
I THOUGHT REVENGE WOULD BE FUN. INSTEAD, I JUST FEEL--
LIKE ZAK'S OUT THERE PLOTTING HIS REVENGE TO AVENGE OUR VENGEANCE?!
NOT REALLY. MORE LIKE...LIFE, JUST NOW. IT GOT REALER SOMEHOW.
BECAUSE IT IS TIME. EXPAND THOSE MINDS, PORK RINDS.

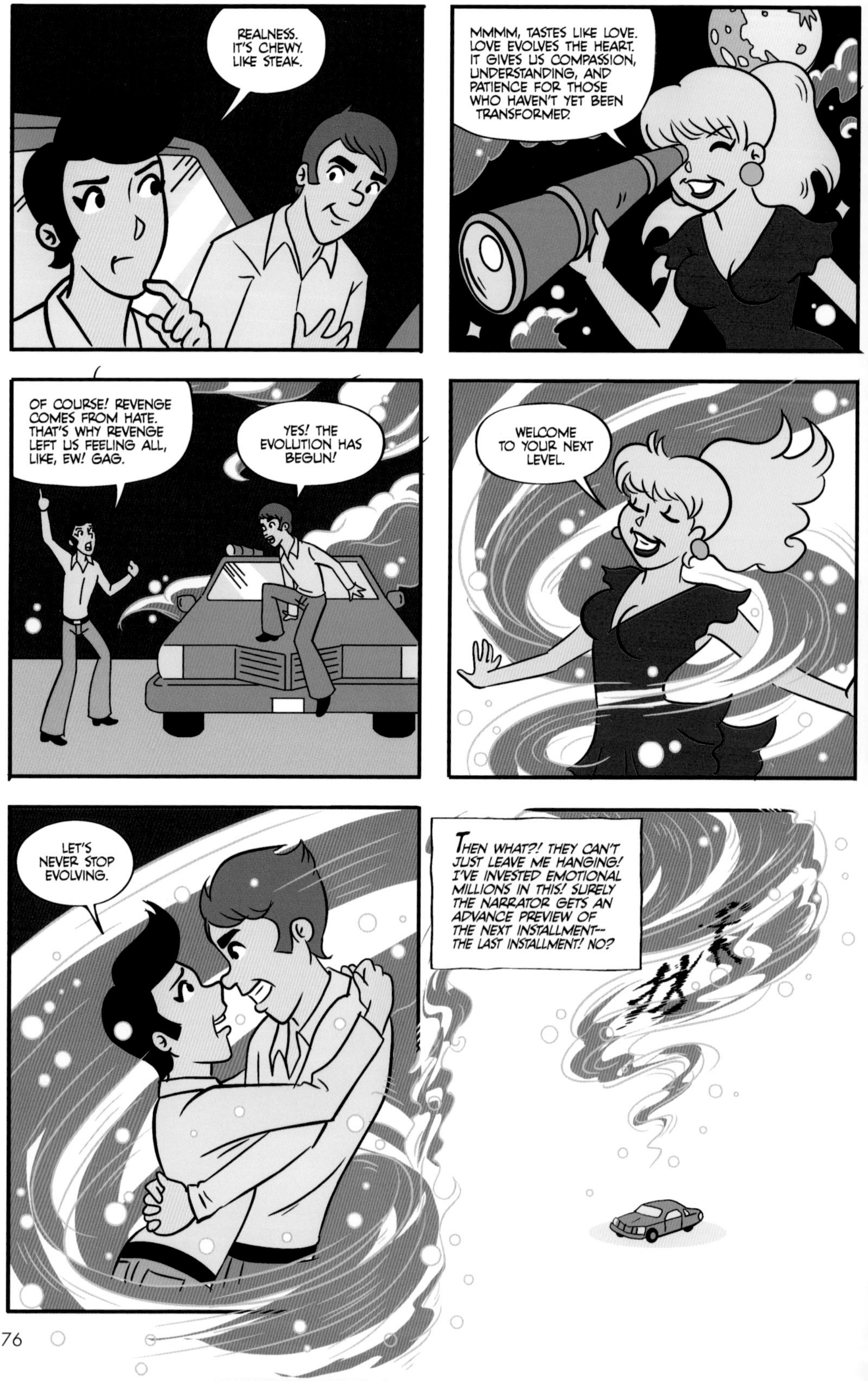
REALNESS. IT'S CHEWY. LIKE STEAK.
MMMM, TASTES LIKE LOVE. LOVE EVOLVES THE HEART. IT GIVES US COMPASSION, UNDERSTANDING, AND PATIENCE FOR THOSE WHO HAVEN'T YET BEEN TRANSFORMED.
OF COURSE! REVENGE COMES FROM HATE. THAT'S WHY REVENGE LEFT US FEELING ALL, LIKE, EW! GAG.
YES! THE EVOLUTION HAS BEGUN!
WELCOME TO YOUR NEXT LEVEL.
LET'S NEVER STOP EVOLVING.
THEN WHAT?! THEY CAN'T JUST LEAVE ME HANGING! I'VE INVESTED EMOTIONAL MILLIONS IN THIS! SURELY THE NARRATOR GETS AN ADVANCE PREVIEW OF THE NEXT INSTALLMENT-- THE LAST INSTALLMENT! NO?

Agent Secrets

6

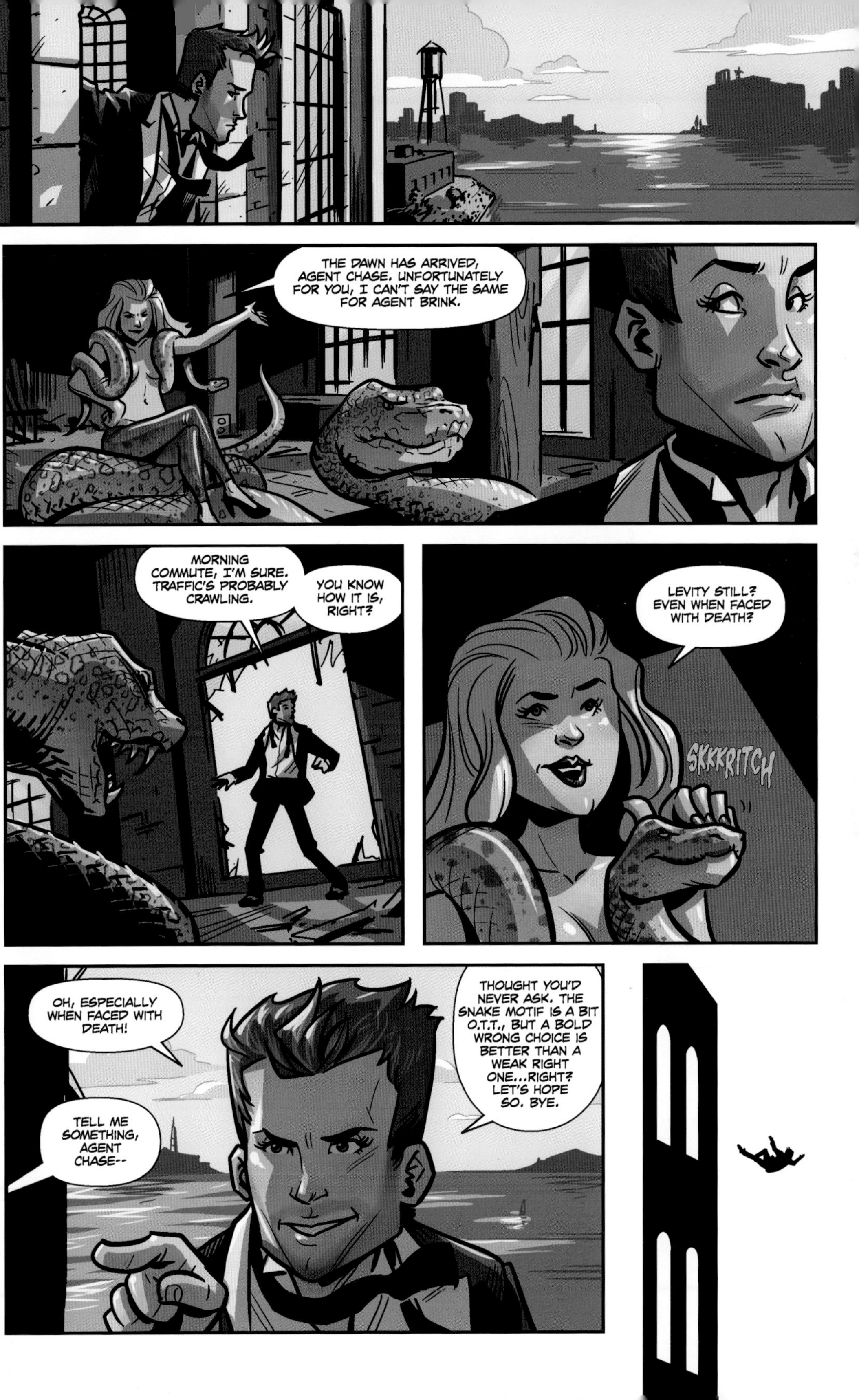
THE DAWN HAS ARRIVED, AGENT CHASE. UNFORTUNATELY FOR YOU, I CAN'T SAY THE SAME FOR AGENT BRINK.
MORNING COMMUTE, I'M SURE. TRAFFIC'S PROBABLY CRAWLING.
YOU KNOW HOW IT IS, RIGHT?
LEVITY STILL? EVEN WHEN FACED WITH DEATH?
SKKKRITCH
OH, ESPECIALLY WHEN FACED WITH DEATH!
TELL ME SOMETHING, AGENT CHASE--
THOUGHT YOU'D NEVER ASK. THE SNAKE MOTIF IS A BIT O.T.T., BUT A BOLD WRONG CHOICE IS BETTER THAN A WEAK RIGHT ONE...RIGHT? LET'S HOPE SO. BYE.

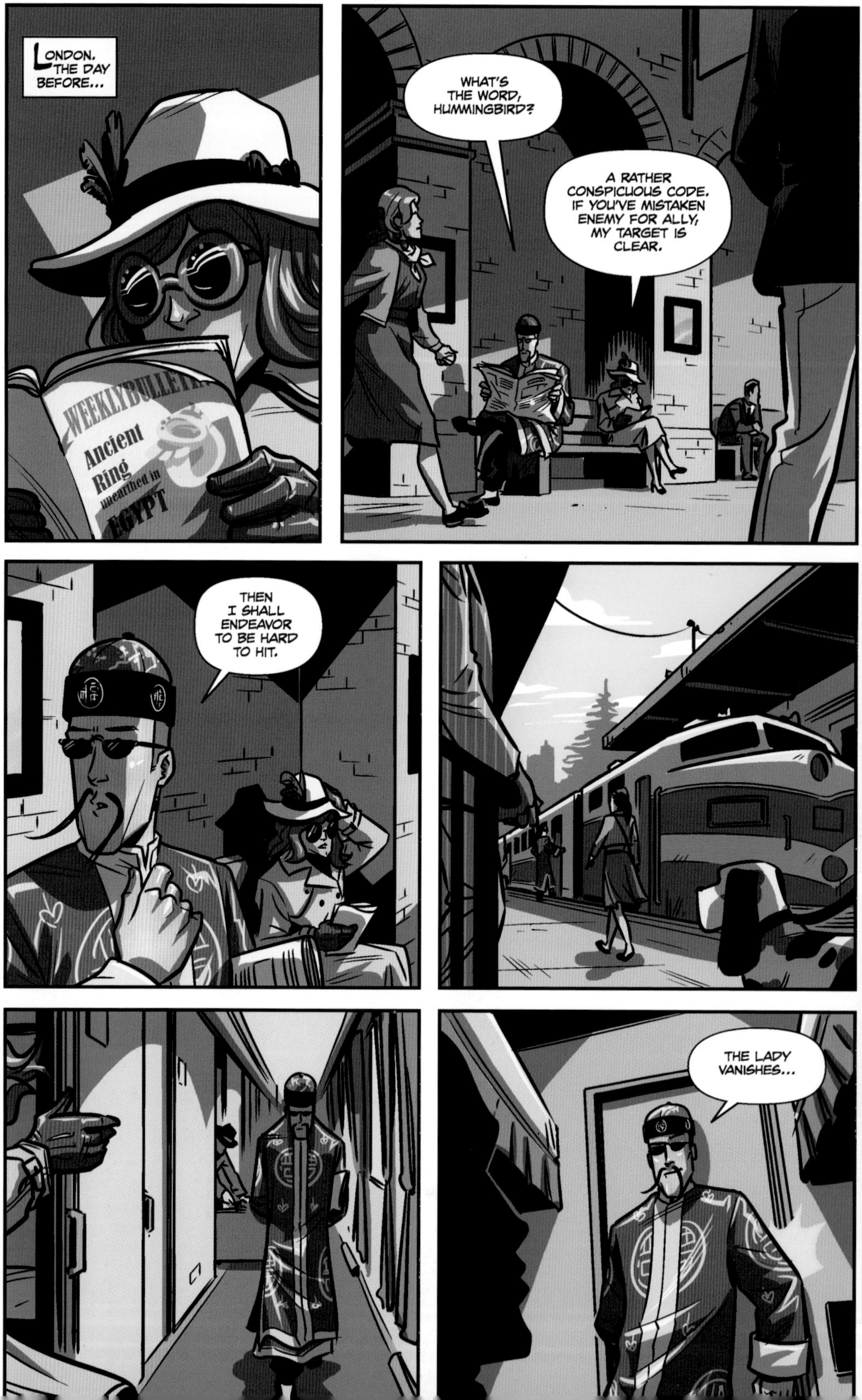
LONDON. THE DAY BEFORE...
WEEKLY BULLETIN
Ancient Ring unearthed in EGYPT
WHAT'S THE WORD, HUMMINGBIRD?
A RATHER CONSPICUOUS CODE. IF YOU'VE MISTAKEN ENEMY FOR ALLY, MY TARGET IS CLEAR.
THEN I SHALL ENDEAVOR TO BE HARD TO HIT.
THE LADY VANISHES...

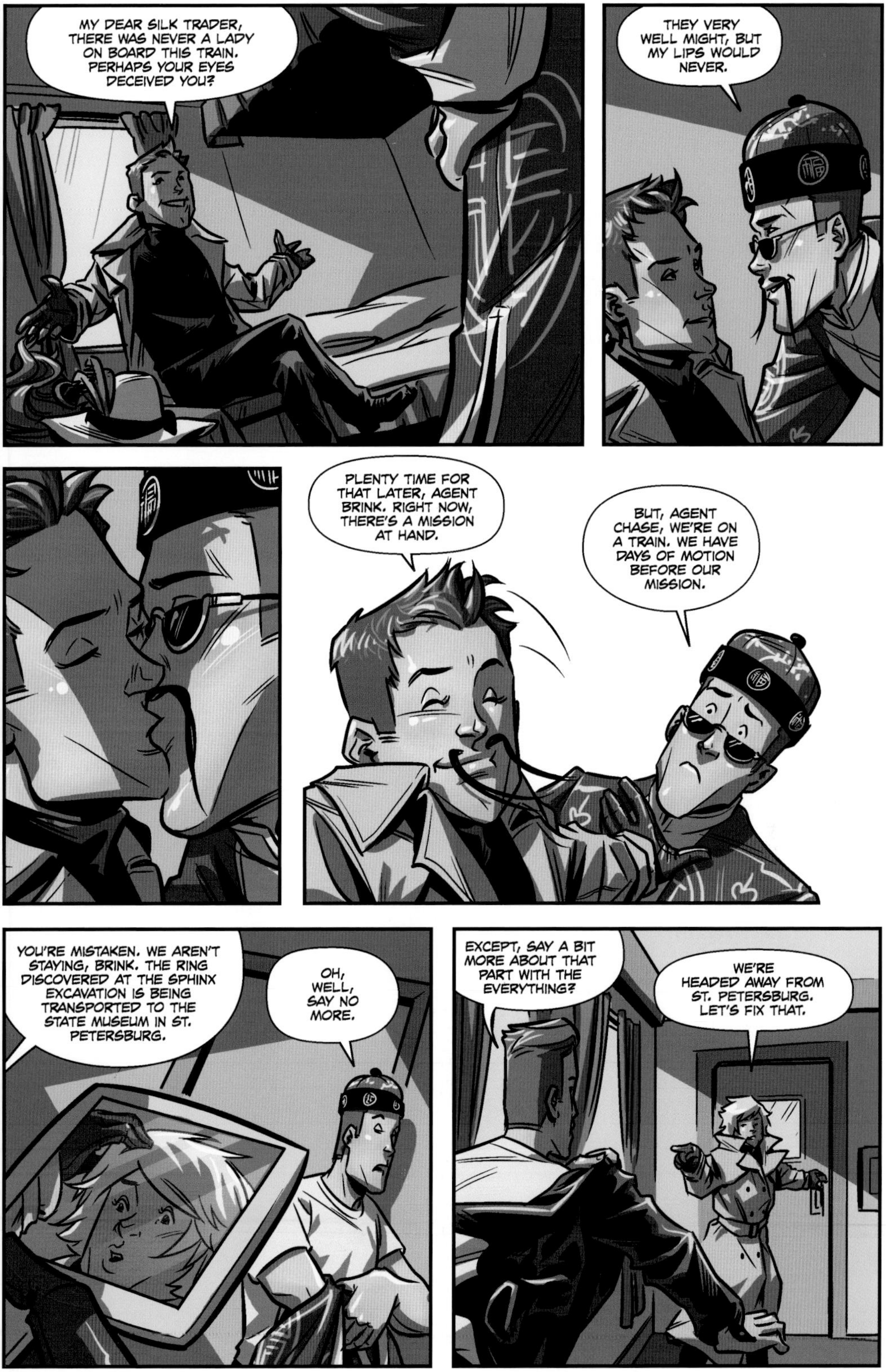
MY DEAR SILK TRADER, THERE WAS NEVER A LADY ON BOARD THIS TRAIN. PERHAPS YOUR EYES DECEIVED YOU?
THEY VERY WELL MIGHT, BUT MY LIPS WOULD NEVER.
PLENTY TIME FOR THAT LATER, AGENT BRINK. RIGHT NOW, THERE'S A MISSION AT HAND.
BUT, AGENT CHASE, WE'RE ON A TRAIN. WE HAVE DAYS OF MOTION BEFORE OUR MISSION.
YOU'RE MISTAKEN. WE AREN'T STAYING, BRINK. THE RING DISCOVERED AT THE SPHINX EXCAVATION IS BEING TRANSPORTED TO THE STATE MUSEUM IN ST. PETERSBURG.
OH, WELL, SAY NO MORE.
EXCEPT, SAY A BIT MORE ABOUT THAT PART WITH THE EVERYTHING?
WE'RE HEADED AWAY FROM ST. PETERSBURG. LET'S FIX THAT.

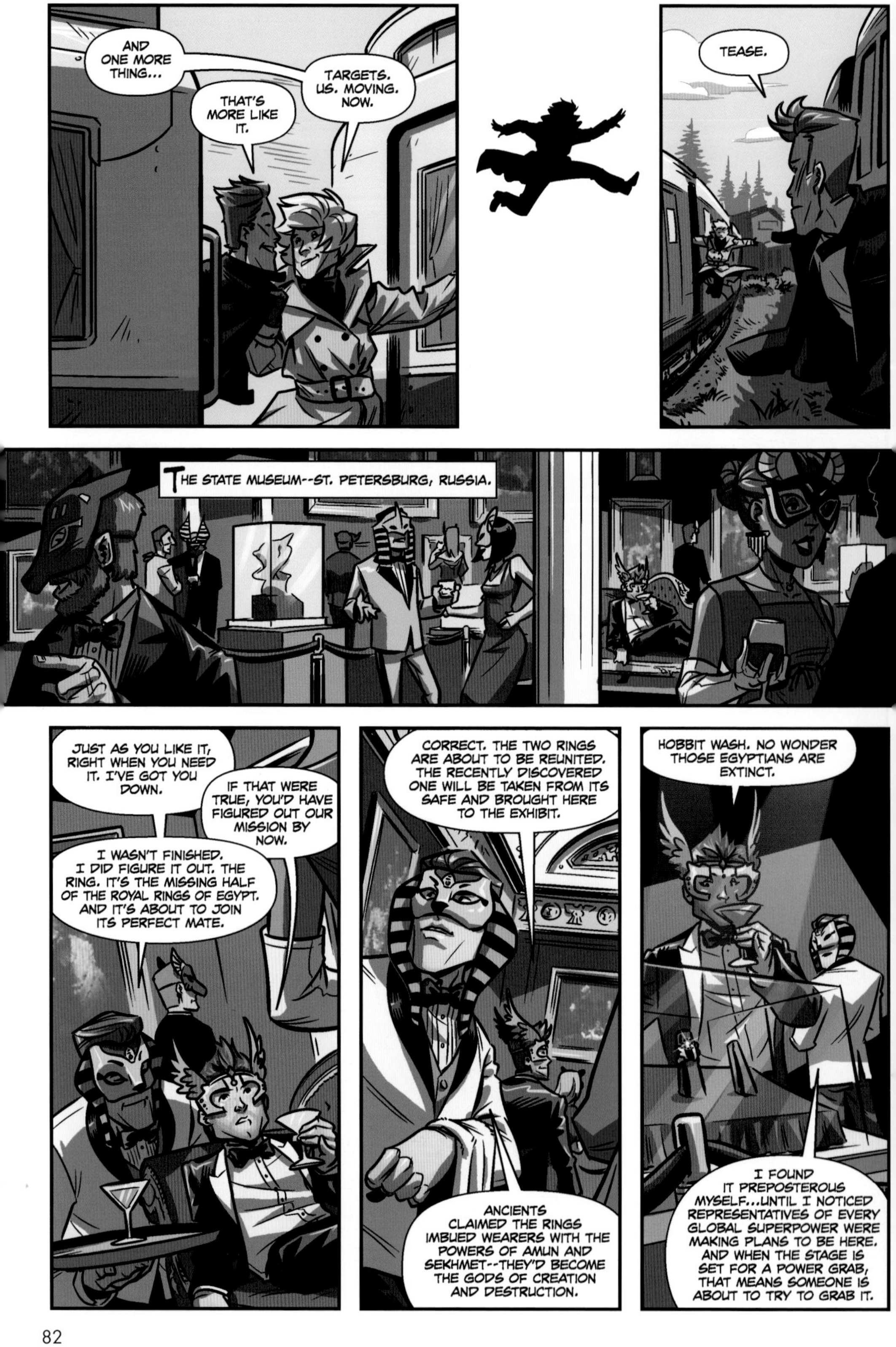
AND ONE MORE THING...
THAT'S MORE LIKE IT.
TARGETS. US. MOVING. NOW.
TEASE.
THE STATE MUSEUM--ST. PETERSBURG, RUSSIA.
JUST AS YOU LIKE IT, RIGHT WHEN YOU NEED IT. I'VE GOT YOU DOWN.
IF THAT WERE TRUE, YOU'D HAVE FIGURED OUT OUR MISSION BY NOW.
I WASN'T FINISHED. I DID FIGURE IT OUT. THE RING. IT'S THE MISSING HALF OF THE ROYAL RINGS OF EGYPT. AND IT'S ABOUT TO JOIN ITS PERFECT MATE.
CORRECT. THE TWO RINGS ARE ABOUT TO BE REUNITED. THE RECENTLY DISCOVERED ONE WILL BE TAKEN FROM ITS SAFE AND BROUGHT HERE TO THE EXHIBIT.
ANCIENTS CLAIMED THE RINGS IMBUED WEARERS WITH THE POWERS OF AMUN AND SEKHMET--THEY'D BECOME THE GODS OF CREATION AND DESTRUCTION.
HOBBIT WASH. NO WONDER THOSE EGYPTIANS ARE EXTINCT.
I FOUND IT PREPOSTEROUS MYSELF...UNTIL I NOTICED REPRESENTATIVES OF EVERY GLOBAL SUPERPOWER WERE MAKING PLANS TO BE HERE. AND WHEN THE STAGE IS SET FOR A POWER GRAB, THAT MEANS SOMEONE IS ABOUT TO TRY TO GRAB IT.

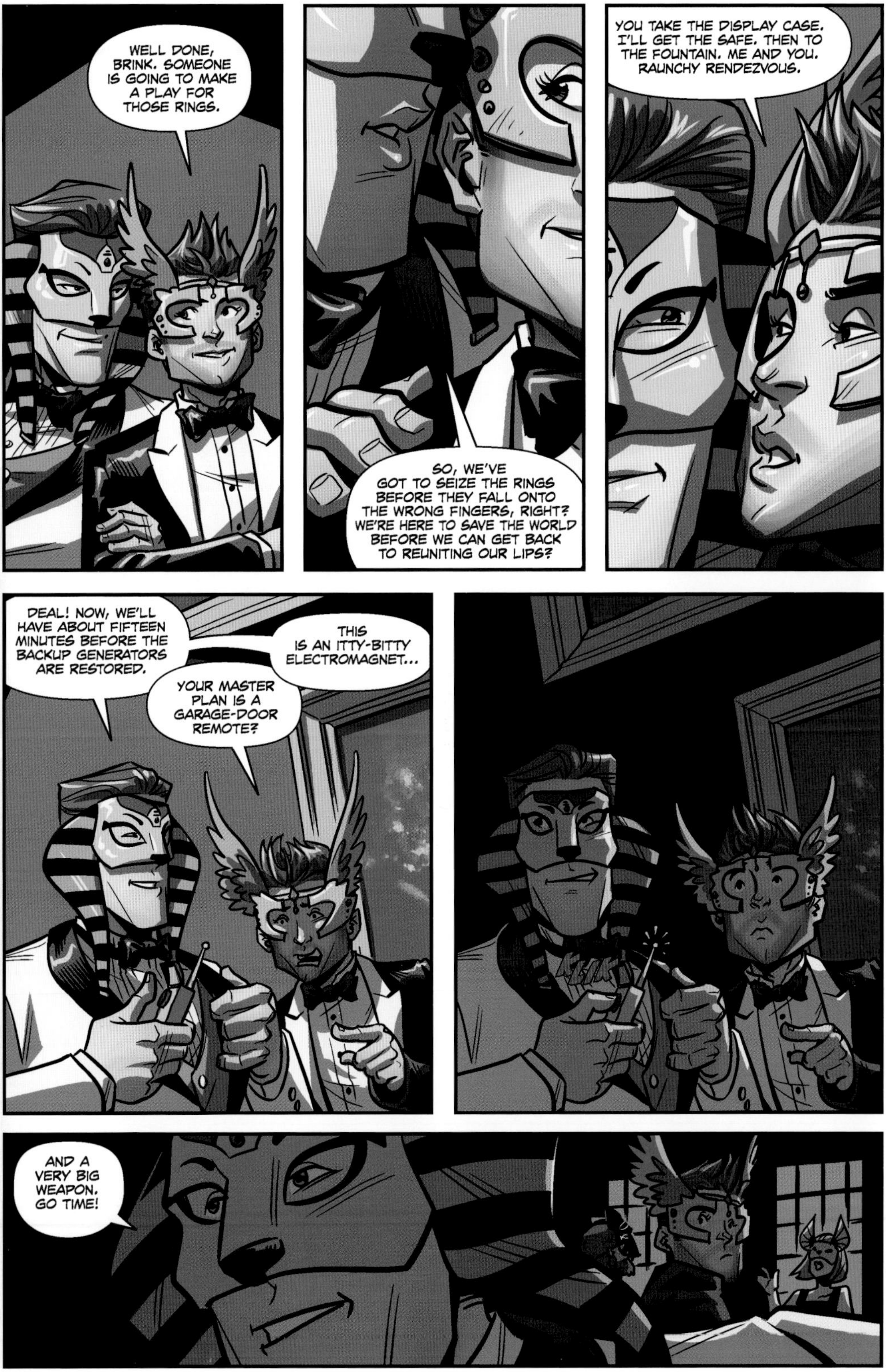

WELL DONE, BRINK. SOMEONE IS GOING TO MAKE A PLAY FOR THOSE RINGS.
SO, WE'VE GOT TO SEIZE THE RINGS BEFORE THEY FALL ONTO THE WRONG FINGERS, RIGHT? WE'RE HERE TO SAVE THE WORLD BEFORE WE CAN GET BACK TO REUNITING OUR LIPS?
YOU TAKE THE DISPLAY CASE. I'LL GET THE SAFE. THEN TO THE FOUNTAIN. ME AND YOU. RAUNCHY RENDEZVOUS.
DEAL! NOW, WE'LL HAVE ABOUT FIFTEEN MINUTES BEFORE THE BACKUP GENERATORS ARE RESTORED.
THIS IS AN ITTY-BITTY ELECTROMAGNET...
YOUR MASTER PLAN IS A GARAGE-DOOR REMOTE?
AND A VERY BIG WEAPON. GO TIME!

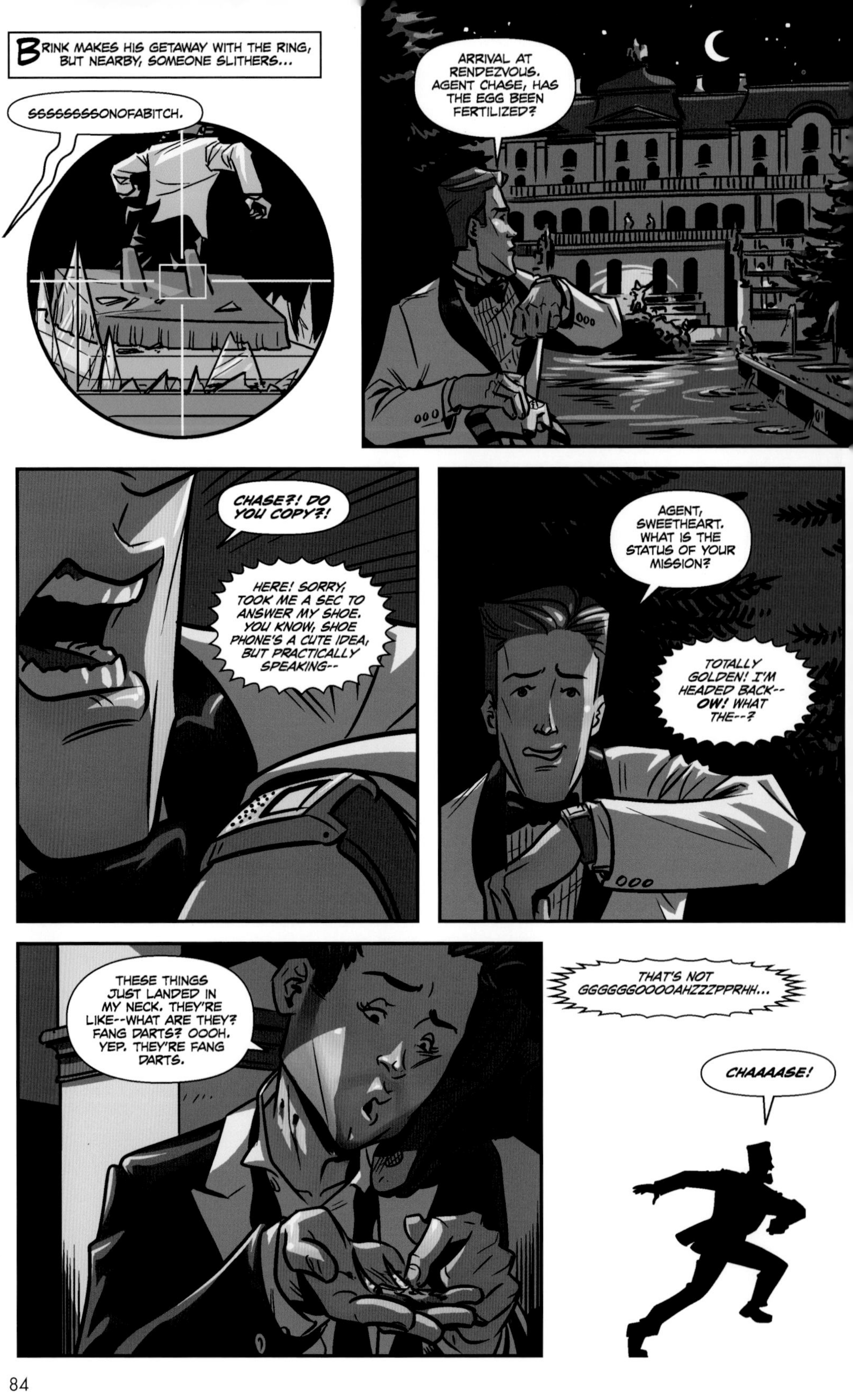
BRINK MAKES HIS GETAWAY WITH THE RING, BUT NEARBY, SOMEONE SLITHERS...
SSSSSSSSONOFABITCH.
ARRIVAL AT RENDEZVOUS. AGENT CHASE, HAS THE EGG BEEN FERTILIZED?
CHASE?! DO YOU COPY?!
HERE! SORRY, TOOK ME A SEC TO ANSWER MY SHOE. YOU KNOW, SHOE PHONE'S A CUTE IDEA, BUT PRACTICALLY SPEAKING--
AGENT, SWEETHEART. WHAT IS THE STATUS OF YOUR MISSION?
TOTALLY GOLDEN! I'M HEADED BACK-- OW! WHAT THE--?
THESE THINGS JUST LANDED IN MY NECK. THEY'RE LIKE--WHAT ARE THEY? FANG DARTS? OOOH. YEP. THEY'RE FANG DARTS.
THAT'S NOT GGGGGGOOOOAHZZZPPRHH...
CHAAAASE!

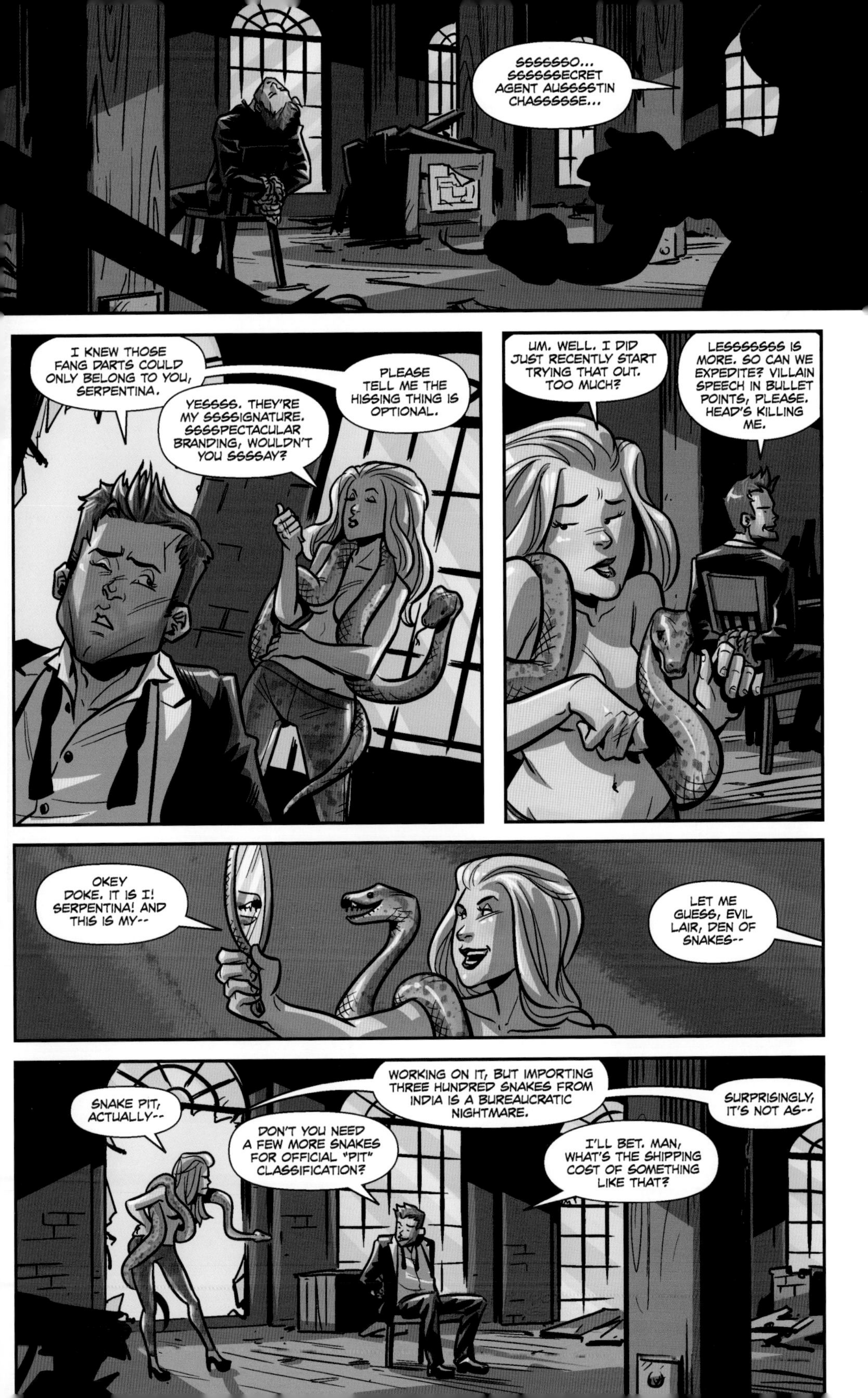
SSSSSSO... SSSSSSECRET AGENT AUSSSSTIN CHASSSSSE...
I KNEW THOSE FANG DARTS COULD ONLY BELONG TO YOU, SERPENTINA.
YESSSS. THEY'RE MY SSSSIGNATURE. SSSSPECTACULAR BRANDING, WOULDN'T YOU SSSSAY?
PLEASE TELL ME THE HISSING THING IS OPTIONAL.
UM. WELL. I DID JUST RECENTLY START TRYING THAT OUT. TOO MUCH?
LESSSSSSS IS MORE. SO CAN WE EXPEDITE? VILLAIN SPEECH IN BULLET POINTS, PLEASE. HEAD'S KILLING ME.
OKEY DOKE. IT IS I! SERPENTINA! AND THIS IS MY--
LET ME GUESS, EVIL LAIR, DEN OF SNAKES--
SNAKE PIT, ACTUALLY--
DON'T YOU NEED A FEW MORE SNAKES FOR OFFICIAL "PIT" CLASSIFICATION?
WORKING ON IT, BUT IMPORTING THREE HUNDRED SNAKES FROM INDIA IS A BUREAUCRATIC NIGHTMARE.
I'LL BET. MAN, WHAT'S THE SHIPPING COST OF SOMETHING LIKE THAT?
SURPRISINGLY, IT'S NOT AS--

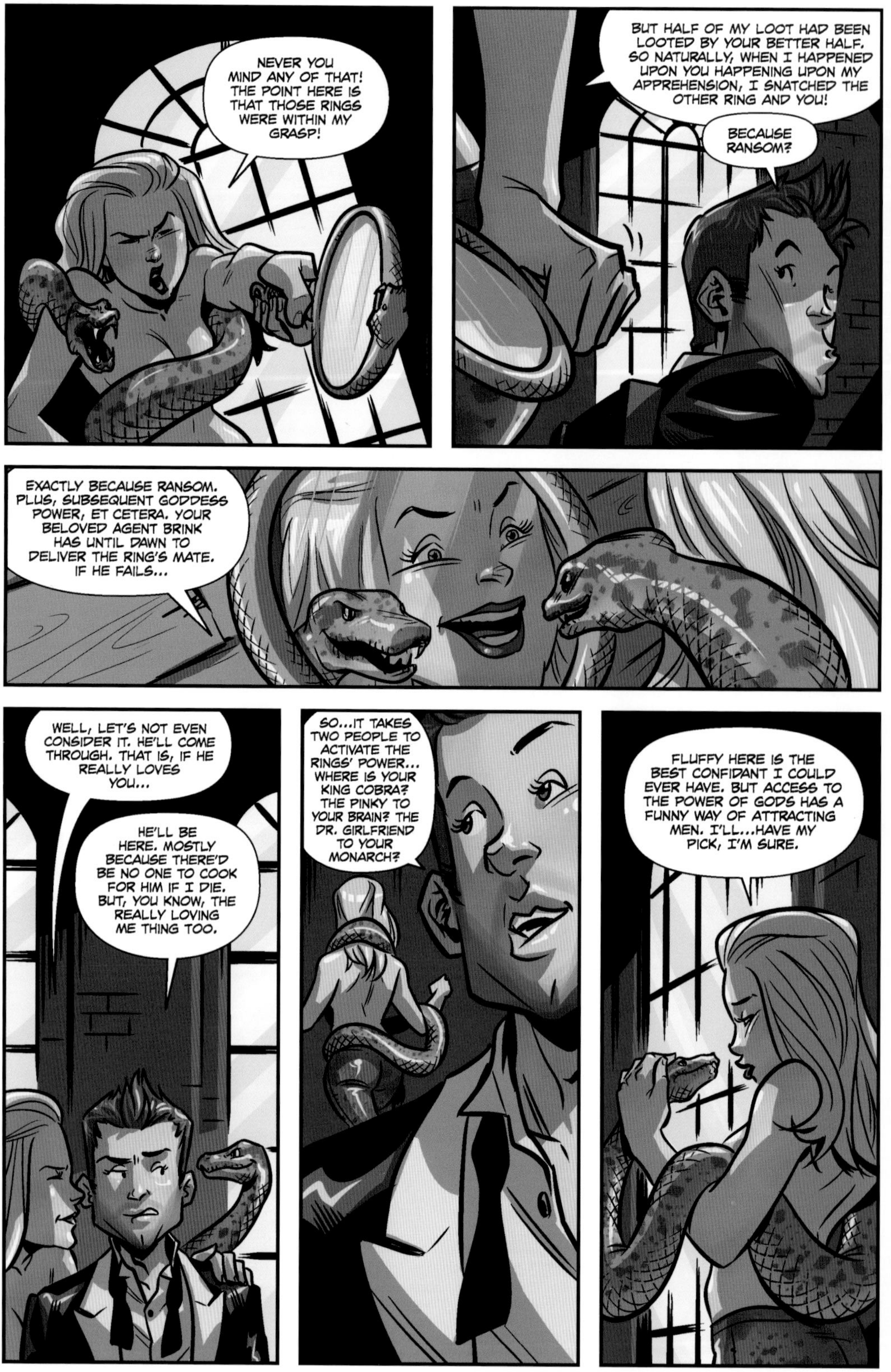
NEVER YOU MIND ANY OF THAT! THE POINT HERE IS THAT THOSE RINGS WERE WITHIN MY GRASP!
BUT HALF OF MY LOOT HAD BEEN LOOTED BY YOUR BETTER HALF. SO NATURALLY, WHEN I HAPPENED UPON YOU HAPPENING UPON MY APPREHENSION, I SNATCHED THE OTHER RING AND YOU!
BECAUSE RANSOM?
EXACTLY BECAUSE RANSOM. PLUS, SUBSEQUENT GODDESS POWER, ET CETERA. YOUR BELOVED AGENT BRINK HAS UNTIL DAWN TO DELIVER THE RING'S MATE. IF HE FAILS...
WELL, LET'S NOT EVEN CONSIDER IT. HE'LL COME THROUGH. THAT IS, IF HE REALLY LOVES YOU...
HE'LL BE HERE. MOSTLY BECAUSE THERE'D BE NO ONE TO COOK FOR HIM IF I DIE. BUT, YOU KNOW, THE REALLY LOVING ME THING TOO.
SO...IT TAKES TWO PEOPLE TO ACTIVATE THE RINGS' POWER... WHERE IS YOUR KING COBRA? THE PINKY TO YOUR BRAIN? THE DR. GIRLFRIEND TO YOUR MONARCH?
FLUFFY HERE IS THE BEST CONFIDANT I COULD EVER HAVE. BUT ACCESS TO THE POWER OF GODS HAS A FUNNY WAY OF ATTRACTING MEN. I'LL...HAVE MY PICK, I'M SURE.

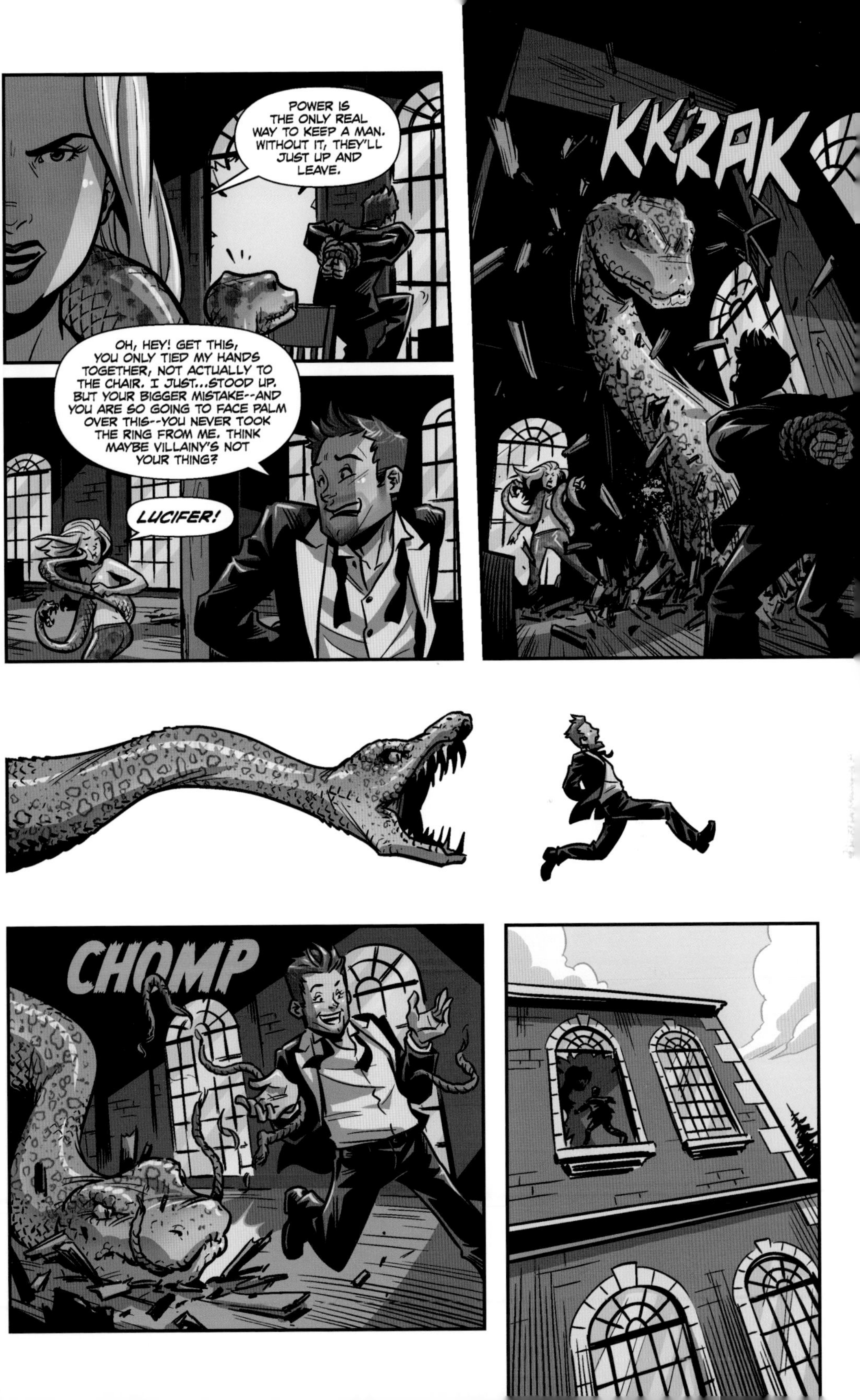
POWER IS THE ONLY REAL WAY TO KEEP A MAN. WITHOUT IT, THEY'LL JUST UP AND LEAVE.
KKRAK
OH, HEY! GET THIS, YOU ONLY TIED MY HANDS TOGETHER, NOT ACTUALLY TO THE CHAIR. I JUST...STOOD UP. BUT YOUR BIGGER MISTAKE--AND YOU ARE SO GOING TO FACE PALM OVER THIS--YOU NEVER TOOK THE RING FROM ME. THINK MAYBE VILLAINY'S NOT YOUR THING?
LUCIFER!
CHOMP

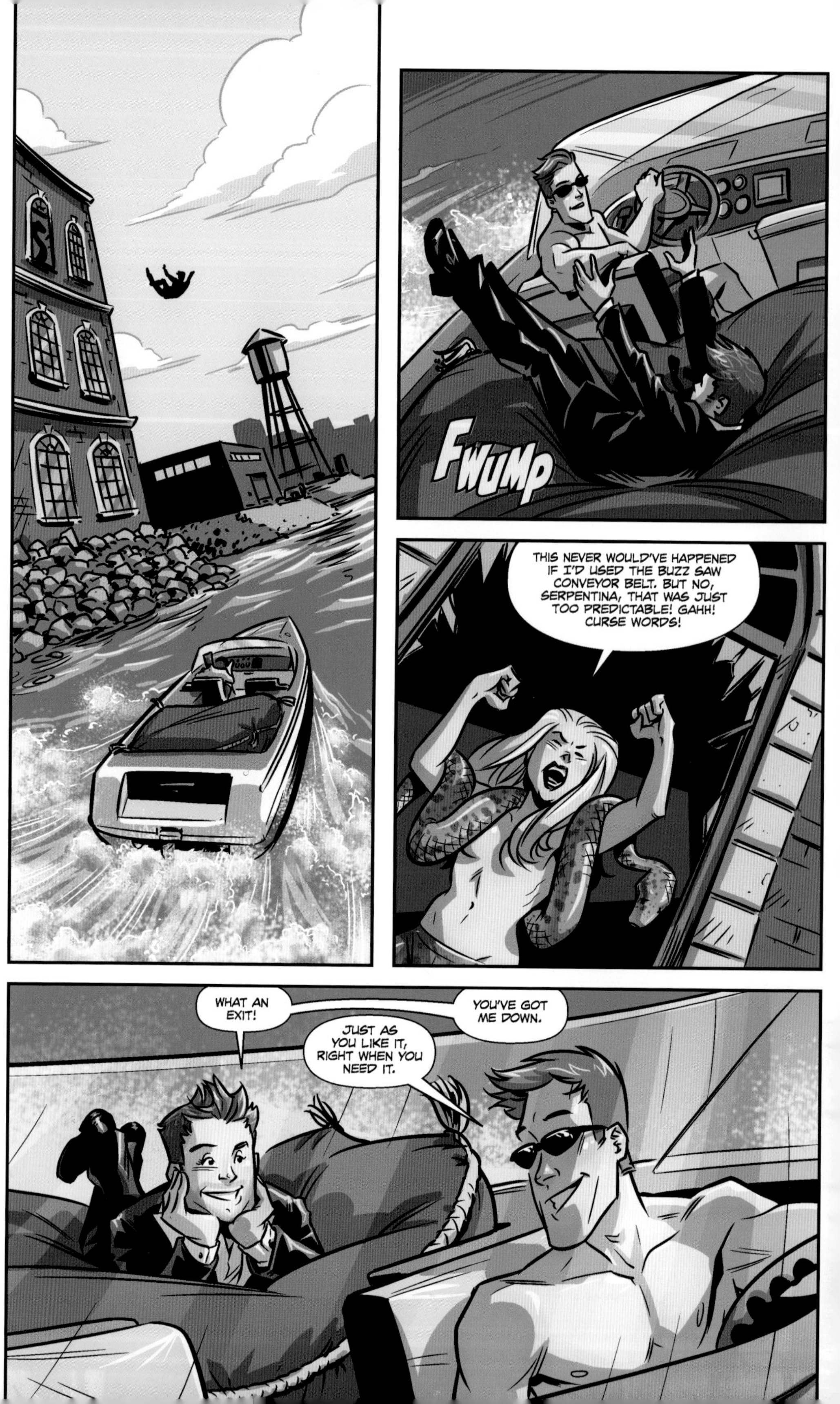
FWUMP
THIS NEVER WOULD'VE HAPPENED IF I'D USED THE BUZZ SAW CONVEYOR BELT. BUT NO, SERPENTINA, THAT WAS JUST TOO PREDICTABLE! GAHH! CURSE WORDS!
WHAT AN EXIT!
YOU'VE GOT ME DOWN.
JUST AS YOU LIKE IT, RIGHT WHEN YOU NEED IT.

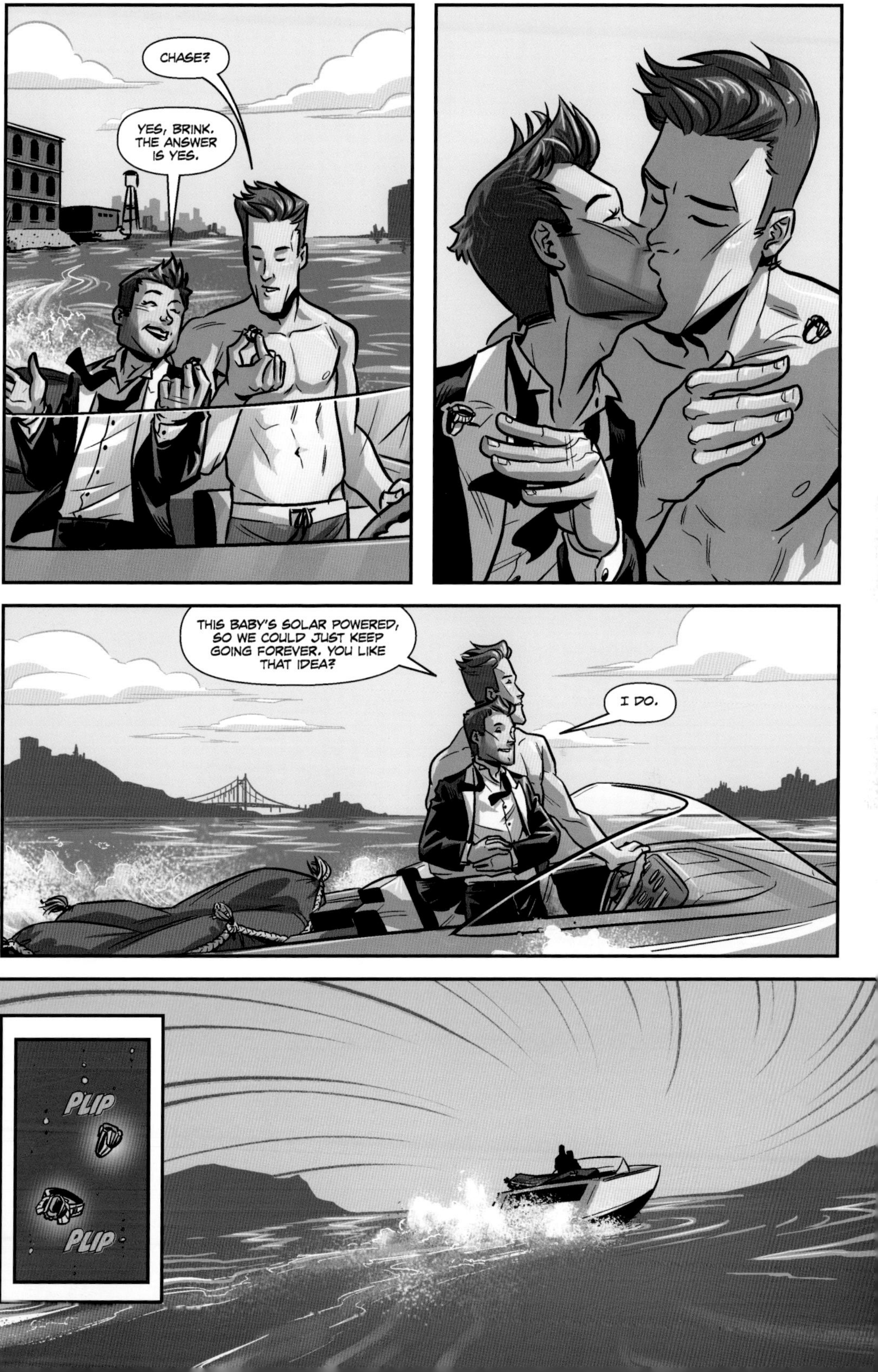
CHASE?
YES, BRINK. THE ANSWER IS YES.
THIS BABY'S SOLAR POWERED, SO WE COULD JUST KEEP GOING FOREVER. YOU LIKE THAT IDEA?
I DO.
PLIP
PLIP

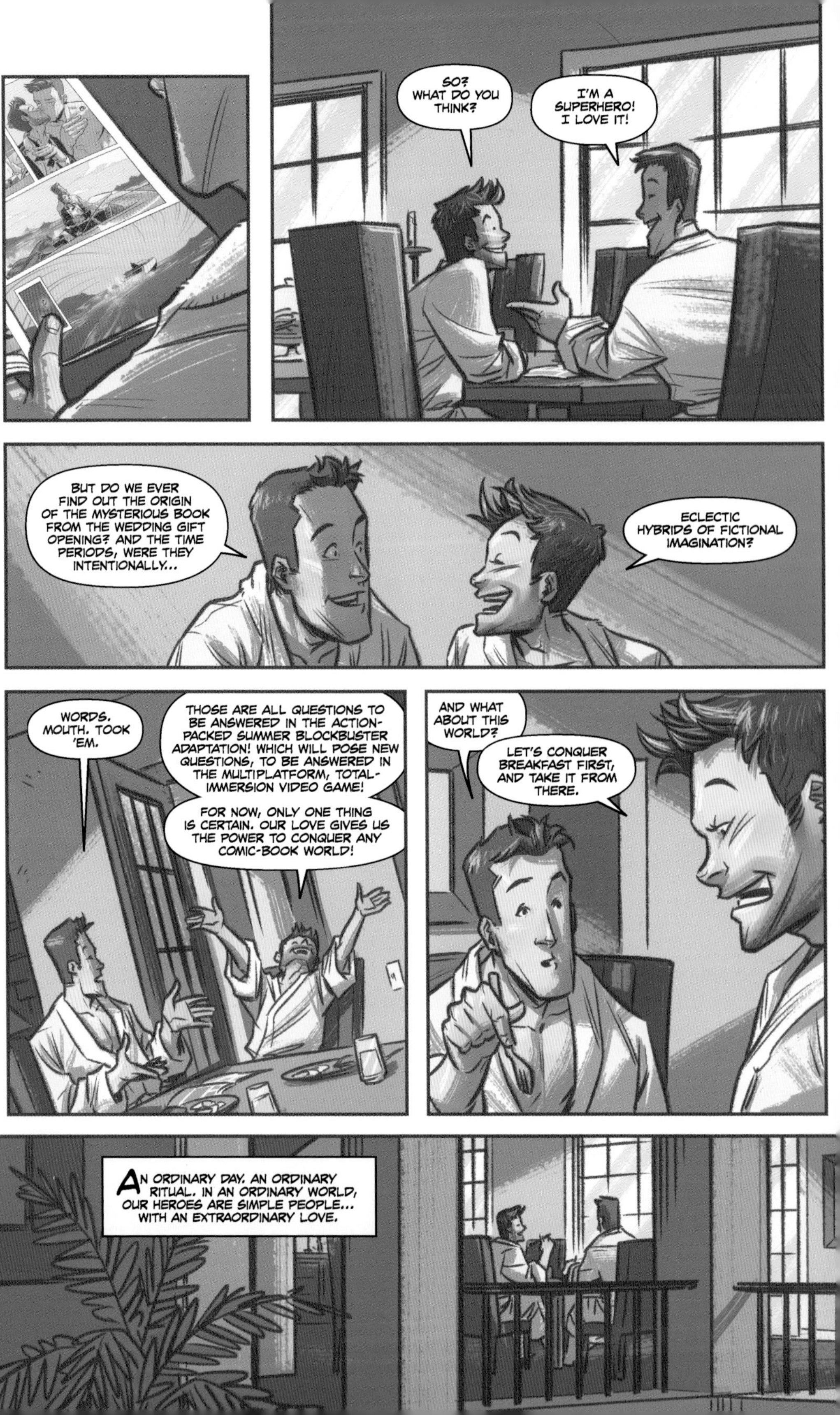

SO? WHAT DO YOU THINK?
I'M A SUPERHERO! I LOVE IT!
BUT DO WE EVER FIND OUT THE ORIGIN OF THE MYSTERIOUS BOOK FROM THE WEDDING GIFT OPENING? AND THE TIME PERIODS, WERE THEY INTENTIONALLY...
ECLECTIC HYBRIDS OF FICTIONAL IMAGINATION?
WORDS. MOUTH. TOOK 'EM.
THOSE ARE ALL QUESTIONS TO BE ANSWERED IN THE ACTION-PACKED SUMMER BLOCKBUSTER ADAPTATION! WHICH WILL POSE NEW QUESTIONS, TO BE ANSWERED IN THE MULTIPLATFORM, TOTAL-IMMERSION VIDEO GAME!
FOR NOW, ONLY ONE THING IS CERTAIN. OUR LOVE GIVES US THE POWER TO CONQUER ANY COMIC-BOOK WORLD!
AND WHAT ABOUT THIS WORLD?
LET'S CONQUER BREAKFAST FIRST, AND TAKE IT FROM THERE.
AN ORDINARY DAY. AN ORDINARY RITUAL. IN AN ORDINARY WORLD, OUR HEROES ARE SIMPLE PEOPLE... WITH AN EXTRAORDINARY LOVE.

THE ORIGINAL OUTLINE

From Brad Bell and Jane Espenson

Our idea is to use the six issues to show Cheeks and Brady overcoming six different obstacles in their new married life. In each issue, the genre of the comic book is chosen specifically to highlight the conflict. A supernatural element introduced in the first issue propels them into the fantasy worlds – a device that we comically puncture in the final issue.

Issue One:

We begin in the naturalistic real world of the series. Cheeks and Brady have been sent a mysterious wedding gift that transforms into a glowing orb or other mystical object. When they trigger it, it sends them into the first alternate universe, in which Cheeks is a supervillain and Brady is a **superhero**. We tell the story of their being attracted to each other (in their secret identities), while battling in their personae, until they are forced to work together to prevent disaster. It's a story about overcoming very deep differences in background and worldview to become a functional couple – stage one of a relationship. Built into the story is a reappearance of the Mysterious Triggering Object, which sends them into...

Early sketches for Brady and Cheeks by Ron Chan, artist for issues #1 and #6.

Issue Two:

Now they are **space heroes** in the vein of Han and Luke, engaged in a battle against an orbiting fortress. This is a story about how to take on challenges. They disagree about strategies in a way that reflects their personalities and their approach to how to handle their lives as gay men. Brady likes to effect change from within, while Cheeks prefers a direct attack. They combine their methods and crash the establishment. Again, the object makes an appearance, sending them into...

Issue Three:

In which they are James Bond-style **secret agents**. A story about communication and trust. They attend a black-tie event to recover stolen artworks. Their communication methods break down. Brady is nabbed by the bad guys. Cheeks has to intuit that Brady let himself get nabbed so that Cheeks could recover the art and rescue him (spectacularly) later.

Brady as Light Fantastic and Cheeks as the Darkness, by Ron Chan.

Issue Four:

Fidelity. Set in an **Archie** comics style teenaged world. Brady and Cheeks as American high schoolers. For the first time, we see another guy making a play for one of them. They resist, setting up the interloper to look a fool in front of everyone at the Big Game, and staying loyal to each other. A romp.

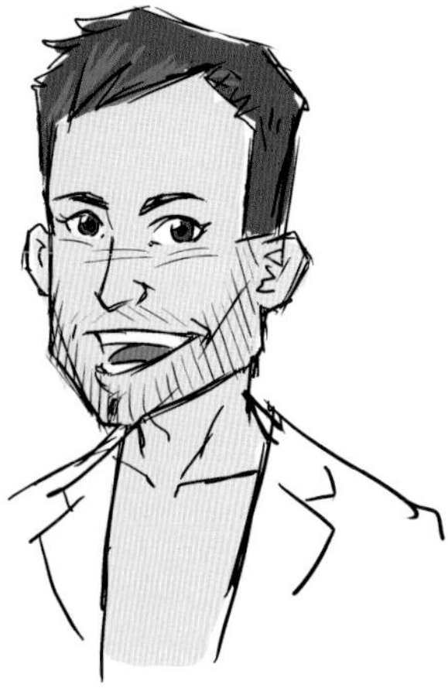

Issue Five:

An English drawing room **mystery**. Cheeks as a Holmesian detective. Brady as his dim-but-earnest assistant. Despite his superior intelligence, Cheeks finds himself tricked into a dangerous situation. Brady demonstrates tenacity in saving Cheeks. Cheeks realizes he has underestimated the value of loyalty – Brady has different gifts that are just as valuable.

Issue Six:

A **swords-and-sorcery** world in which Cheeks is menaced by a dragon. Brady rescues him, only to learn that Cheeks wanted to slay his own dragon. We have gone from a story about them respecting their differences to one about celebrating their similarities. When Brady learns this lesson, the mysterious object (which has been providing the transition between issues) appears again and returns them to the real world where we see that the entire series, including the wedding-gift prologue, has been a comic book that Cheeks is writing. Brady praises it, except that he "doesn't get the part about the wedding gift."

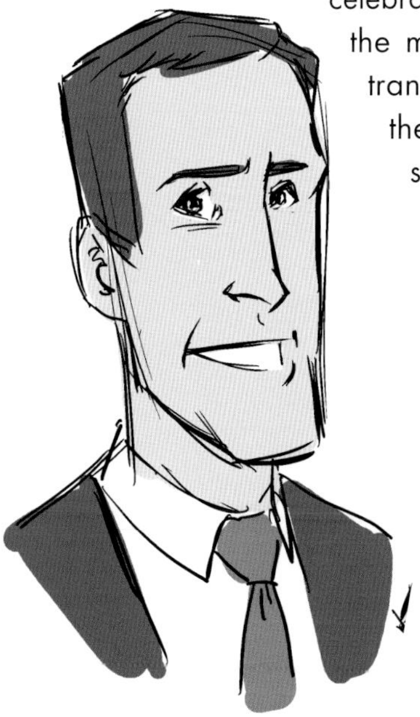

Character sketches by Ron Chan.

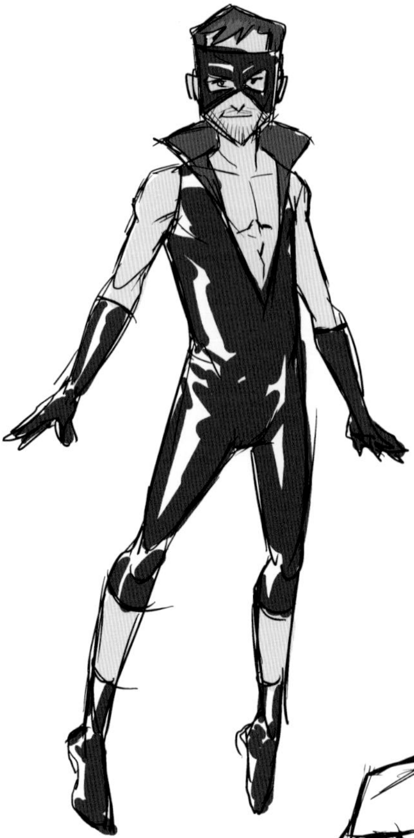

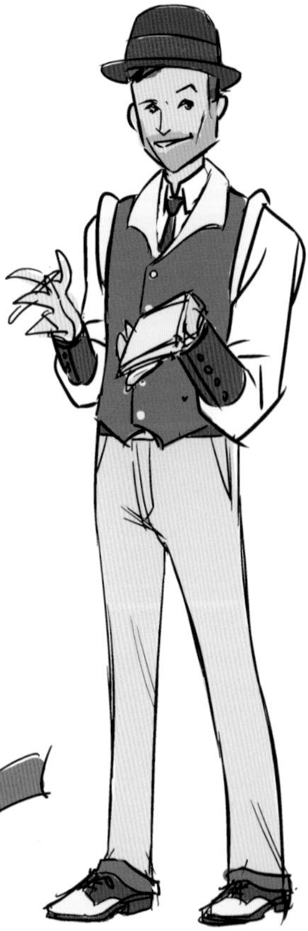

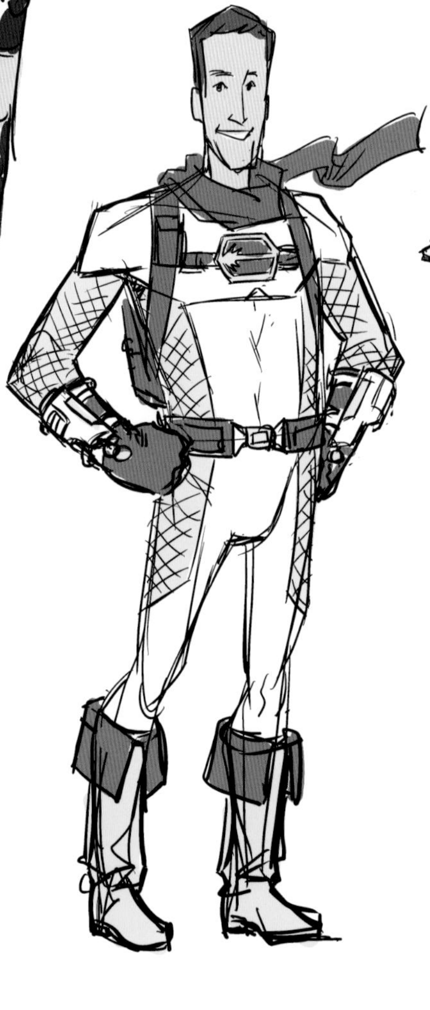

Revised designs and Cheeks's Chet Deckfin.

THE HISTORY OF ISSUE #2, PAGE 11

On July 4, 2012, Jane and Brad took the first pass at a rough outline for issue #2. Page 10 was described as follows:

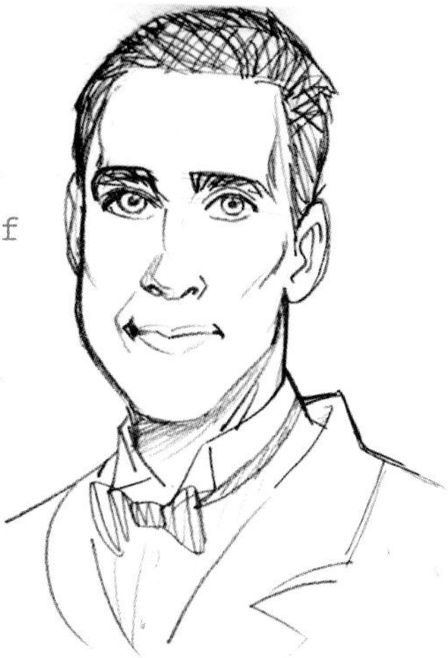

PAGE TEN

Brady jumps and then catches Cheeks -- and they realize that it took two of them to make this plan work. They celebrate. Yay! Good plan! Go us! So...now how do we get to town?

> **Brady:** Together.
> **Cheeks:** No, I mean, we're naked.

A passing peasant girl -- Haley -- ogles them and makes appreciative comments.

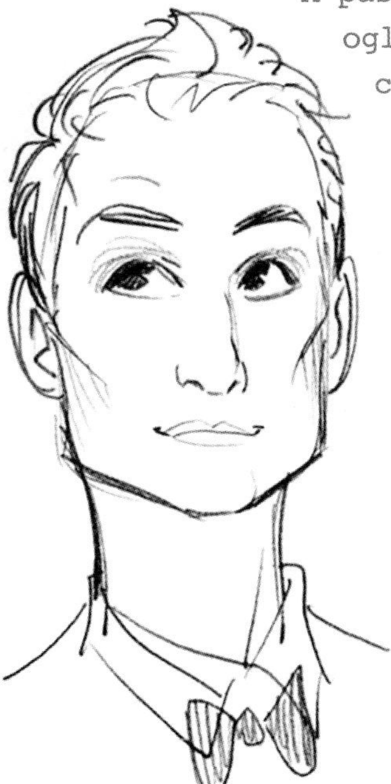

On July 9, Brad wrote ten and a half pages of the twelve-page script, breaking off right before Haley's appearance. He sent it to Jane, and the following e-mail exchange resulted:

This and following pages: Various likeness sketches by issue #2 artist Natalie Nourigat.

From: B. Bell
To: Jane
Sent: Mon, Jul 9, 2012 5:39 pm
Subject: Ish 2

I don't know if this is
any good...it strays just
a bit from the outline
but is mostly the same. I
got to them escaping and
then -- nothing. I have
no idea. Hope this helps.
Let me know what you
think.
xoxo

On Jul 9, 2012, at 9:37 PM, Jane Espenson wrote:

This is GREAT! I'm getting into it now!
I'll have it back to you late tonight or
early tomorrow.
Love it!

**On July 10, Jane added what had now become the second
half of page 11. Panels 1 and 2 here were written by Brad,
panels 3 to 5 were added by Jane:**

PAGE ELEVEN:

Panel One: We look down, above
Cheekston, who is still hanging
onto the rope. In the background is Prince Kelly, on the
ground, arms extended to catch
Cheekston.

    CHEEKSTON
    Fine. I get it. Just
    catch me, okay?

Panel Two: Cheekston is again in Prince Kelly's arms, Princess style. Only this time, they smile sweetly at one another. Framed in a medium shot, avoiding any nudity.

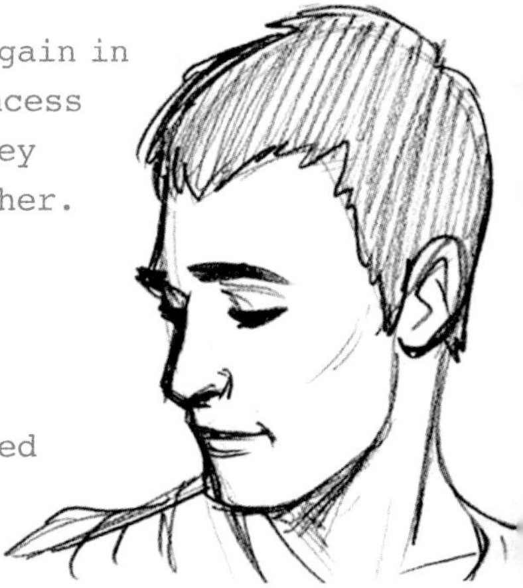

PRINCE KELLY
Looks like you needed me after all.

CHEEKSTON
We needed us, dear prince.

Panel Three: They're still there -- Cheekston in Kelly's arms, smiling at each other -- faces a little closer together.

VOICE (FROM OUT OF PANEL)
Get a chamber!

Panel Four: Reveal a PEASANT GIRL (HALEY), passing by wheeling a keg of ale in a barrow. The guys stare at her.

PEASANT GIRL
Whoo! Make out! Make out!

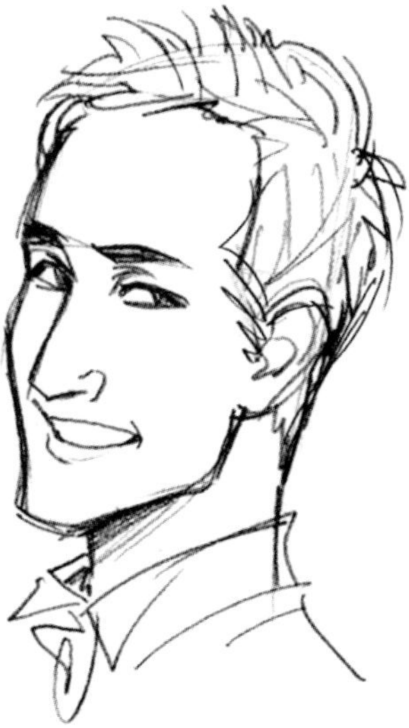

Panel Five. Still, there they stand, Kelly holding Cheekston. The girl is gone.

CHEEKSTON
So rude!

PRINCE KELLY
Mayhaps we should get out of here before that guard misses us.

CHEEKSTON
Mayhaps.

Then, the script went back to Brad for more polishing. By July 17, this was the script:

PAGE ELEVEN:

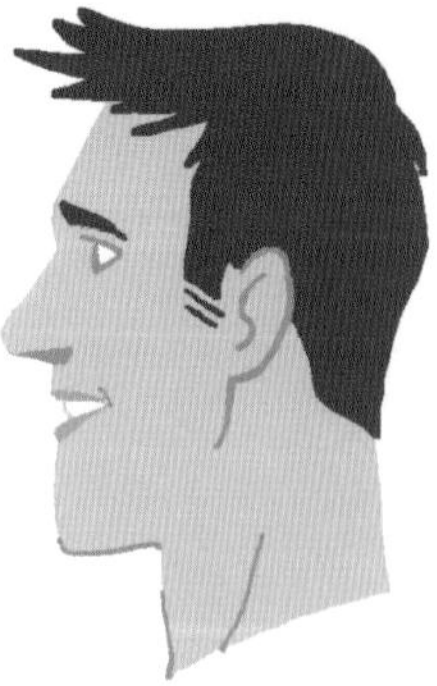

Panel One: Prince Kelly is landing on the ground in a crouch. Above him, Cheeks still clings.

    PRINCE KELLY
    Oof!

Panel Two: We look down, above Cheekston, who is still hanging onto the rope. In the background is Prince Kelly, on the ground, arms extended to catch Cheekston. We note a pen with chickens nearby in this area -- it may be visible throughout this page's panels.

    CHEEKSTON
    Fine. You're freakishly tall. I get it. Just catch me, okay?

Panel Three: Cheekston is again in Prince Kelly's arms, Princess style. Only this time, they smile sweetly at one another. Framed in a medium shot, avoiding any nudity.

    PRINCE KELLY
    Looks like you needed me after all.

    CHEEKSTON
    We needed us, dear prince.

Panel Four: They're still there -- Cheekston in Kelly's arms, smiling at each other -- faces a little closer together.

    VOICE (FROM OUT OF PANEL)
    Get a chamber!

Panel Five: Reveal a PEASANT GIRL (HALEY), passing by wheeling a keg of ale in a barrow. The guys stare at her, eyes wide and uncertain of how to act.

PEASANT GIRL
Yes! I ship it! So hard! Make out! Make out!

Panel Six: Still, there they stand, Kelly holding Cheekston. The girl is gone.

CHEEKSTON
Gotta love the fans.

PRINCE KELLY
Mayhaps we should get out of here before that guard misses us.

CHEEKSTON
Mayhaps, yes. Mayhaps.

On July 19, Dark Horse editor Sierra Hahn sent this note:

From: Sierra Hahn
To: B. Bell; Jane E.
Sent: Thu, Jul 19, 2012 4:50 pm
Subject: Husbands #2 -- script

Hey guys -- This is fantastic. So effin' funny and charming. A few tiny notes, and we're good to go! [...]

PAGE 11

Panel 4 -- Haley's line confused me -- "I ship it!" Is she referring to the beer? I is confused.

Brad replied, in part:

From: B. Bell
To: Sierra; Jane
Sent: Thu, Jul 19, 2012 6:10 pm
Subject: Husbands #2 -- script

Hey Sierra,

Yay! Glad you like Issue 2. Those notes are simple and good fixes. Thank you.

As for Haley's "I ship it!" Shipping is Internet fanspeak. It means to support or have a fan-like interest in someone's relationship. (Relation-SHIP)

:D
Cheers,
Brad

At that point, the script was handed over to the artist. But the writing wasn't done. Here is one last e-mail, sent from Jane and Brad, responding to the pencils from artist Natalie Nourigat.

On Aug 31, 2012, at 5:37 PM, Jane Espenson wrote:

I'm with Brad and we love these! Idea: when Haley wheels by at the end, can we put chickens in her barrow, to establish where those roosters came from? Just a thought!

And with that, the final version of page 11 was set free to sail the seas of posterity.

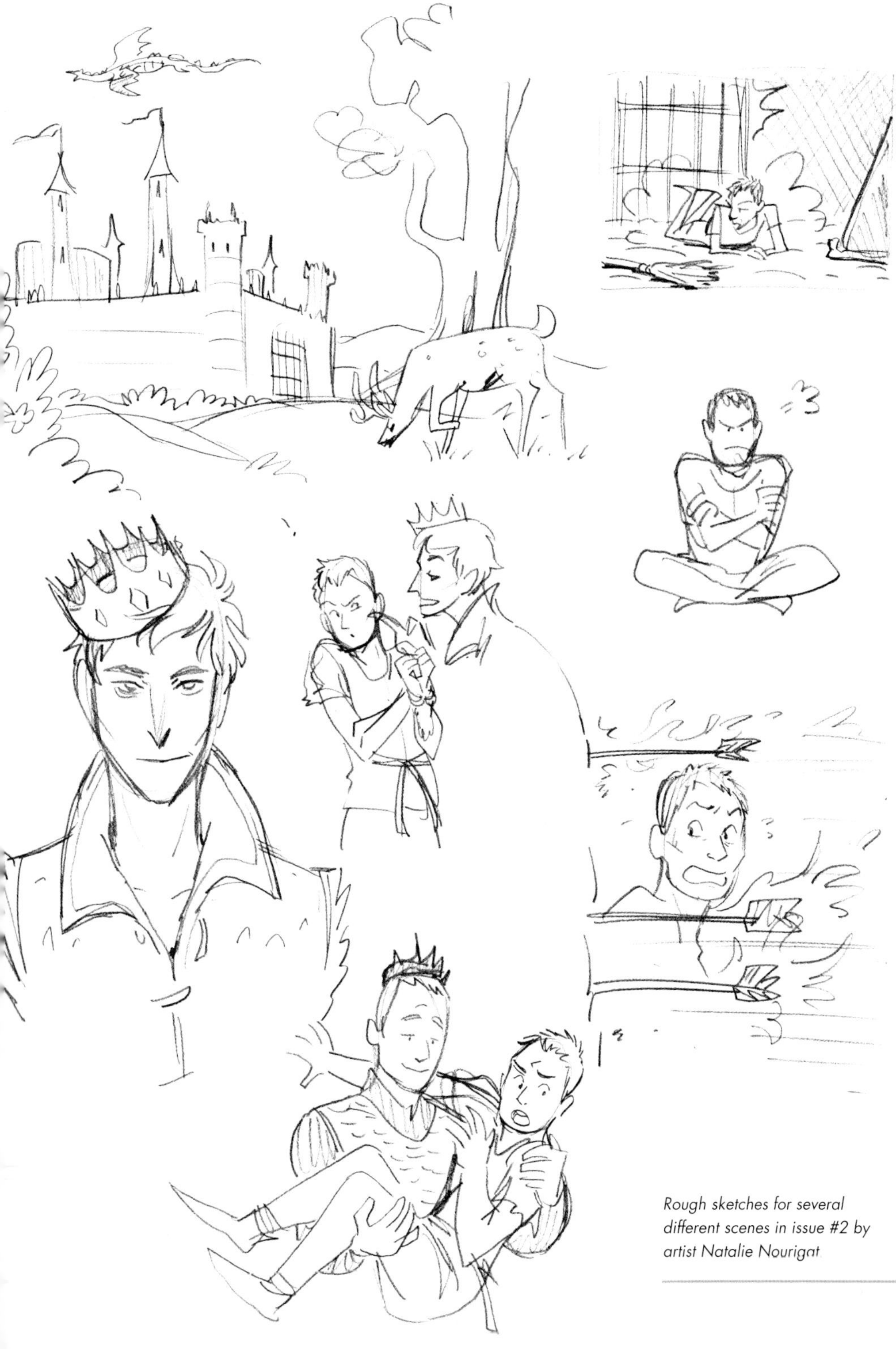

Rough sketches for several different scenes in issue #2 by artist Natalie Nourigat.

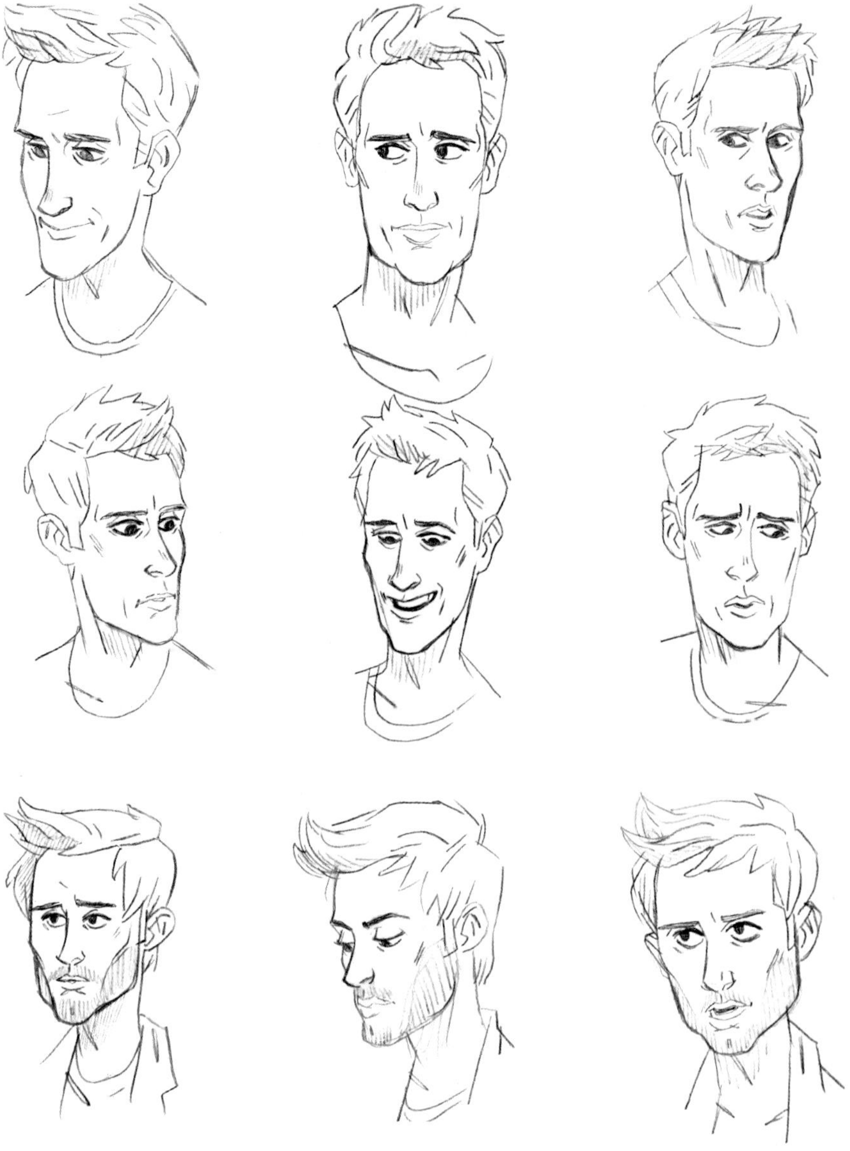

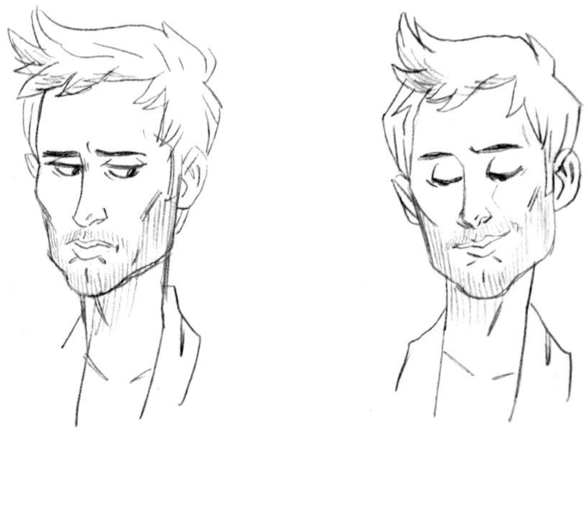

Practice sketches of likenesses and expressions of Brady and Cheeks by M. S. Corley.

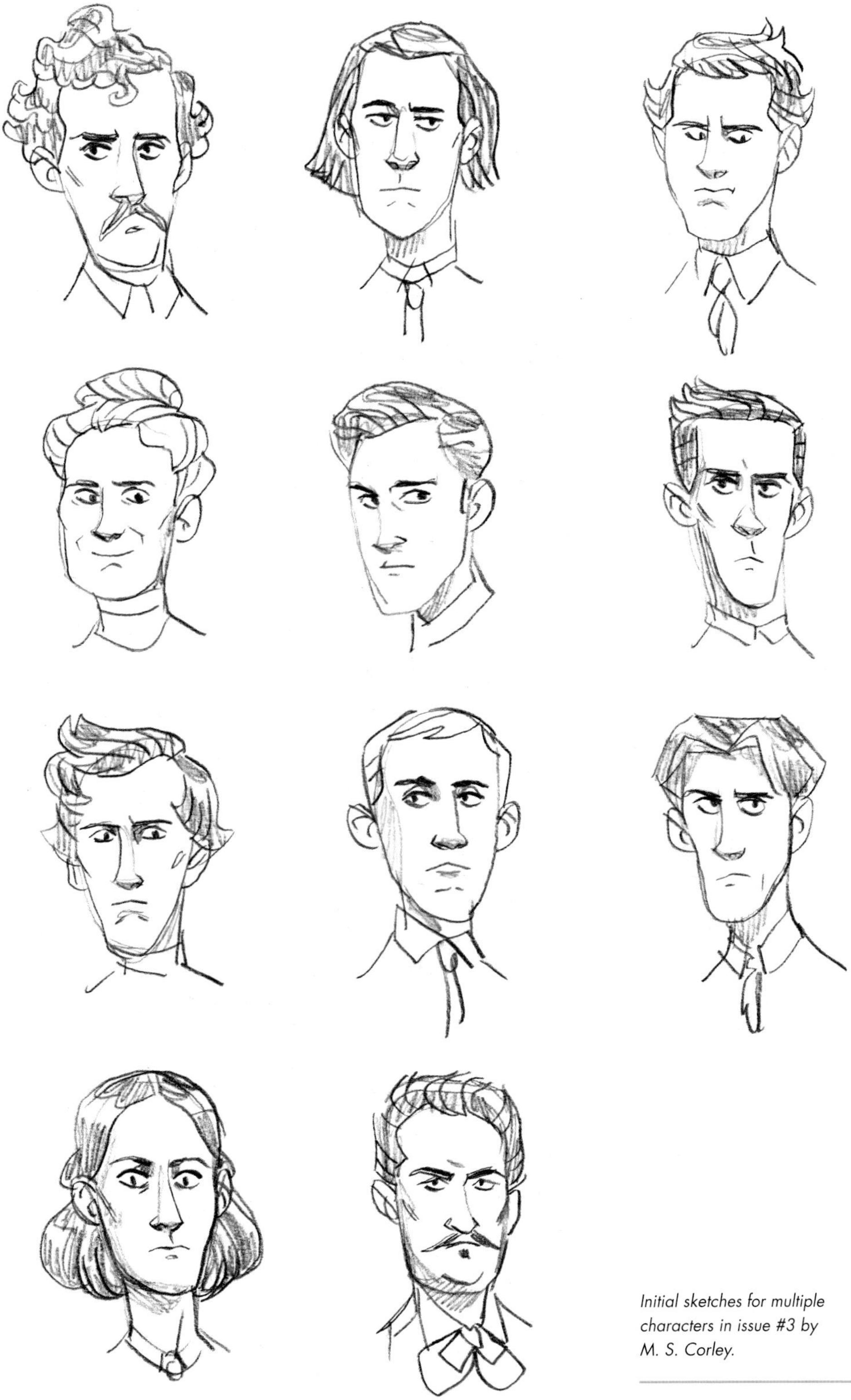

Initial sketches for multiple characters in issue #3 by M. S. Corley.

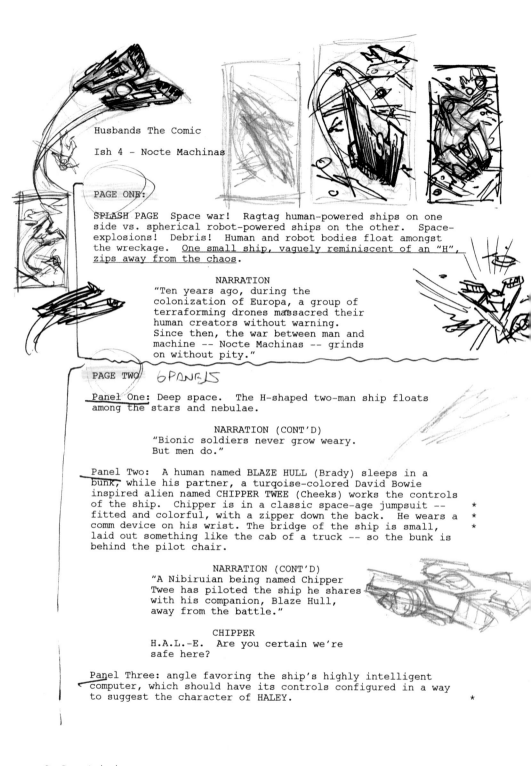

Husbands The Comic

Ish 4 - Nocte Machinas

PAGE ONE:

SPLASH PAGE Space war! Ragtag human-powered ships on one
side vs. spherical robot-powered ships on the other. Space-
explosions! Debris! Human and robot bodies float amongst
the wreckage. One small ship, vaguely reminiscent of an "H",
zips away from the chaos.

                    NARRATION
          "Ten years ago, during the
          colonization of Europa, a group of
          terraforming drones massacred their
          human creators without warning.
          Since then, the war between man and
          machine -- Nocte Machinas -- grinds
          on without pity."

PAGE TWO   6 PANELS

Panel One: Deep space. The H-shaped two-man ship floats
among the stars and nebulae.

                    NARRATION (CONT'D)
          "Bionic soldiers never grow weary.
          But men do."

Panel Two: A human named BLAZE HULL (Brady) sleeps in a
bunk, while his partner, a turqoise-colored David Bowie
inspired alien named CHIPPER TWEE (Cheeks) works the controls
of the ship. Chipper is in a classic space-age jumpsuit --   *
fitted and colorful, with a zipper down the back. He wears a   *
comm device on his wrist. The bridge of the ship is small,   *
laid out something like the cab of a truck -- so the bunk is
behind the pilot chair.

                    NARRATION (CONT'D)
          "A Nibiruian being named Chipper
          Twee has piloted the ship he shares
          with his companion, Blaze Hull,
          away from the battle."

                    CHIPPER
          H.A.L.-E. Are you certain we're
          safe here?

Panel Three: angle favoring the ship's highly intelligent
computer, which should have its controls configured in a way
to suggest the character of HALEY.   *

*Ben Dewey's sketches
over the issue #4 script.*

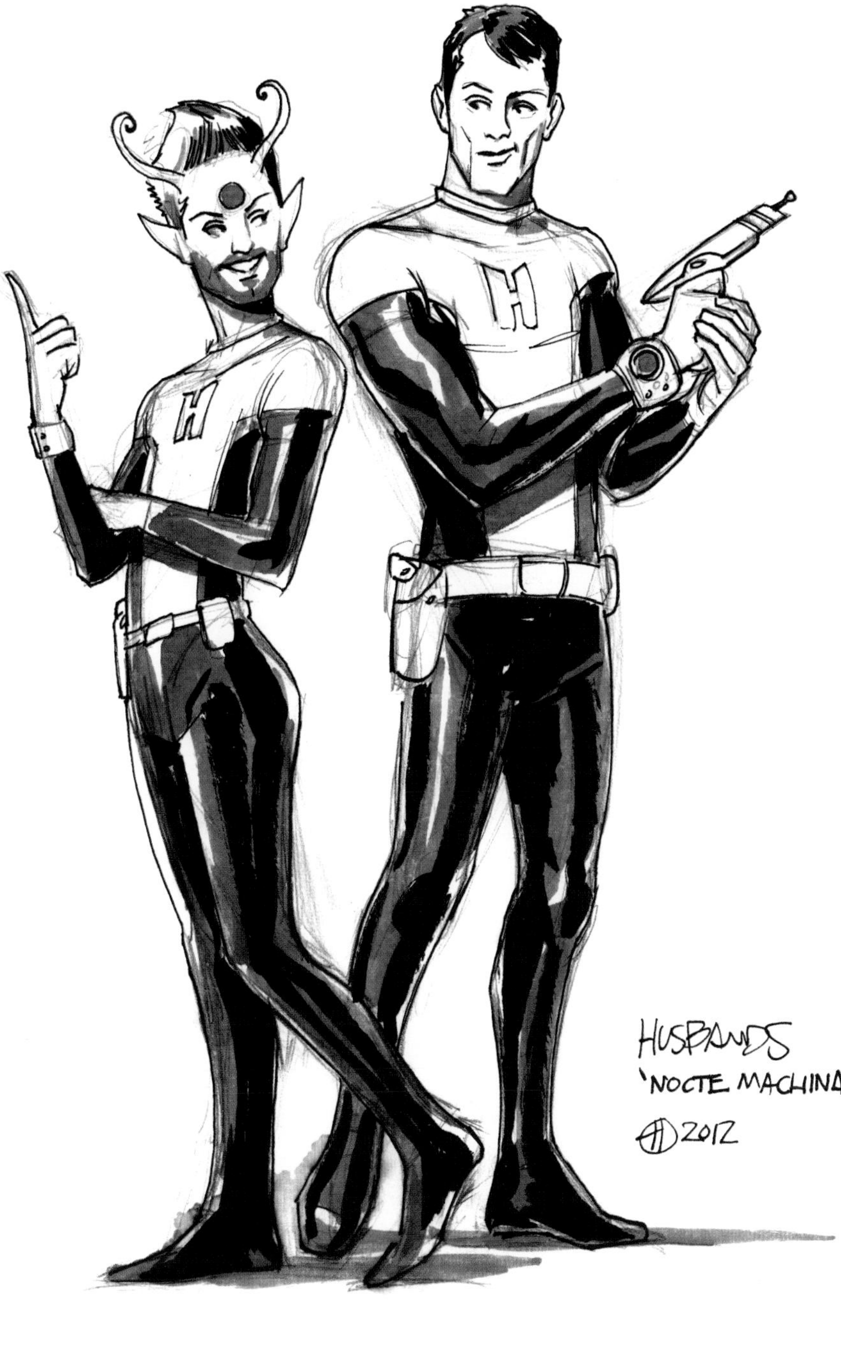
HUSBANDS
'NOCTE MACHINAS'
2012

Ben Dewey created this initial sketch for the characters Chipper Twee and Blaze Hull.

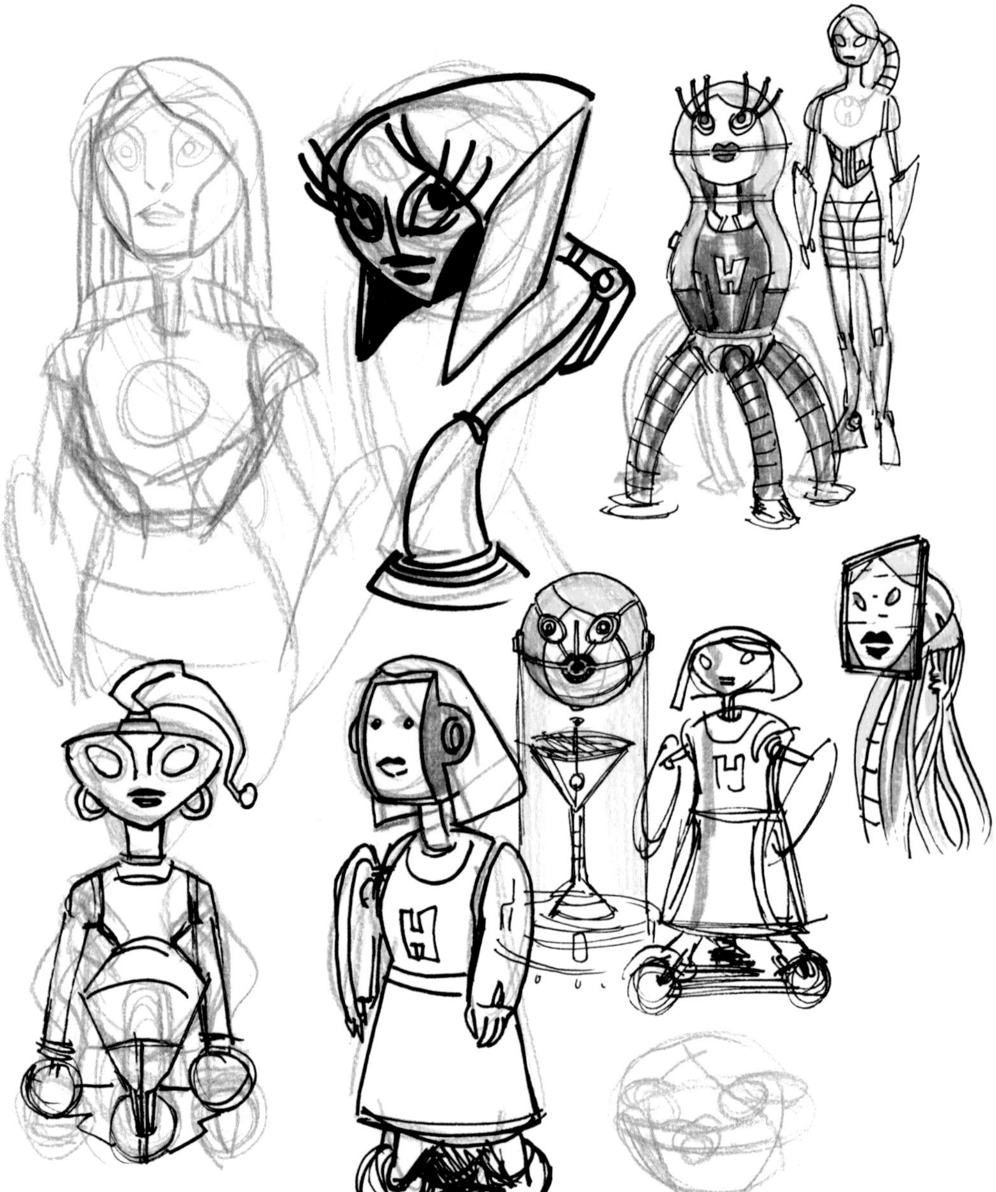

Haley's robotic character in issue #4 grew from these many concepts provided by Ben Dewey.

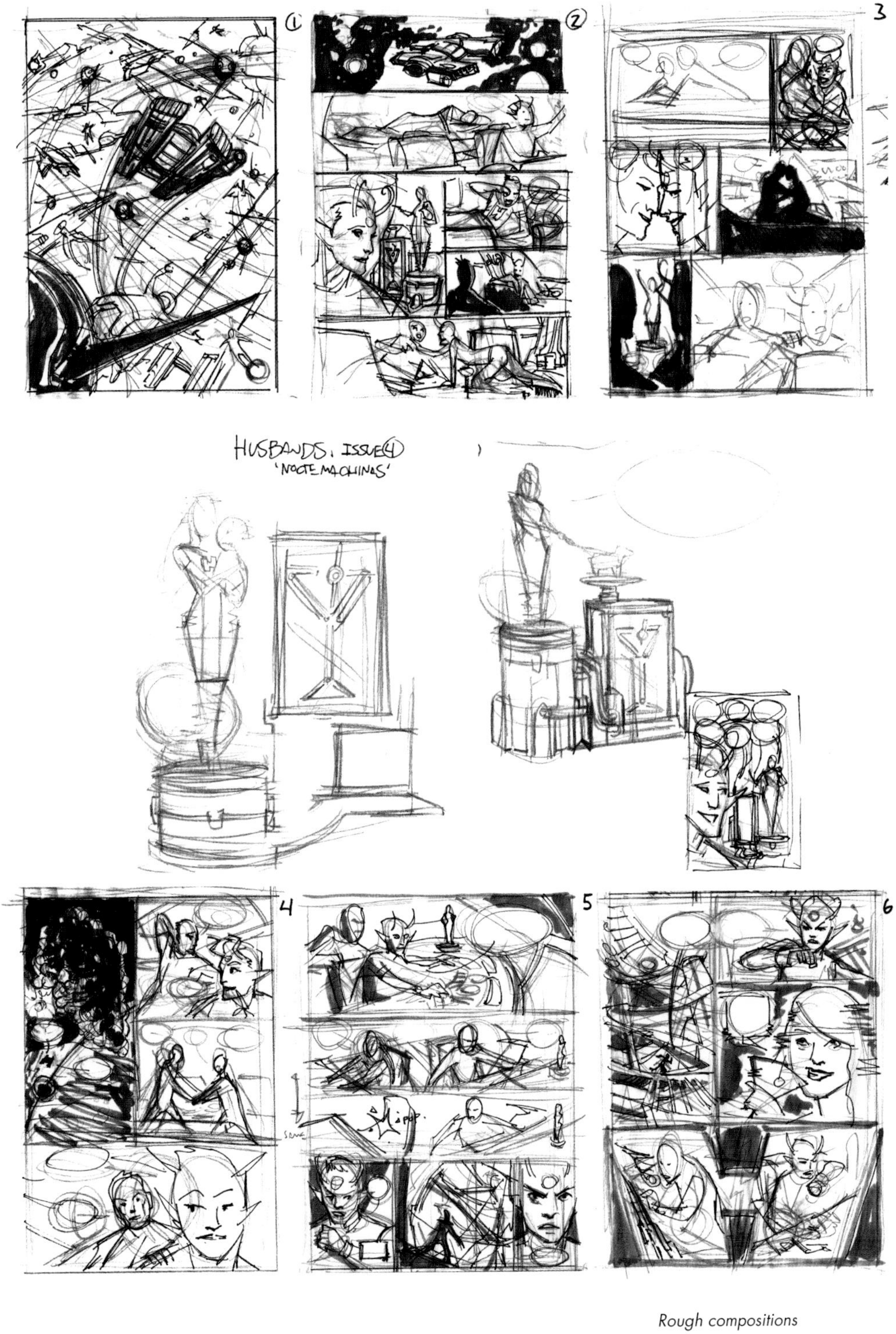
1
2
3
HUSBANDS. ISSUE 4
'NOCTE MACHINAS'
4
5
6

Rough compositions by Ben Dewey.

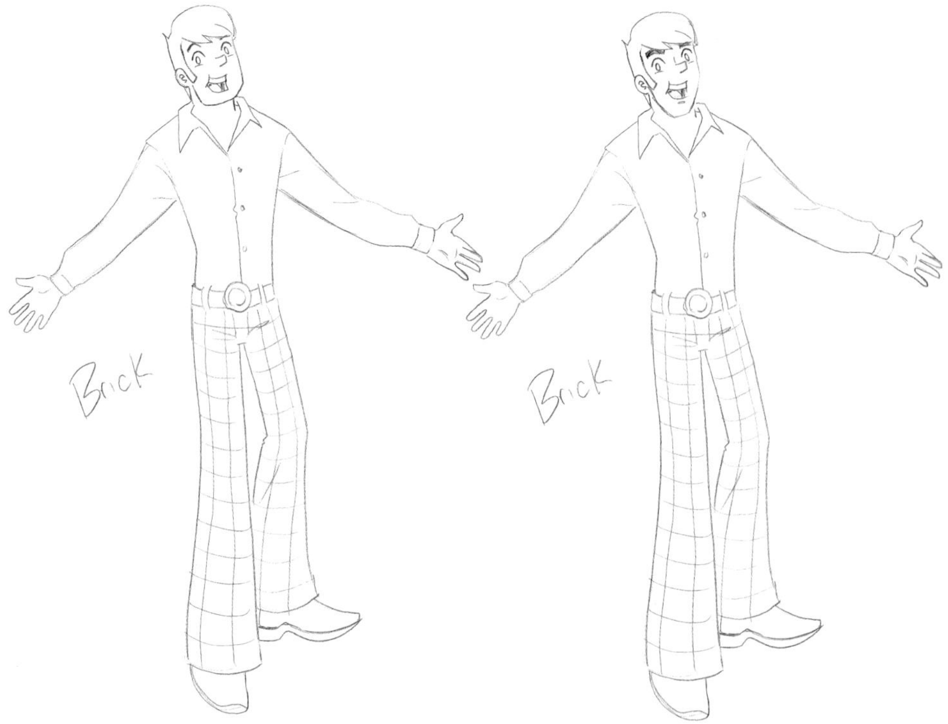
Brick
Brick

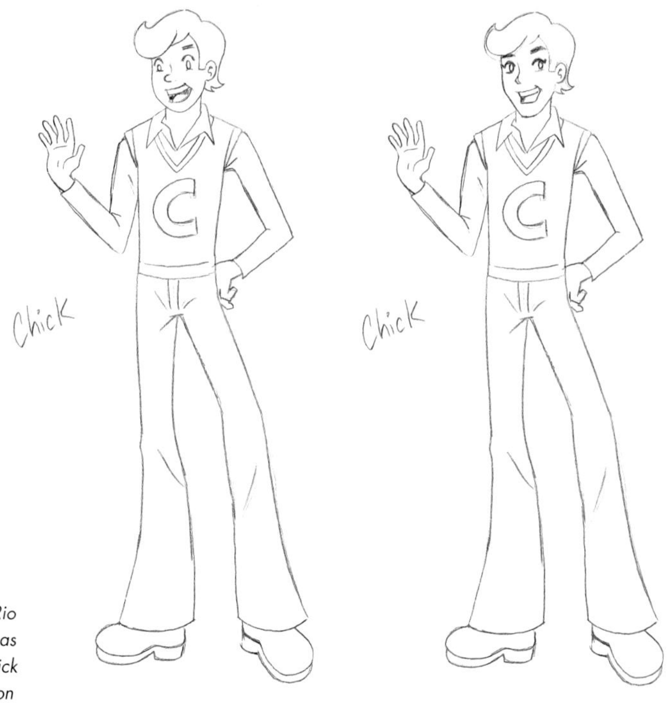
Chick
Chick

For issue #5, artist Tania del Rio re-created Cheeks and Brady as the Archie-style characters Chick and Brick. Initial designs are on the left, with revisions on the right.

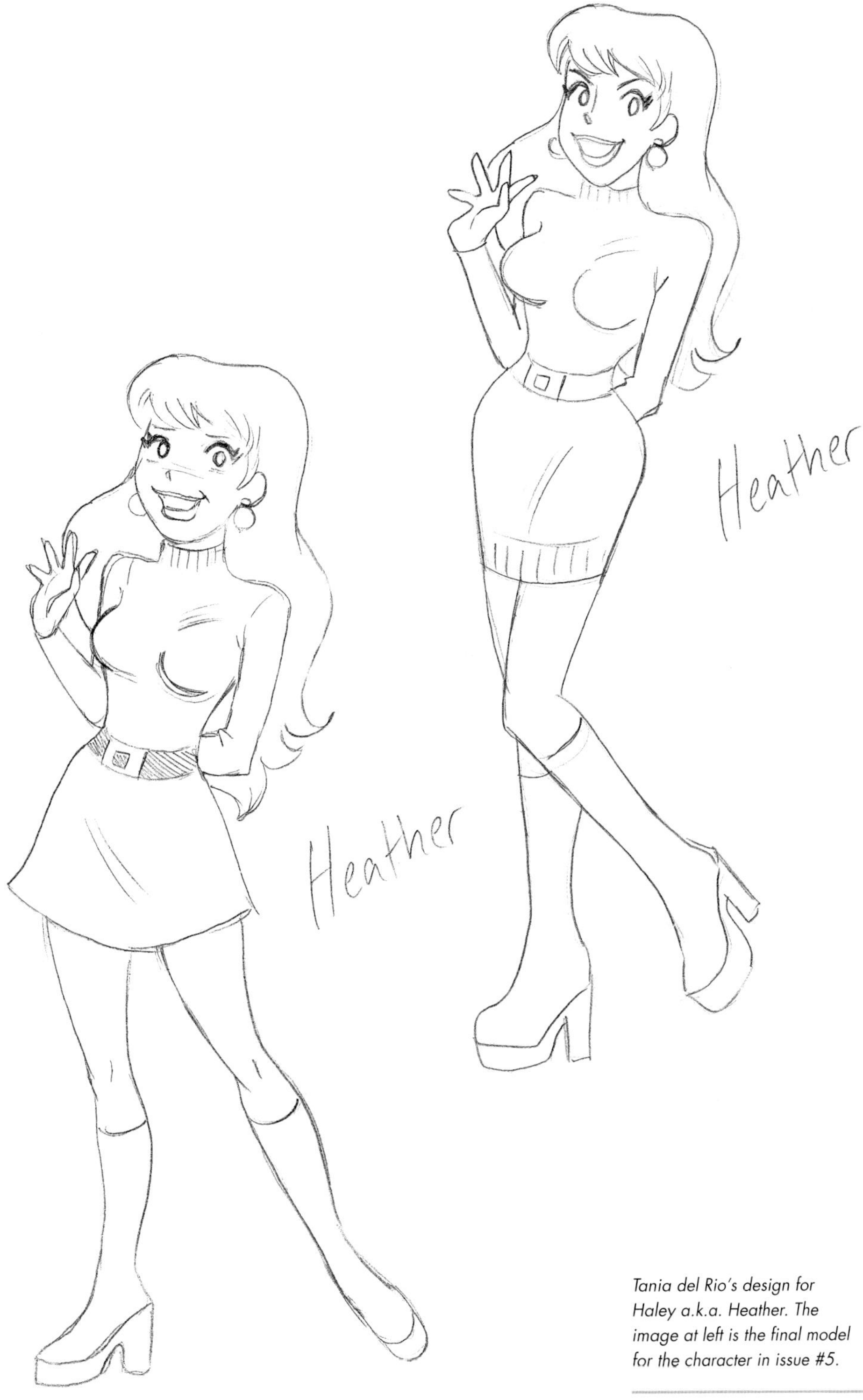
Heather
Heather

Tania del Rio's design for Haley a.k.a. Heather. The image at left is the final model for the character in issue #5.

AFTERWORD

This book, like all good books, is a subversive thing. At first glance, it's hilarious, with gorgeous artwork and sexy men, hooray! But it's part of a revolution, in the fight which keeps rearing its head—especially at election time—with religion and the Right obsessing over us. Now, we've got Jane and Brad fighting back. And they're leading the way with the greatest weapon of all.

With joy.

To hell with polemics! Jane and Brad, or Brad and Jane—I've never asked which one's the top—disarm the reader with happiness, hoots, and dazzling smiles. Hidden underneath, there's a lovely lick of anger, but they've got enough style and skill to turn that yell into a grin. When you're laughing this much, who can stay angry?

To be gay in the twenty-first century is a political act. And if *Husbands* is our manifesto, then I say we're winning. Vote Jane! Vote Brad! What wonderful *Husbands* they make.

—Russell T. Davies

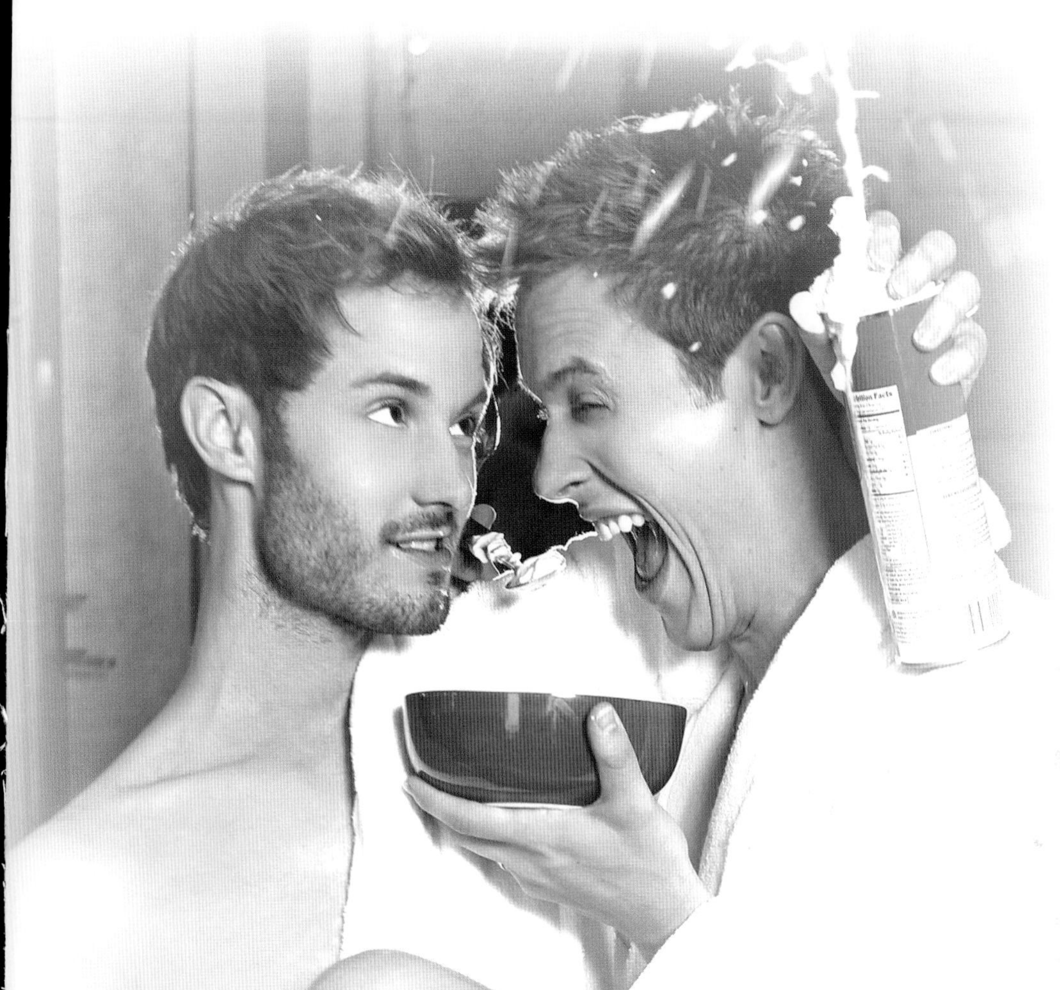

ALSO FROM DARK HORSE COMICS

 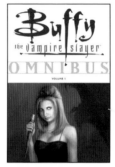

BUFFY THE VAMPIRE SLAYER OMNIBUS
VOLUME 1
ISBN 978-1-59307-784-6 | $24.99
VOLUME 2
ISBN 978-1-59307-826-3 | $24.99
VOLUME 3
ISBN 978-1-59307-885-0 | $24.99
VOLUME 4
ISBN 978-1-59307-968-0 | $24.99
VOLUME 5
ISBN 978-1-59582-225-3 | $24.99
VOLUME 6
ISBN 978-1-59582-242-0 | $24.99
VOLUME 7
ISBN 978-1-59582-331-1 | $24.99

BUFFY THE VAMPIRE SLAYER: PANEL TO PANEL
ISBN 978-1-59307-836-2 | $19.99

ANGEL OMNIBUS
Christopher Golden, Eric Powell, and others
ISBN 978-1-59582-706-7 | $24.99

TALES OF THE SLAYERS
*Joss Whedon, Amber Benson, Gene Colan, P. Craig
Russell, Tim Sale, and others*
ISBN 978-1-56971-605-2 | $14.99

TALES OF THE VAMPIRES
Joss Whedon, Brett Matthews, Cameron Stewart, and others
ISBN 978-1-56971-749-3 | $15.99

BUFFY THE VAMPIRE SLAYER: TALES HARDCOVER
ISBN 978-1-59582-644-2 | $29.99

FRAY: FUTURE SLAYER
Joss Whedon and Karl Moline
ISBN 978-1-56971-751-6 | $19.99

**SERENITY VOLUME 1: THOSE LEFT BEHIND
SECOND EDITION HARDCOVER**
Joss Whedon, Brett Matthews, and Will Conrad
ISBN 978-1-59582-914-6 | $17.99

**SERENITY VOLUME 2: BETTER DAYS AND
OTHER STORIES HARDCOVER**
*Joss Whedon, Patton Oswalt, Zack Whedon, Patric
Reynolds, and others*
ISBN 978-1-59582-739-5 | $19.99

**SERENITY VOLUME 3: THE SHEPHERD'S
TALE HARDCOVER**
Joss Whedon, Zack Whedon, and Chris Samnee
ISBN 978-1-59582-561-2 | $14.99

DR. HORRIBLE AND OTHER HORRIBLE STORIES
Joss Whedon, Zack Whedon, Joëlle Jones, and others
ISBN 978-1-59582-577-3 | $9.99

DOLLHOUSE VOLUME 1: EPITAPHS
*Andrew Chambliss, Jed Whedon, Maurissa Tancharoen,
and Cliff Richards*
ISBN 978-1-59582-863-7 | $18.99

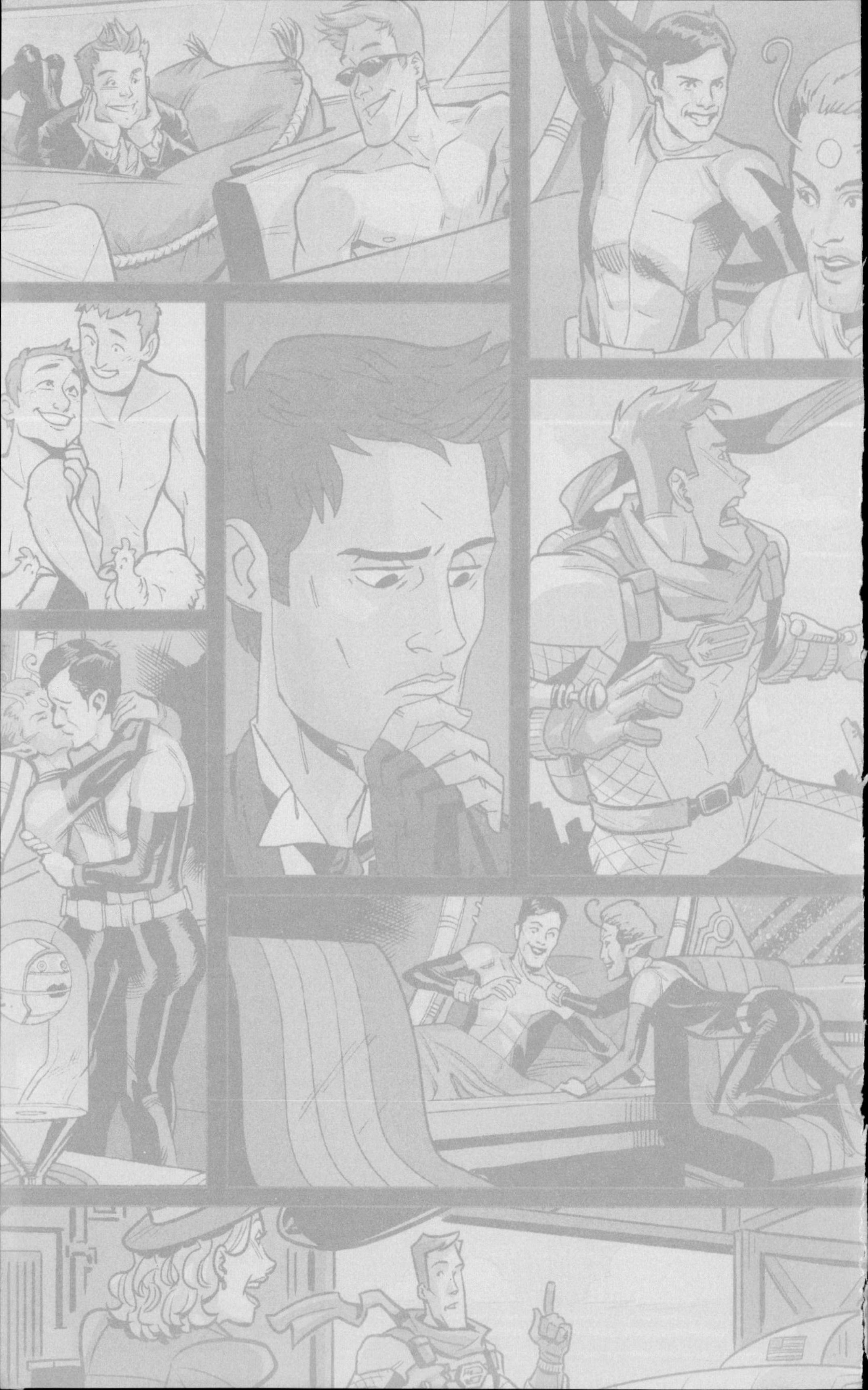